TWENTY-FIRST CENTURY CHALLENGES TO PUBLIC MANAGEMENT

TWENTY - FIRST CENTURY CHALLENGES TO PUBLIC MANAGEMENT

Edited by
SATYAVAN BHATNAGAR

KALPAZ PUBLICATIONS
DELHI-110052

Twenty-First Century Challenges to Public Management

ISBN: 81-7835-561-2

Published in 2007 in India by
Kalpaz Publications
C-30, Satyawati Nagar,
Delhi-110052
E-mail: kalpaz@hotmail.com
Phone : 9212729499

Lasser Type Setting by : Rudra Computer Graphics, Delhi
Printed at : Salasar Imaging System, Delhi

CONTENTS

PREFACE

Human being and his collectivities are always in a state of flux. Change and challenge confront them at every step of their life, putting their ingenuity to test perpetually. India has been no exception to this universal law of nature. Though it has been experiencing changes and also confronting challenges since times immemorial, yet the rate and intensity of change that have overtaken it since the dawn of Independence have been both colossal and unprecedented. This is for the reason that never before in the annals of its long history has such a tremendous task of restructuring of society from a feudal order to democracy ever been undertaken. It is therefore but obvious that upheavals and challenges of every type would come in its way. Another factor that has further accentuated the challenge is the unimaginative degree of developments that the previous century has ushered in almost every walk of life everywhere in the world.

It was with a view to pinpointing some of the challenges that public management has been face to face in the twenty-first century that the Chandigarh-based Senior Citizens' Council for Human Resource Development organized recently a number of seminars wherein the issue was seriously debated among its members (mostly comprising the retired university professors, civil servants and other professionals). This book, a compendium of fifteen papers, is the outcome of that learned exercise. While the entire gamut of change and challenge could not be compressed in this canvass because of its too wide a sweep, efforts have however been made to touch upon as many and as diverse areas as possible, taking due care that no major aspect of public management is left out.The topics covered range from such generic areas as political system, governance and the economy to such specific subjects as education, health services, management and water resources. Further, the authors have tried to focus on the problems in their respective areas and the nature of the challenges that they pose to the decision-makers at their appropriate levels. Hope, the book would go a long way in giving a fillip to the national debate on the challenges that confront the nation in this particular field at the dawn of the twenty-first century and might perhaps help induct greater earnestness among the decision-makers.

As mentioned above, this book is the brainchild of the Senior Citizens' Council for Human Resource Development, more especially of its Chairman, Dr. B.P. Mathur who conceived the idea of such an exercise and hammered it to its logical conclusion. The project might not have been put through had Professor Shital Prakash not taken pains to pursue it at every stage of its development. We owe a debt of gratitude to both of them.

Equally indebted are we to those learned authors who spared some of their valuable time for the thought-provoking papers that constitute the soul of this work. But for them, this project would not have seen the light of the day. Being the Editor, I am personally thankful to Professor D.D. Narula who not only contributed a series of three highly learned papers on the economic state of the nation but has also taken pains to go through each and every word of the manuscript and made valuable suggestions that have gone a long way in improving the quality of the Book. Finally, we put on record our deep sense of appreciation to Messrs Kalpaz Publications who bestowed an artistic get-up on the book and made it possible to place it in the hands of the readers.

Chandigarh
13 April 2007

Satyavan Bhatnagar
(Editor)

LIST OF CONTRIBUTORS

Arora, Parvinder, (Dr.) University Business School, Panjab University, Chandgiarh.

Bhatnagar, Satyavan. Formerly Professor of Political Science and Director, Correspondence Courses, Panjab University, Chandigarh.

Ghuman, B.S. Professor and Chairman, Department of Public Administration, Panjab University, Chandigarh.

Kaushik, S.P. Formerly Professor of Surgery, Post-Graduate Institute of Medical Education and Research, Chandigarh; Professor and Head, Department of Surgical Gastroentero Logy, Sanjay Gandhi Post-Graduate Institute of Medical Sciences, Lucknow; Professor Head Department of General Surgery Government Medical College, Chandigarh.

Mathur, B.P. Formerly Deputy Comptroller and Auditor General of India; Chairman, Audit Board of India, and National Institute of Financial Management, Faridabad.

Mathur, S.S. Formerly Professor and Chairman, Department of Education, Panjab University, Chandigarh.

Mathur, Sanjay. Managing Director, FOSECO, Pune.

Mittal, S.P. Formerly Principal Scientist, ICAR.

Narula, D.D. Formerly Member-Secretary, Indian Council for Social Science Research and Professor of Economics, Rajasthan University, Jaipur.

Sharma, S.L. Dean, Institute of Correctional Administration, Chandigarh; Dean, faculty of Arts, Panjab University, Chandigarh and Formerly Profesor and Chairman, Department of Sociology, Panjab University, Chandigarh.

Vaidya, S.C. Professor of Finance Management, Business School, and Director, IAS Coaching Centre, Panjab University, Chandigarh.

Veer Singh. Dean, University Instruction and Professor of Law, Panjab University, Chandigarh.

Introduction

Challenge and man are eternal fellow travellers, the former chasing the latter wherever and in whatever situation he may be placed. It is another thing that man has the ingenuity and the energy to successfully face the challenge. However, the fact is that the latter does not cease chasing him. The secret of their company is that man by nature cannot sit idle; he must keep himself occupied ceaselessly with one activity or another. When he does so, he tends to encounter, more often than not some sort of a problem that beckons him to grapple with. The more unfamiliar or novel an activity that he undertakes, the greater are the chances of the encounter taking place. Such situations that thus put him to test constitute, what we describe a challenge.

The intensity of the challenge and how one perceives it varies from individual to individual. There are individuals who fear facing any type of challenge, howsoever minor it may be, whereas there are others who have been endowed with such a marvellous attitude of mind that even the hardest of the problem cannot cow them down. There are yet another type of people who, unlike the former find the peaceful go of life insipid and listless. Instead, they want it to be hectic, always full of challenges. In fact, they love to face them. If at any given point of time there is no problem or challenge before them, they would even create one for them. By nature, they are at war with the *status quo*, always finding fault with it and like to effect changes in it one way or the other.

The nature and intensity of the challenge also vary from time to time, depending upon the society's level of knowledge in general and of science and technology in particular and also on the level of its overall development at any given point of time. In good old days, such petty things as how to light the fire or to produce the foods grains posed problems too daunting for him. But to us, they appear too trivial, the reason being that today we are so well equipped with all sorts of knowledge and also that science and technology have placed at our disposal such a fantastic range of tools and techniques that we do not feel unnerved if any problem howsoever challenging it may be, comes in our way.

What is true of the individual is also true of society at large, the only difference being that while at the individual plane, it is the lone person that faces the challenge; at the societal level it is the ingenuity of the collectivity that is at test. The nature and dimension of the societal challenges are also more subtle and complicated. Speaking in the context of the modern day developments, the twenty-first century has brought in its wake challenges that are unique in many ways. Most of them are in fact the by-product of the changes that we have experienced in various walks of life, more specifically during the past half a century or so. Ironically, modern science and technology that we take pride in for having pushed it to newer heights has itself turned out to be a new source of anxiety to us. In passing, we may allude to such new problems as pollution, depletion of the ozone zone, the AID'S and the like.

Next to science and technology, the most outstanding (nay, the earth-shaking) development of the previous century was the end of colonialism and consequent emergence of a number of countries in Asia, Africa and Latin America as independent political entities. Their liberation, by itself was an event of utmost significance in the sense that there lay ahead new challenges for those that got political independence and even for their erstwhile colonial masters. While for the former it ushered in a new era of hope and opportunity for a better future ahead, for the latter it was a timely warning that they should be prepared to accommodate the new nations in the public management of the world at large. Seizing the new opportunity, no sooner did most of the newly liberated countries get freedom from the foreign domination than they designed and put into operation ambitious development plans for an all round development. Some of them executed these programmes with a fair degree of success whereas quite a number of them miserably flopped, perhaps due to the reason that they were unable to face the onslaught of the anti-reformist forces, released in the course the implementation of those programmes. As a result, they were left with no other alternative but to abandon them, relegating their people to the older situation of socio-economic stagnation.

If the first three decades following the mid-twentieth century witnessed the success and failure of the development drives of these countries, how democracy failed to make a debut there and so on and so forth, the closing decades of that century marked such startling events as the fall of the Berlin Wall, to be followed by the collapse of the Soviet Union and its dramatic breakdown. Almost simultaneously, the various Communist regimes of Eastern Europe and elsewhere crashed down one after the other in quick succession. In this way, the communist ideology that had thus far posed a challenge to liberal democracy beat a retreat, paving the way for the return of the market to the center-stage of the politico-economic management of the world. Liberalization, privatization and globalization became the new *mantra* of the state policy everywhere. India was no exception. It too adopted this *mantra* under the leadership of Dr. Manmohan Singh.

These developments gave birth to new issues that in turn posed a challenge to everyone. The rise of the market was an event of profound significance. Its thrust was so sharp and sweeping that it not only gave a near death blow to the regime of highly controlled and state-regulated economy but it also overshadowed every aspect of the governance of society. China, even though a communist regime could perhaps sense the temper of the times to come much ahead of others, and had thus opened her doors for foreign capital and had taken such other steps towards the marketization of her economy. Another notable impact of the market was the weakening of the concept of state sovereignty. Cross border economic blocs that had emerged in the wake of the overarching market ideology in various parts of the globe gave a fillip to the softening of the rigidity of the state borders. The harbinger of this transnational development was the European Union (EU). Following the lead given by it, countries after countries stepped out of their narrow state boundaries and coalesced with one another to develop their economies by relaxing their tariff-related policies and also lending cooperation to one another in myriad other ways. In a way, this development in particular transformed the very face of the globe. Those things that were considered thus far impossible came to be translated into a reality.

As for us, we had gone by the turn of the century miles ahead of many a developing country. Not only our democracy had developed deeper roots but our economy too had become quite robust. These achievements combined with long strides we had taken toward the development of science and technology, particularly in the field of information technology had raised our international stature. A perceptible change of attitude towards us was noticed among those who had a stake in world politics. Where they used to look at us as one of the numerous developing countries, still engrossed in the basic problems of poverty and disease, now rate us as a fast emerging regional power. Their hitherto Pakistan-centric approach underwent a diametric change. Most of them began to compare us with China and other developed economies of Asia. Thus, we acquired a new world stature and that has added strength to our voice. Our diplomatic representatives are looked upon with greater respect and their viewpoint listened to more attentively. Pakistan that had so far been adopting highly belligerent postures towards us too softened her attitude. War mongering was pushed aside, though temporarily and instead agreed to negotiate peace with us. However, India's growing stature also became a cause of heartburn for some, especially for those in South Asia. Pakistan for instance still blows hot and cold in one breath. Where it has joined hands with us in promoting peace in the sub-Continent and has even taken in tandem with us a number of confidence-building measures (that process is still under way and hopefully it might acquire a snow-balling speed in the days to come), it has not stopped extending active support to the terrorists, her numerous assurances to the contrary notwithstanding. She does not even cherish our moral commitment to Afghanistan to lend a helping hand to her in her endeavour to rebuild the war-ravaged country. While the hidden intentions of both Pakistan and China have been too familiar to us, Bangladesh and Myanmar too indulged into the game of clandestinely encouraging and giving a fillip to forces inimical to our interests. Our claims to the permanent membership of the United Nations Security Council or our having sponsored a nominee for the Secretary-Generalship of the UN was not taken kindly by many countries including most of our neigbours.

At home, our effort to recast our economy on new global lines also attracted the ire of such forces as trade unions, the leftist ideologues and other conservative sections of our political class. Not to speak of their lending tangible support to this meaningful venture, they tried to disrupt it badly. Another insurmountable roadblock in the way of this ambitious venture was the bureaucracy. It has become well neigh impossible for us to bring home to our *'babus'* that the new economic-centric model of democracy demands a direction and control pretty different from the one that Max Weber had suggested long ago. Their continued hesitation, nay their refusal to read the writing on the wall has not only dampened the enthusiasm of those who wish to accelerate the pace of change but has also created potent hindrances in their way. The mutuality of interests of the bureaucracy and the politician also brings the latter into play and then both combine together to frustrate the entire effort to reshape the things in a more modern way. Unless these forces are suitably tamed, we might lose pace with the rest of the developed world.

Thus, we find that public management is fraught with challenges at every step of our march towards modernity. It is with a view to identifying those challenges that the Chandigarh-based Senior Citizens' Council for Human Resource Development thought in terms of pinpointing them. In that connection, a series of seminars were organized at its headquarters wherein its members and other seasoned scholars and professionals gave serious thought to the issues of public management and also tried to see how these challenges can be effectively met. What has finally emerged out of these learned discussions has sought to be encapsulated in the course of this book.

At the outset, Satyavan Bhatnagar scans through the wide canvass of the Indian political system, primarily focusing his attention on that chain of developments that led to the birth and stabilization of democracy in this country. In this connection, he highlights how the various challenges that came in the way of this novel experiment (of establishing this too intricate a form of government and that too on such a massive scale and against so heavy odds) making special mention of how the huge sections of the depressed and the deprived people were sought to be pulled into the main stream of articulate citizenship, how the opposition of those people whose vested interests were hit hard was quelled, and more significantly how the demands of the newly inducted citizenry were met by such measures as the Right to Information, public interest litigation, strengthening of the institutions of the Panchayati Raj and the like. After having done so, he pays attention to those challenges that these developments have brought to the fore, making a pinpointed reference to the havoc caused by the unholy coalition of the bureaucracy, politician and the muscleman; the resistance of this coalition to all types of reforms in the structure and processes of the governance; the inadequacy of the effort to meet the fast growing demand of the enlightened people for qualitative civic life such as good educational and health institutions; infra-structure in terms of the energy, roads, railways, ports, air lines, irrigation and the like; and above all employment. He laments that the effort being put in to meet these requirements is not only too tardy but is also hampered at every step. In case this effort fails to keep pace with the increase in population and more particularly with the escalation of the aspiration of the people (and he is too pessimist that the gap between the demand and its fulfillment is not going to be narrowed down under the given conditions, instead it might yawn further), the Indian democracy will be caught in too ticklish a situation. Herein lies the biggest challenge to it. He winds up his paper on a very optimistic note to the effect that democracy is the only political institution that is equipped with such in-built structures and processes as have the capability of meeting any challenge, however potent it may be by immediately pressing them into action and adapting the functioning of the system to the requirements of the time. He further underlines that happily enough we have left no stone unturned to equip it with all such types of structures and processes. And therein lies the secret why our democracy has been able to withstand so many storms in the past and hopefully it will do so in the days to come as well.

Coming down to the specifics, B.P. sMathur takes up the challenge to governance. He too feels that both the structure and the procedures of governance have become over the years too outdated to deliver the goods, especially when viewed in the context of the change in the goals that the government has of late chosen to pursue. He observes that it is widely perceived that India's poor development record on economic, social and moral fronts is largely due to poor governance. He laments that bureaucracy (the kingpin of the system) has become 'unresponsive to popular demands, embroiled in red tape and formalism, and officials are power hungry and corrupt.' With a view to giving direction to the Indian system of governance, he relates in detail the international experience how the various countries, more specifically the UK, New Zealand and the USA that too had at one time or another faced the same problem, had tackled it and streamlined their systems by incorporating the principles of New Public Management. He recommends that our government too should lay emphasis on '(i) decentralization of authority within governmental units and devolution of responsibilities to lower levels of government, (ii) downsizing of public services and privatization and corporatization of activities; (iii) reexamination of what government should both pay for and do, what government should pay for and not do, and what it should neither pay nor do; (iv) consideration of more cost-effective ways of delivering services; (v) customer orientation; (vi) benchmarking and measuring of performance, and (vii) reforms designed to simplify regulations and reduce its cost.'

Reflecting upon the state of our economy in the first decade of the twenty-first century (in the following three chapters), D. D. Narula identifies 'eradication of poverty, elimination of hunger and malnutrition and provision of adequate employment' as three principal challenges that it is face to face today. The first Chapter of the series is divided into three sections. While Section I is devoted to the GDP (its growth rate, its structure and use-value composition), Section II makes a broad comparison of the development strategies of India and China, in their historical settings. In the final Section, Narula examines the impact of high growth rates on poverty and employment. The second chapter comprises two sections only (Sections 4 and 5). While the former deals with different aspects of development strategy such as foreign trade, foreign direct investment, capital account convertibility, the World Trade Organization (WTO), etc. the latter discusses issues of saving and investment, infrastructure (both physical and social), financial sector, public-private partnership, non-farm development, rural industrialization, small scale industry, special economic zones, hunger, starvation and malnutrition and employment-led growth. The last Chapter of the series again consists of two sections (6 and 7). The former brings out the widening social-economic inequalities, conspicuous consumption and their demonstration effects and the impoverishment of the vast masses, both rural and urban. Its final section highlights the development dilemmas, where a federal polity and multi-party coalition government of diverse interest groups faces the challenges of inclusive development. Devolution of adequate powers and finances to Panchayats and the effective use of Right to Information and peoples' participation are likely to present challenges to our democracy, forcing it either to perform or to perish.

The study finds that while in the 1980's the growth rate of GDP had accelerated, it had slackened in the1990s, again picking up since 2003-04. A major drag on the growth rate is the low growth rate of value-added in agriculture, which is the chief source of wage-goods for the poor. The rate of its growth would be only at one-third of what was stipulated in the Tenth five-year plan period, reasons being the failure of land reforms and decline of public investment in rural infrastructure. Further, slow growth of rural non-farm sector, especially rural industrialization, export of foodgrains, steep rise in prices of foodgrains and failure of Food Corporation of India to operate the targetted public distribution system efficiently, account for the failure of high growth rate of GDP, not affecting poverty. The depressing scene in agriculture has, in turn adversely affected the per capita availability of cereals and pulses, making it fall to the level of the 1960's. A redeeming feature, however, is the higher reduction of poverty in some of the poorer states, such as Assam and the North East, Chhatisgarh, Orissa, Jharkhand and

Bihar, possibly due to migration of workers to better-off states, during the eleven- year period, 1993-94 to 2004-05. To come to the growth rate of employment, the 61st quinquennial survey reveals that it has been less than 2 percent p.a. for the economy as a whole, during the post-reform period with employment in the primary sector growing sluggishly and services sector employment growing the fastest and employment in the secondary sector also growing rapidly. Further, casualisation of labour and the use of contract labour have marked an increasing trend during the period. The growth process has favoured the male skilled workers whereas women employment has been adversely affected. The National Rural Employment Guarantee Scheme that was launched with so great fanfare in February 2006 has created nation-wide fervour and expectations among the people. However, a survey of its working in three states, namely, Jharkhand, Bihar and Kerala revealed that the scheme had been working well in Kerala whereas the Jharkhand government had not yet prepared its State component, and the Bihar government had not yet appointed the necessary staff for making it operational.

The study further highlights (in Chapter IV, Section 4) that FDI reached its highest level in 2005-06, of under $8 billion. However, the outward flow of FDI, due to acquisitions and mergers by Indians and NRI's, has already exceeded the inward flow, resulting in a negative net FDI Foreign portfolio investment, which now exceeds FDI, forcing the Reserve Bank of India (RBI) to consider measures to control it. A surplus on capital account and a deficit on current account, India had a surplus balance of payments, principally due to the remittances of Indian workers abroad, of which India was the largest recipient in 2005-06. RBI is proceeding cautiously on the question of capital convertibility, being fully conscious of the pitfalls and dangers involved. The World Trade Organization (WTO) has failed to persuade the USA and the European Union, on reduction of their subsidies to agriculture and thus the Doha round is almost wrecked. China, India, Brazil and South Africa – the G4 – have joined together to foil attempts by USA and EU to adopt various stratagems to defend their privileged position and to defend the interests of the developing countries. The study further shows that much higher domestic savings would be needed to finance the 11th plan, if 9 percent growth rate of GDP, as visualized in the Approach Paper, is to be achieved. RBI had shown its deep concern regarding the Participatory Notes (PN's) as a part of foreign institutional investment. It has also cautioned banks on loans for real estate and personal loans. Since Khadi and Village Industries Commission has signally failed to introduce technology in the rural industries, the study pleads for handing over the technology, extension and training functions to Krishi Vikas Kendras, and other competent and committed NGOs and private parties. As for the special economic zones, since these have fomented a serous controversy regarding the acquisition of agricultural land for industrial development; the agriculturists need to be made stake-holders and the issue needs to be discussed widely. Further, on the educational front, besides universalisation of elementary education, development of higher education and research is emphasized; the problem of health being intimately related to nutrition, the stress is laid on adequate and nutritious food. Recommendations of the National Farmers Commission are detailed.

Finally, the study highlights the grim contrast of the rising affluence of the upper and the middle classes, their expensive and imitative western life styles and the degrading poverty, hunger and disease-prone majority of the population. The development dilemmas as stated earlier are a serious challenge to the polity and economy. The trade-off between employment and growth needs to be worked out, if the conflict between the classes and the masses has to be resolved in a peaceful way. This would help enrich both democracy and economy.

In Chapter VI B.S. Ghuman illustrates how 'mega events like liberalization, globalization, privatization and decentralization, increasing media and citizen oversight and information technology' have impacted the process of the governance of society, forcing Public Administration to widen its traditional focus from bureaucracy to the performance of the Non-Governmental Organizations, the day-to-day behaviour of the market and the like. One of the conclusions that he dwells upon is that the administrative ministries and bureaucracy have made consistent efforts to thwart the implementation of new initiatives in the field of the economic governance. He begins his paper with a theoretical framework of the basic concepts. After having done so, he proceeds ahead to trace out the various steps taken to shift the thrust of the economy from its traditional regimented model to the market-oriented liberal model, all with a view 'to attain a higher rate of growth on sustainable basis through efficiency and productivity originating from relaxation of government controls over production, investment and prices in the domestic economy and progressively opening up of the Indian economy to foreign trade, capital and technology.' With that end in view, reforms relating to the exchange rate, interest rate, fiscal and monetary policies were introduced in a phased manner. He also details out how sweeping changes were introduced to relax the regimented regime of strict state control not only from the industries (thirteen of them were liberated from it) but also from the ranks of the public sector enterprises by making provision for the market forces to play some role; how the infrastructure sectors particularly telecommunication, power and roads which were traditionally the monopolies of the state sector were also opened to the private sector; and how external liberalization (i.e. globalization) was stretched to cover such areas as trade, foreign exchange, capital and technology. Happily, the process of economic liberalization is nearing completion and it seems to be irreversible in this country as well. But unfortunately the corresponding changes have not been able to keep pace with the changes in the economy, though the efforts are still under way. He dwells at length how efforts have been made to adapt the administrative structure to the new temper of the times. However, a quick perusal of ten years' experience of the Indian economy during post-liberalization phase reveals a gap between rhetoric and reality. In support of his contention, he cites, firstly how the annual growth rate of industrial sector during 1990's and early 2000s has fluctuated between 1 percent and 12.3 percent and similarly how the annual growth rate of export has oscillated between 2.7 percent and 35.3 percent; secondly, how the economic laws governing both internal and external sectors simultaneously have not helped the Indian industries to improve efficiency and productivity, instead how the multinational corporations (MNC's) entered in India in a big way and took over most of the lucrative industrial activities, pushing many domestic industrial units into sickness; and thirdly, how the administrative ministries and bureaucracy have made consistent efforts to thwart the implementation of new initiatives in the field of the economic governance. Above all, the trickle down effect has also not worked well (more and more people have gone down the poverty line), employment scenario too has not shown any appreciable improvement, and regional disparities have also widened. In the end, Ghuman makes some policy recommendations how the situation can be improved.

Moving further one stumbles against the poor 'Work Culture' that constitutes one of the big hurdles in the way of the public management. Veer Singh begins his paper on this theme with a highly lamenting remark, saying, 'Historically, Indians have had a poor work culture and efficiency. Output of an Indian worker is considerably low in comparison to the Japanese, Germans and other communities. Therefore, in spite of being very rich in terms of bountiful natural resources, India has been a very poor country for centuries. On the other hand, Japan which is poor in terms of natural resources, is one of the strongest economies in the world today because of the habit of hard work, discipline of its human resources.' He attributes the poor work culture of the country to such causes as 'primordial value system and the change resistant tradition, feudal power structure, corruption and ineffective socio-legal control mechanism.' As for the remedies, he suggests a few correctives, both informal and formal. The former include education, religious and social awareness, social reform movements and the role of the NGO's, while the formal correctives refer to the revamping of the management systems and build-up of social capital and effective legal control mechanism.

Yet another stumbling block is corruption that S.L. Sharma discussed at length in his paper, Corruption: A Social Scientific Analysis. Highlighting the sweep and the intensity of corruption, he remarks 'Few will dispute the fact that corruption has assumed epidemic proportions in present times and that warrants careful diagnosis and effective action in right earnest. The challenge is both enormous and grave.' He handles the subject mostly in its theoretic perspective, starting from its conceptual definition and going over to its rise and spread in society with particular reference to India, its social causes and consequences and the combating strategies. He laments, 'What is alarming about corruption is not just its rising graph and its pervasive spread but its social acceptability. Notably, attitudes of both officials and the people towards corruption have drastically changed . . . What is even worse, corruption has begun to acquire respectability of a sort. It is being hailed as an instrument of efficiency. . . . It has become a way of life. All the same, it signals a perturbing development. For, when an evil becomes acceptable as a good it must ring disturbing bells.' As for the combating strategies, he highlights several policy positions ranging from the 'fatalists' to 'moralists' and to the 'statists.' While the fatalists are pessimists, the moralists plead for the change in the value system, animated value reform campaigns and value planning in education. The statists bank heavily on legal and administrative solutions, suggesting strict anti-corruption legislation, its ruthless enforcement, exemplary punishment to its offenders, strengthening of the vigilance commission, administrative reforms, transparency in administration, measures to determine accountability and incentive pay structure for civil servants. Summing up he says, 'Taken singly, each of the above discussed policy positions is incapable of tackling the problem of corruption. That is so because corruption is multidimensional and an intricately embedded phenomenon that cuts across the polity, economy and society. What is therefore required is a multi-pronged attack on it. As such there is a need for a combined strategy with judicious use of the above referred policies measures implicit in them.'

Another highly challenging issue that forms the theme of the following three chapters is education. While S.S. Mathur takes up the management aspect of education, Kaushik and Bhatnagar discuss, Medical Education and Distance Education respectively. Mathur feels concerned that even though India has made astounding progress in various fields, education and health including, planners, administrators and social scientists are still baffled about how to achieve the cherished goal of making India a truly advanced welfare state in the shortest possible time. It is in this context that they build a management model, the main refrain of which is to effect a change in the mindset of the administrators and planners of education which, in his opinion constitutes the *raison d'etre* of development. How to bring about that change is sought to be achieved through five different directions. The first such direction brings home to all those concerned with education that universal education does not always result in making everyone of the students who attend school becoming functionally literate; that education is not only concerned with the diffusion of information but should be knowledge based and skill oriented; that much of the education depends on the emphasis on common sense rather than on forcing the students to achieve high scores in the memory related tests and examinations; and that good management of teaching-learning depends on watching and listening. The second direction emphasizes sound system for the selection of the personnel for efficient educational management while the third direction relates to the change in the mindset of the management. A manager must be straight and forthright in expressing his views without any fear or favour. The fourth direction calls upon the managers and administrators to help bring about social equity. It is in this context that he refers to the system of reservations for the backward and down-trodden classes in services and in educational institutions and remarks that no doubt this policy has raised the status of so-called schedule and backward castes, but it has benefited only a limited number of the socially neglected classes. Our administrators still of the opinion that by extending reservations to higher percentages and to more classes they will ensure social and economic equity. This mindset needs to be radically changed. Finally, Mathur wishes the educators to adopt a dynamic approach to the educational system so that it may capture the spirit of the new times and adapts itself to the fast changing environments of the country. He emphasizes that we cannot cope with the forces of modern and progressive world with the old notions of our educational system. Much dynamism needs to be shown in winning the battle against repressive and divisive forces. They bolster his thesis with reasoned and highly cogent arguments, drawing support here and there from the learned authorities on the subject, appropriate research articles, government reports and the like.

—

S.P. Kaushik dwells upon the medical aspect of education. The burden of his paper is that if Alma Atta Declaration of 'health for all by the year 2000' has not been achieved, 'quality control of medical personnel remains a core issue in development of health care services in any country and particularly in India.' He explains in detail the various drawbacks that this particular area of medical services suffers from. He begins with the admission of students to the medical colleges and laments that despite clear-cut guidelines about the fairness of admissions on merit basis, 'backdoor entries are made by foul means. This results into a group of students with sub-standard merit.' Mandatory reservation of seats for certain categories of candidates marks the beginning of the dilution of merit and that ultimately tells upon the quality of the finished product. To avoid this situation the state should either provide all kinds of support to the depressed sections of society so that their wards may also be able to compete with the rest of the aspirants on equal footing or it should accord reservation to them only at the entry point and not beyond. Proceeding further, he comes to the merit of the medical faculty upon which depends the quality of the product that an institution turns out. Here too a lot of bungling takes place in their recruitment. Money power, connections, patronage, inbreeding, promotion by seniority, lack of the system of lateral entry at various points are some of the factors that impinge upon the quality of the medical faculty. 'The end result is . . .that if both the faculty and the students don't have the best available merit and healthy work culture, it should be difficult to imagine the quality of outgoing product.' On the top of it we do not provide for any regular system of training programme to both the under-graduate and the post-graduate students or for the in-service personnel. As for the clinical proficiency, patient care and research, our medical institutions have lagged behind in laboratory based and experimental research. Despite the fact that hundreds of research papers are published year after year, yet we could not make any mark on the international front. As for the infra-structural support, the equipment is usually old, outdated and not necessarily in good functional condition. Above all, we do not provide for any dependable system of regulatory control that may monitor from time to time the quality of the medical personnel particularly with regard to their participation in continuing medical education programmes, compulsory audit of one's results, record keeping, ethical monitoring and periodic rectification by competent authorities. He concludes, 'Unless society can ensure that only the best talented students get the opportunity to enter the basic medical and/specialized courses and are trained by the best available faculty, under the best possible support systems and environments, it would not be justifiable to expect better health care delivery and performance.'

Satyavan Bhatnagar lauds the remarkable manner how Distance Education has been sharing the burden of the conventional system in not only providing education to an ever increasing number of students but also in assisting the massive work force to equip itself with newer skills and techniques befitting the requirements of a fast industrializing society. He traces the development of this stream since its inception way back in the sixties of the last century when it had made its debut in the country in the form of the institutes of Correspondence Courses with a view to helping the conventional colleges/universities to absorb the flood of students. He goes over to highlight the problems that it faced at the hands of the conventional educators and how Open Universities stepped in to share the burden of the existing institutes. After having discussed the teething problems of the system, he dwells upon how it has geared itself to cope with the new challenge that the fast emerging industrial society has hurled at it, namely how to train and retrain the huge workforce of the nation in the newer skills and techniques so that it may be possible for the existing personnel to redeploy themselves from one place to another with the added advantage of not displacing them from their desks and workshops. This hidden potential of this stream of education/training has conferred upon it so great an element of respectability that numerous industries and other private institutions have gone in to undertake this job of training and retraining. Commendably, India has of late emerged as a great hub of outsourcing services even in the filed of education through this mode, thereby adding another feather in the cap of Distance Education.

The following three chapters are devoted to yet another vital area of public management, namely the management of the corporate world. S.L. Sharma, Mathurs and S. Vaidya and Arora discuss this issue at great length. Sharma dwells upon the management of change. He feels that though waves of change have always been sweeping the society from time to time, the prevailing wave is remarkably different from the earlier ones. What distinguishes it from the earlier waves is 'the velocity of its causative forces, the rapidity of its pace and the globality of its sweep'. Today every institution is faced with the challenge of change. Those of them that do not adapt themselves with the changing temper of the times are left out of the race. The crux of the matter is how to cope with the change. There are two perspectives, liberal and Marxian. The former aims at 'managing organizational change while the latter seeks to organize the marginalized and alienated sections of society for their empowerment'. Focusing his paper on the management of the organizational change, Sharma dilates upon three major concerns, namely why to change; what to change and how to change. He is of the view that the need to change arises because of the lack of fit between an organization and its surrounding ethos. If the surrounding ethos buzzes with change, how can an organization escape it? If it does not do so, it is bound to lose the race. As for the nature of change, a thorough study of the organization alone can pinpoint the critical area(s) where there is a scope for change. There are four broad areas where change can be required, namely technological, institutional, personnel and cultural. He points out that it may be 'easier for an organization to adopt the latest technology but not the latest philosophy.' Besides new advances in manufacturing technology and managerial philosophy, there have emerged some new social sensibilities, the most important of which is the concern for egalitarianism. Rising concern for environment and ecology is another social sensibility. Yet another is the upsurge of civil sensibility. He emphasizes 'it will help an organization to be in sync with the emerging social sensibilities of our times to incorporate them into its internal milieu.' As for the strategies how to bring about change, Sharma suggests the middle course of 'an inclusive and integrated approach.' Elaborating it, he says, "It is inclusive in that it lays stress on involving all concerned, including the top, the middle and the bottom level functionaries. It is inclusive also in that it puts premium on a shared vision and multilevel communication. It is integrative in that it sets its focus on commencing systemic and attitudinal changes simultaneously. It is integrative also in that it underlines the need for reconciling the corporate commitment with family commitment of the functionaries. Last of all, it is integrative in that it integrates internal marketing with external marketing."

What type of leadership modern organizations require is the issue that S.S. Mathur and Sanjay Mathur discuss in their paper that follows next. They begin with the premise that the conceptual approach to the nature of leadership as well as that of the organization has changed over the time. At one time, the impression was that leaders are born but today the thinking is that leaders are built as per the requirements of the organizations, more specifically as per their social environments in which they function. Correspondingly, with the change of the time a new language of organizations is emerging. Today, organizations are dropping the title of the 'manager' and replacing it with such terms as team leader, project coordinator, leader partner, facilitator, etc. For, organizations are no longer considered as 'arrays of human resources but as communities of individuals.' Quoting Handy, they observe that there are three new concepts that govern organizations today. First, subsidiary, meaning thereby that the higher-level body should not assume responsibility of what could easily be handled by the lower-level units. The duty of the leader is to ensure that the latter are encouraged to exercise the responsibility entrusted to them rather than do it themselves. Second, earned authority, that is the leaders are given time to prove their worth. Third, virtuality, that is organizations are a dispersed lot in the sense that most of the things that they do may be got done very conveniently from outside on contract basis. ' The organization is a box of contracts rather than a home for life for its entire people.' In such a situation, the leader should develop belief in him, passion for his job and love for his people as also for his opposites. He must also bear in mind, first that knowledge is changing very fast, second that today's work is mostly knowledge based and, third that it is imperative on his part that he must adapt his organization from time to time, preferably by unbundling it. 'A good leader delights in changing'. Above all, he must develop emotional intelligence.

The third paper in the series relates to the corporate responsibility towards society, incidentally a hot issue of debate these days in this country. S. Vaidya and Arora discuss it at length, though in its theoretical perspective. Their basic premise is that profit maximization or for that matter wealth maximization is no more the only criterion for evaluating a business. Instead, the interests of the shareholders as also of the others who have a stake in the business need to be duly taken care of. This is what is described as Corporate Social Responsibility. The idea of the corporate social responsibility (CSR) is not new to the corporate world, though different people might have interpreted it differently at different places and under different circumstances. It may or may not have any direct relationship with the economic performance of the corporate entity and there might have been different motivating forces as well. The fact remains that corporates do take CSR initiatives on their own. The current paper is a review of different studies on different aspects of CSR. The primary focus of the paper is on the meaning and the concepts as identified by different authors as also on the research issues in the field of CSR and what drives the business for CSR initiatives.

In his paper that follows next, S.P. Mittal makes a strong case for the conservation of the water resources not only in the country but also in the world as a whole. His argument is that 'a very tiny portion of planet's fresh water is available in lakes, rivers, atmosphere, soil and vegetation.' He further observes that despite long strides in agriculture that we have taken in recent years, no less than 42 per cent of the cultivable area is still rainfed. The irony is that even though we get plenty of rain every year, most of the rainwater runs down the stream. If we make a suitable effort to harvest the run off water, more land can be brought under assured system of irrigation. It is in this context that he relates his experience how rainwater has been effectively harvested in the Shivalik Hills (Punjab) with the help of the earthen dams. It was in the village, Sukhomajri that the maiden experiment of Integrated Watershed Management was conducted way back in year, 1978. An earthen dam, 12 metre high was constructed with a view to storing 5.6 ha m rainwater that earlier flowed down the hilly catchment area of 9.2 hectare. The laudable success of that experiment made the State Government to direct the Departments of Forest, Agriculture and Soil Conservation to go in for the construction of more such dams. Remarkably, within a short period of time, no less than 200 such earthen dams came up in the states of Himachal Pradesh, Haryana and Punjab. The assured supply of irrigated water that these dams provided gave a big boost not only to the production of the conventional crops like wheat and *bajra* but also encouraged the farmers to proliferate their cultivation to such fodder crops as *barseem* that in turn made them step into the realm of the dairy industry. It is interesting to note that the production of milk marked a four-fold increase in a very short period of time. It hardly needs to be emphasized that these dams by themselves would not have paid such rich dividends had their management not been entrusted to the communities that were benefited from them. It is the participatory management of the government and the people that enhanced the utility of these water resources. For, once the beneficiaries are given a feel of collective management, they could realize their true importance of such valuable assets of the community. But to involve them in such a venture is not an easy task. They had to be convinced of vast potential, hidden in them. To achieve that objective it was further essential that complete transparency was maintained right from the stage of their conception and construction to that of their management. Only then they would feel attracted to them and lend their due cooperation. Credit goes to the departments concerned that that after having built these dams they passed on their management to the water-users' societies, called the Hill Resource Management Society. Thus we find that these earthen dams have changed the very face of the hill terrain that hitherto suffered the chronic problem of soil erosion and utter poverty of the people. Today, the whole pattern of their life is totally revolutionized.

1

INDIAN POLITICAL SYSTEM AT THE DAWN OF THE TWENTY-FIRST CENTURY

Satyavan Bhatnagar

I

The state constitutes the largest laboratory of public management. If the state is politically stable, its public policy is progressive, its economy is robust and, above all it keeps its doors and windows open for the refreshing gustoes of new ideas and thoughts that sweep the minds of the people as also its institutional fabric, the atmosphere of freedom and progress that it would thus generate ensure sound management of all institutions that function within its domain. For, it is the overarching role of the state as also the free play of the various human forces and factors that provide the wherewithal to sound public management. As for India, we have been striving hard ever since the dawn of Independence to provide to the nation an institutional arrangement, based on sound public management so that we may ensure for the incoming generations a healthy atmosphere of freedom and progress. Happily, that sustained effort has begun to bear fruits as we find all around us. In the sections to follow we narrate the long story how we wove, step by step the new institutional fabric, based on sound principles of democracy, development and public management and also the challenges we are still face to face and how we propose to overcome them.

II

Way back when we implanted democracy in India, many an eyebrow was raised. Those opposed to the decision did have a point of view and perhaps quite a potent one. They were of the opinion that any form of government where people have a role to play can never hope to be successful unless the general lot of the population is socially cohesive, economically reasonably well-off and politically articulate. But in our case, all these pre-requisites werer sadly missing. Obviously, the apprehension of those opposed in this view was thus quite justified. But at the same time it was also true that democracy alone provided that institutional arrangement as could help us realize our long cherished dreams of a progressive and developed society, marching shoulder to shoulder with other advanced nations of the world. We could not, therefore afford to wait for the conditions to ripe, instead we had to take a calculated risk, as our visionary constitution-fathers very justifiably did and went whole hog for democracy. We adopted it not only as a form of government but also as a way of life.

However, this decision was too tall for us, the reason being that the socio-economic infrastructure required for the success of democracy, as alluded above was practically non-existent in this country. Rampant illiteracy, utter backwardness and deep-rooted conservatism that our masses suffered from were too inimical to ensure its proper growth. But determined as we were to make this experiment a success, we went in, to begin with, for adult franchise, keeping all suggestions to the contrary at bay. To facilitate the task of the bulk of our electorate that was not in a position even to decipher the names of the persons, offering their candidature at the polls, we devised the novel system of providing election symbols to the latter. Having taken such preparatory steps, we conducted the first-ever general election both for Parliament and State Legislatures (1951-52), a massive exercise indeed, having never been gone through on such a large scale any where in the length and breadth of the globe. Though some of the stray accounts of the electoral conduct of the poor illiterate voters were quite funny, the enthusiasm that the rank and file of the populace evinced in that exercise was unparallel in the annals of the world history.

That resounding success notwithstanding, the fact still remained that our society suffered from numerous handicaps that demanded our attention on top priority basis. The most important among them was the highly stratified nature of our society. The lower rungs of it comprised vast number of such people as were not only poor, illiterate, ignorant and conservative but also suffered from myriad types of discrimination at the hands of their well-off and better-placed brethren. Those sections were yet to be pulled up and brought into the mainstream of articulate citizenship. Realizing their miserable plight, we chose to concentrate most of our development effort on them so that they too could come at par with their better-off brethren and compete against them on equal footing in every walk of life. Taking a holistic view of the situation the strategy that we worked out comprised, *inter alia* (a) mass-scale schooling that helped their future generations to become articulate citizens; (b) due protection to their socio-economic interests through such measures as weighted representation in the elected decision-making councils and reservation of a certain percentage of vacancies/seats in every avenue of employment and educational institution; (c) alleviation of poverty by providing them employment through the above mentioned out-of-the-way reservation quota, varied types of direct as well as indirect financial assistance and, above all provision for multi-pronged subsidies for foodstuffs, agricultural inputs, energy and the like; and (d) democratic decentralization, with a view to involving the mass citizenry in the decision-making apparatus of the nation, through the agency of the gram panchayats and other sub-district level democratic institutions. These varied measures were taken with the hope that in due course of time these sections would cease to be handicapped both socially or economically and thus come up to the level where the traditionally well-off had perched themselves for centuries.

Today, we find that even though some of these measures might not have achieved the desired degree of success, the fact remains that we have almost attained the goal. For what we find today is that the masses are no longer that much illiterate, ignorant or even conservative as they once used to be. They are far more articulate, politically enlightened and even economically better off. Ever escalating political graph of public opinion bears witness to this development.

Ardent consciousness that these sections of society have developed over the years with regard to their interests and to the importance of their numerical strength that all of them (*Dalits*, backward castes, tribal and the like), combined together possess, has made them gather a sizeable socio-political moss. (If today caste has become a very potent political factor in India to the chagrin of many of us, it is precisely for the reason that it provides a handy forum for these sections in particular to assert themselves, both socially and politically.) Whenever and wherever they find their interests being side-tracked, they get worked up and come out on the streets. That speaks for the rising tide of protests, *dharnas*, demonstrations and the like. Their fast growing might has left hardly an aspect of life that might have escaped the impact of this rising force. In politics, no political party can ever hope to have a stake in a legislature unless it negotiates space with them. (Sainth, P. 161) In civil services too they have got their share reserved, merit or no merit. Earlier, this out-of-the-way favour was shown to them at the entry point. But the recently enacted Eighty-fifth Constitutional Amendment has extended this benefit to the higher cadres as well. It would not be a surprise that some day (not very far) when they may coerce even the private enterprise to show some accommodation for them.

Thus, the balance of power seems to be shifting in their favour very fast. This is manifest in the way the things that were considered to be impossible a few decades back are now being made possible. To quote one recent instance. Way back in the fifties and sixties of the last century, large tracts of land were acquired in various parts of the country for purposes of establishing public institutions such as hydel projects, steel mills and the like. In the process, hundreds of farmers were thrown on the wayside. Nobody bothered for them. As a result they had to suffer silently unknown misery for decades. Now when they have become conscious of their interests, they would not take the things lying down. They are very much up and doing. The other day a chunk of them, belonging to the Jharkhand-Orissa belt on whose land the Bhilai Steel Plant had been erected came out on the streets, demanding due compensation with retrospective effect. At one stage, their agitation took an ugly turn, forcing the police to open fire on them, resulting in the death of thirteen protesters. Everyone who mattered in decision-making stood on his toe. *(The Tribune,* Chandigarh. 13 January 2006). Not only did that particular section of the oustees succeed in getting their due but they also showed a way for the others. In due course of time, this agitation snowballed into a country-wide movement, clamouring for adequate compensation to all such persons whose lands are acquired for any purpose, whatsoever. It was in the wake of this movement that ugly situation was created at Sigur and Nandigram (West Bengal) towards the close of the year 2006. The ferocity of the agitation and the manner how various political parties vied with one another to extend their patronage to this newly emerging constituency have put a question mark on the fate of not only the Special Economic Zones (SEZ) but also on the larger issue of industrialization. As a result, active thinking is under way to find out how to balance suitably the interests of the farmers whose lands are acquired, on the one hand and to maintain the tempo of industrialization, on the other. Another equally relevant issue that may be referred to in this context is that of the reservation of quota for these sections in the higher cadres of the various civil services as also in the higher educational institutions. They had been pressing this demand again for the last few decades. But it remained a cry in wilderness. Now when they have gathered a clout in the decision-making apparatus of the state, they have got this demand too conceded with a spirit of vengeance.

III

All this may be true, yet it is also a fact that our public life has come in recent years to be highly infested with such social evils as corruption, murder, loot, deceit, debauchery, strife, violence and the like. Justice appears to be highly elusive and the government servants (police and judicial officers being no exception) care two hoots for the common man. Everyone is busy fostering his own nest one way or the other. It has become a game, free for all. This state of affairs poses a big challenge to the nation today

None of these facts can be disputed, much less refuted. However, a counter question may legitimately be posed, namely what has pushed us to such an impasse? We have been one of the oldest peoples of the world, tracing our origin back to antiquity. Why has a crisis of such a magnitude overtaken us at this particular juncture of history? This issue does not seem to have been examined in depth. To me it appears that all these ills have been the natural by-product of the twin-process of development and democracy that has emboldened every thinking person (even a mediocre) to reason and question the rationale of every decision. If we were not pushed to such a miserable state earlier it is precisely for the reason that never before in history had such an experiment of the Himalayan size had ever been conducted in this country. When a mass of people as fantastic in strength as one billion embarks upon their historic journey towards political development and modernity some degree of tumult and turmoil is but natural and especially so when they have chosen to tread the democratic path. Interestingly, the type and extent of the socio-economic turbulence or political instability that we have had to face in the course of this *'samudra manthan*" (the process of this social churning) is far less in comparison to what Europe of yesterday or China of today had to undergo.

The happier aspect is that these ugly developments have not shaken our confidence in democracy (unlike what we witness elsewhere in the developing world). All this speaks for the manner how we have nursed this nascent plant over the years. Today, we can confidently vouchsafe that we have arrived at a stage when this system can take due care of the ills that we suffer from not only at this juncture of history but also in future. As mentioned earlier, the growing pressure of the public opinion would act as a great bulwark against them. There are certain positive developments that lend credence to our optimism in this regard.

At the outset we may refer to the Right to Information. Interestingly, many an olden democracy of the West has not so far conceded this privilege to their citizens. One of its direct fall-outs will be that it would make the governing process more and more transparent and that in turn would further reinforce people's faith in democracy. To dilate, until recently decision-making was the guarded privilege of a handful of the moneyed and the highly educated elite. They would take decisions behind the heavily curtained doors of their offices and the bureaucracy would not let any body peep behind them. The hoax of secrecy and sanctity, mischievously devised by them helped them exploit the common man. Today, this Right has given the final burial to whatever little of secrecy that had been left shrouded in decision-making, rendering the whole process completely transparent. Nothing can now be kept away from the gaze of the public. However, the full potential of this Right shall be known only when every Tom, Dick and Harry will begin to ask for information about the various decisions and how those decisions have been implemented and if not implemented, then why. It would make it difficult for those charged with that responsibility to save their skin. The *babus* have already begun to feel the heat of this development, as is evident in their game of creating one hurdle after another to obstruct its smooth implementation. But the day seems to have passed when such dirty tactics of theirs would be able to curb the growing spirit of democracy

Computer technology that has recently been introduced in the administrative structure and processes is another case in point. It would further drive a nail into the high-handedness of the *babus*. (Jagmohan. p. 44). We are already a witness to the fact that wherever computers have been introduced, not only the delivery of governmental services has become more efficient but also the administrative processes have become less cumbersome and simpler. The too unduly large role of the *babus* has also been dented to a great extent. Happily, a countrywide massive campaign has been initiated to induct this technology in all government offices.

Attention may also be drawn to the efforts that have of late been under way to strengthen the Panchayati Raj Institutions. Ever since these have come into being way back in the mid-fifties of the last century, both the Union and the State Governments had not looked kindly to them. Even though the 73rd Amendment to the Constitution has called upon the latter in particular to invest in them the powers of local governance both in letter and spirit and that they should curtail their interference in their working to the bare minimum. But all these pleas had so far fallen on deaf ears. However, of late things appear to have changed. More and more powers are being decentralized to them and a serious effort is also under way to make them function more effectively. Again, the driving force behind this move can justifiably be attributed to the increasing pressure of public opinion from the grass roots. The newly elected members of the Panchayati Raj Institutions, bubbling with enthusiasm as they have been, are impatient to play the role assigned to them by their electorate. They are more than duly conscious of the functions and powers that have been assigned to them by the Constitution and other statutes and if any one of these is withheld from them, they would spare no effort to wrest it from the higher authorities, may they be the political elite or the bureaucracy. They brook no interference from them.

In the context of these developments we may raise the issue even at the cost of repetition, as to why have so many scams have of late been coming to light? Have these been committed only yesterday and is it because people have become so dishonest just overnight? Were their immediate predecessors more honest than them? Neither of these conjectures appears to be true. The fact is that most of these scams, if not all of them have been the legacy of the past. It is only today when public with zealous exercise of its democratic rights, has become so vocal and the public life, correspondingly more transparent that it has become difficult to hide them any longer. Somewhere some weak link in the chain of the scam masters does give way before the pressure of the public opinion. If that were so, the day does not appear to be far when we would get them duly punished (today we could unearth the scams but not take the scam masters to the gallows), thereby restoring the long lost fear of the law.

The fast growing pressure of public opinion, especially when it emanates from all the diverse sections of the citizenry, would ensure that the interests of the common man are no longer jeopardized. It is but obvious that as more and more people get enlightened about the role that they can play in public life, the more cautious would be the conduct of the powers that be. Such institutions as Judiciary, Election Commission, Parliament and State Legislatures, etc that have been entrusted with the onerous task of safeguarding the interests of the people will be more vigilant of their responsibility and would function with greater vigour.

IV

To come to the causes of social degeneration, we are of the firm view that it can justifiably be attributed (though we may not rule out the other possibilities also) to what we describe as the phenomenon of 'over-government', implying that the state plays much larger role than what can justifiably be assigned to it. How this phenomenon crept into our political system and how it became all-pervasive makes an interesting account. Way back when in the early years of the Independence the nation was haunted by acute scarcity of goods and services (foisted on us partly by World War II and partly by the Partition of the country) we were left with no other option but to entrust the state with the responsibility of managing the procurement and distribution of essential goods. Once initiated into that new sphere, the state went on enlarging the scope of its activities with unabated speed. In due course when the development process went into strides, it assumed the bigger responsibility to plan and execute the various new programmes of socio-economic reconstruction, thereby adding yet another dimension to its functioning. However, that development was not something of an unusual phenomenon as it may sound to us today, for the then world, saturated as it was with the Marxian ideology postulated the state to play such a massive role. Pandit Jawahar Lall Nehru (then at the helm of affairs), himself being an ardent votary of that ideology, put the state zealously at the center-stage, entrusting it with all types of responsibilities. The regimes that followed further lent weight to the policy of state control, ultimately pushing the country to a situation where the state had to handle every conceivable human activity, ranging from education to employment, from the weaving of *khadi* to the manufacturing of steel, from the provision of energy to the sale of foodstuffs, from local transport to civil aviation. The state thus having arrogated to itself the right of the common man to feather his needs himself, unleashed the dangerous cult of '*mai baap*', thereby robbing him of his instinct of hard work and making him utterly dependent on the government.

Another dangerous corollary of that development was that the ever-expanding sphere of the government paved the way for the participation (nay, meddlesomeness) of the legislators and other politicians in the process of governance. The massive recruitment of thousands of workers required to man the various operations of social reconstruction that the government had to go in for, opened the door ajar for them. They saw in it an excellent opportunity to sneak their way into it. To facilitate their task, they aligned with them, to begin with the higher rungs of bureaucracy. Combined together, both of them inducted hundreds of their 'men' and 'women' into the government service and extended to them full protection against any type of disciplinary action that might be proposed against them. Thus pampered, the *babus* turned into an indisciplined lot, haughty and arrogant. Having taken into their head that they are not accountable to anyone, they would freely and fearlessly hoodwink the common man under the garb of highly complicated and cumbersome office procedures (that too is their deliberate manipulation), ultimately turning the government offices into dens of corruption. (Arun Shorie. pp. 25-42). Today, the situation has deteriorated to such an extent that if the government moots any reform in the system, the *babus* feel highly perturbed and oppose the move tooth and nail. (An inside account of the story how far the *babus* can go in defence of their cause has most aptly been portrayed by none other than the former Minister for Disinvestments, Arun Shorie in his recent book, '*Governance and the sclerosis that has set in.*' pp. 24-42). We may also cite the manner how the employees of the Airport Authority of India tried to obstruct the process of privatization of the Delhi and Mumbai airports. If some of the ambitious programmes in this direction have fallen by the wayside, it is this unhealthy coalition of the *babus* and the politicians that is solely responsible for this disruption.

Yet another fall-out of that development was that that duo of the politicians and the bureaucracy has made themselves, as hinted above indispensable for the common man. He cannot live without their assistance, nay without their patronage. He requires their help and assistance at every step of his day-to-day living. Until recently, he required their *sifarish* (recommendatory letter) to obtain food permits, gas and telephone connection, a two/four wheeler and so on and so forth. Though that situation has improved to a great extent (courtesy the private sector), he has not yet been fully delivered from their clutches. Even today he needs their support to meet such of his vital needs as driving licence, housing plot, construction loan, admission in some government educational institution, and above all employment in some government office and equally important a posting to his convenience. The upshot of their indispensability lies in his seeking their help whenever he is involved, inadvertently or willfully in any illegal activity. It is an open secret that those who are closer to them freely indulge in such activities with one ulterior motive or the other. For, they know (nay, they are cock sure) that a word from their 'mentors' to the officer concerned would be sufficient to get them exonerated of the offence, howsoever serious it might be. These 'unholy' acts of the politicians/legislators in general and their capacity to rescue their well-wishers in particular have further magnified their image as the true benefactors of the people. On their part, they take pleasure and feel proud of doing so. Unfortunately, their involvement in these activities has of late become so prominent and so much engrossing for them that most of the legislators do not pay much heed to their primary sphere of duty, namely law-making. That explains the twin trend of cutting out their participation in the deliberations of the legislative body to which they have been elected as honourable members and of the constantly shortening span of the legislative sessions.

This type of conduct of the legislators provides encouragement (nay, instigation) to many an unsocial element to freely indulge in unlawful activities. This speaks for the reason why the clever guys take pains to cultivate the legislators as well as the *babus* and one of the strategies that they generally employ is that when the election to Parliament/State Legislature draws at hand they work hard day and night, leaving no stone unturned to ensure the victory of the candidate of their choice. Once he is elected, they get rest assured that nothing untoward would ever happen to them and if somehow they were involved in some trouble, their 'benefactor' would get them released 'honourably'. How aptly *The Hindustan Times* remarks in one of its editorials, "If there is a single incentive in this country for anyone to yearn for political connections, it is to protect oneself from the law if and when required." (23 February 2006) Placed in such an 'eminent' position as the legislators are, it would be more appropriate to describe them as 'patrons', for they are the only ones who come to our rescue in times of need. Conversely, what use is the patron otherwise? (Dipankar Gupta. p. 95) Would it not be safe to conclude that under this given situation if one objectively tries to go into the depth of any of the social ills one may not be surprised if one stumbles at its root against either a politician or a bureaucrat? If these so-called high-ups were properly tamed, many of the social ills that have debased the standards of our public life would be taken care of.

All these negative fall-outs of the phenomenon of the over-government make it highly imperative that this phenomenon may be suitably curbed at the earliest. For, we tend to agree with MacIver who very aptly remarks, "We do not sharpen pencils with an axe". (MacIver. *The Modern State*. P.149). The role of the state therefore need be drastically cut down to the bare minimum. Many of the functions that the state performs today (as, for instance the establishment and maintenance of the public sector undertakings; purchase, sale and the distribution of the food grains; production, transmission and distribution of energy; shipping, road transport, civil aviation; higher education; specialized health services and many more such things) can be conveniently passed on to the private sector. The market forces can take care of them suitably. As for the interests of the economically handicapped persons, these can be protected by providing to them financial aid, bank loans, subsidies and the like.

In the same manner, the management of some of the services and institutions that would still remain vested with the State and the Union Governments can be decentralized to the local governing authorities, such as the municipal corporations/boards and the Panchayati Raj Institutions. The current system of the concentration of all aspects of governance in the hands of the higher tiers of the government has also been responsible to a very great extent for the present dismal state of affairs. Though loud claims are made day in and day out that an ambitious process of the decentralization of power and policy-making to the sub-district level institutions has been under way. No denying that some serious efforts are being made but sadly these are far from being substantial. For, what they are engaged in is the strengthening of the local finance and the gearing up of such services as roads, transport and tele-communication; expansion of the educational and the health services and the like. These efforts would certainly go a long way in improving the quality of life in the countryside but the cherished goal of decentralization of authority would remain a distant dream. Only recently, the Union Minister for Panchayati Raj, Shri. Mani Shankar Aiyyar made an open confession in a public gathering at Bhatinda (Punjab) that these institutions have become a paradise for the bureaucracy and that little was being done to invest them with the true spirit of democracy. (*The Tribune*, Chandigarh. 26 and 27 April 2006). Crux of the matters lies in the power of decision-making. So long as it is not decentralized to these institutions both in letter and spirit, the local populace will not have a feel of self-governance nor will it develop a sense of involvement in the larger process of governance of the country. But unfortunately this is a suggestion that is too unpalatable to both the higher-level politicians and the superior bureaucracy, the reason being that it would divest both of them of the vast patronage and powers that they presently enjoy by virtue of their being the dispenser of an endless variety of services and benefits to the people at the grassroots. That would mean a big setback to them because they would then be no longer in a position to project themselves as the *'mai baap'* of the lay masses.

Once the phenomenon of over-government is suitably curbed, our public life would get cleansed to a very great extent. When most of the day-to-day needs of the common man are catered to by the market or are met by the local leaders, the common man would no longer require the assistance, much less the patronage of either the politicians or of the bureaucracy that, in turn would clip their presently long fluttering wings. Not only would it clear much of the mess from our public life but our administrative structure and processes too would get streamlined. The *babus* who have developed a cheek to defy their superiors because of the over-arching hand of their 'political patrons', would not be able to do so any longer and would thus attend to their duties more seriously.

The curbing of the phenomenon of over-government, in the second place would, incidentally, take away much of the shine of the coveted membership of the legislatures, for in the new reformed set-up they would no longer enjoy the patronage and host of other benefits, attendant thereon. Corruption would then get a serious jolt. More so for the reason that not many people and especially those whom lure of money and patronage (and not the motive of social service) throws them in the electoral fray would offer their candidature at the hustings. Only the serious ones, those who are genuinely interested in assisting the law-making process would come forward to contest the elections. Incidentally, the reduction of their number would further have a bearing on the heavy expenditure that the candidates incur in order to win elections. Both these developments would be quite healthy in so far as the toning up of the health of our public life is concerned. Above all, the unhealthy coalition of the politicians, the bureaucracy and the musclemen that constitute the main source from where corruption emanates today, would also wear out. When the first two are made to lose the lustre and the importance of their office, the third would automatically get redundant.

When public sector undertakings would stand abolished (one of the main objectives of the reformatory process), the state would cease to dole out millions of rupees that are presently spent year after year for meeting the deficit on account of their malfunctioning. This would be the third main advantage that would accrue from the curbing of this phenomenon of 'over-government'. It is no longer a secret that the payback of the huge deficit incurred on the maintenance of these undertakings has become a perpetual headache for the Union as well as the State Governments. The long awaited relief that would thus be made available to them would go a long way in liquidating the heavily piled up debt on this account.

Happily, the whole gamut of these problems has of late become a matter of serious concern for the government. Already steps have been taken to wind up some of the public sector undertakings. Hopefully, the process would acquire greater momentum in the days to come, the opposition of the Leftist forces notwithstanding. As for the administrative reforms, these too have been engaging the attention of the Union Government and especially of the Prime Minister, Dr. Manmohan Singh. It is at his initiative and direction that an Administrative Reforms Commission has of late been constituted to give a comprehensive look to the whole situation. Let us hope that it takes care of most of these issues.

The most important development in this context is that there has of late been a widespread feeling among all the saner sections of the public opinion - the academicians, the administrators and the politicians that the additional flab that the governmental set-up at all levels has gathered over the years needs to be cut down drastically. In democracy, nothing works faster than the ideas. "Voice', emphasizes Amartya Sen, "is a critical component of the pursuit of social justice." (*Argumentative Indian.* p. xiii). To begin with, a few individuals conceive and give expression to some new ideas. By and by, these ideas gather momentum, gradually reaching a stage when a concrete shape is given to them in the form of legislative proposals that ultimately get into the statute book. There have been scores of cases when some of the most irritating developments have been taken care that way. By way of an illustration, we may refer, first to the problem of defection (*aya rams* and *gaya rams*) that at one stage had assumed so dangerous proportions that the State Governments had begun to change hands just over night, destabilizing the whole governing process of the country. The second important issue that was taken care related to the volume of the ministries. Their size not only at the state level but also at the Union level had of late become too large to be either financially sustained or administratively justified. The chief ministers were coerced to appoint every second member of the legislature as their ministers. Yet another issue that was forced to be tackled under the pressure of the public opinion is the reckless construction of houses and shopping complexes on public land by the unscrupulous elements in collusion with the corrupt officials. Nobody would ever bother whereas the common man had been left as an idle spectator of that development. All these three problems when acquired dangerous proportions were suitably taken care of. *Thus, we find that it is only in democracy where people when develop political consciousness, mount pressure on decision-makers and it becomes difficult for the latter to defy it. Things must take their normal course.* Happily, as Amartya Sen (to quote him again) rightly points out, "In a limited way, public voice has already begun to show its effectiveness." (p. 37). One can very optimistically remark that if affairs of such a serious nature have been taken care of, we are sure that all other social ills, as referred to above would also be suitably managed. It is only a question of time. Let this optimism not wear out.

V

However, we are got to be vigilant with regard to certain issues that stare at us with so dangerous postures. One of them pertains to the development of those facilities that contribute to good and enlightened citizenship. As we ought to be conscious that time has come for the fructification of all those hard efforts that we have been consistently putting in over the years to induct the hitherto left out masses into the mainstream of articulate citizenship. Before they swell the mainstream by their numbers and choke its smooth flow, we must ensure that we make an adequate provision for such amenities as education, health, employment and the like that they will frantically look forward to. Unless suitable policy measures in this direction are adopted and implemented in time, they would feel frustrated and it will not be astonishing if their frustration precipitates into ugly situation. There is a greater possibility of their treading that path, the reason being that the normal grievance-redressal machinery as constituted under the law appears to have lost its older thrust and efficiency.

The judiciary that constitutes the kingpin of that machinery has unfortunately been caught in a strange paradoxical situation. While on the one hand, its wheels are clogged in the quagmire of the long circuitous judicial rules and procedures, on the other the pressure on it has been constantly mounting up. As a result, it is no longer in a position to deliver justice to the common man as efficiently as is expected of it. However, there is no denying that its role in taking care of the macro level major issues has been quite commendable. In fact, judiciary alone provides a bulwark against the high-handedness of the executive wing of the government. Ironically however, these issues are too big to bother the common man, the reason being that they do not provide any succour to him from his day-to-day problems. What concerns him most is how efficiently his various daily needs are met? What type of treatment is meted out to him when he visits a government office in connection with one of his problems or another, how speedily the local police post registers his FIR or how promptly the courts dispose of his civil and criminal petitions? These and many such issues provide to him the barometer to judge the efficacy of the political system. But unfortunately, the performance of the system on this account has somehow been far from satisfactory, with the result that he takes a very dim view of the governmental apparatus of the state. An empirical survey conducted by the *Hindustan Times* in the context of the court judgment in the Jasicalal murder case, revealed that only 2.7 per cent of the respondents had faith in the law enforcement machinery of the state. (*The Hindustan Times*. 26 February 2006). Prof. Madhva Menon aptly remarks, "With an escalating figure of violent crimes, accumulating arrears of 30 million cases, a conviction rate of less than 10 per hundred prosecutions and a higher level of corruption in the processing of crimes, the system or whatever is left of it, presents a pathetic picture of frustration, helplessness and anger among the people." (Quoted by Jagmohan. p.145). If timely steps are not taken to arrest the erosion of the confidence of the people in the state machinery, there is all the possibility of the common man developing a sense of alienation from the system at large. *This is too serious an issue to be pondered over by every thinking mind of the country in general and by the decision-makers at all levels in particular.*

As for the present situation with regard to the basic needs of the common man, we find that these are utterly inadequate in so far as their present requirement is concerned. And if we take into consideration the way our population is exploding day by day and the manner how their aspirations and expectations are escalating, the situation becomes all the more grim. This warrants us to redouble our efforts in this direction.

A couple of years ago, the Planning Commission, Government of India had constituted a committee on INDIA VISION, 2020. The report that it submitted recently provides meaningful glimpses of the present inadequacies on these accounts. The relevant excerpts of some of their findings may be reproduced, as under:

Education: "India's education system has expanded exponentially over the past five decades, but its current achievements are grossly inadequate for the nation to realize its potential. The net enrollment rate in primary schools is around 77 per cent and in secondary schools it is around 69 per cent . . . . The drop-out rate was 40 per cent at the primary level and 55 per cent at the upper primary level in 1999-2000. These high drop-out rates from both primary and secondary school, combined with low enrollment rates at the higher levels deprive tens of millions of children of their full rights as citizens. Out of approximately 200 million children in the age group of 6-14 years, only 120 million are in schools and net attendance in the primary level is only 66 per cent of the enrollment. Further, less than 7 per cent of the children ever pass the 10th standard public examination." (P.81)

Health: "India's significant achievement in the field of health have been made possible by the establishment of a huge rural health infrastructure, along with the formation of a master health care manpower consisting of over five lakh trained doctors working under plural systems of medicine, and a vast frontline of over seven lakh nurses and other health care workers; 25,000 primary and community health care centers; and 1.6 lakh sub-centres, complemented by 22,000 dispensaries and 2,800 hospitals practicing Indian systems of medicine and homeopathy. *This infra-structure remains under-equipped, under-manned and under-financed to cope with the challenge of eradicating major threats to human life*. (Emphasis added).

" The inadequacy of the current health care system is starkly illustrated by the fact that only 35 per cent of the population have access to essential drugs. . . . Infant immunization against measles and DPT for children under 12 years is only 60 per cent and 78 per cent. . . ." (P.93)

Employment: "India's labour force has reached 375 millions approximately in 2002. . . . Projections based on these parameters indicate that India's labour force will expand by 7 to 8.5 million per year during the first decade of this country, and will increase by a total of about 160-170 million by 2020, i.e. 2.4 per cent per annum.

"Total unemployment in India has been estimated to be about 35 million people in 2002. . . . (P.71) A clear consensus in now emerging that major changes in economic policy and strategy will be needed to meet the country's employment needs. . . . (P. 72) Achieving full employment would require a reorientation of national priorities, technology policy and government action." (P. 73)

These stark realities appear to have driven the present UPA government to a bold initiative to tackle these pressing problems. The few measures that it has adopted in that direction include, *inter alia,* the National Rural Employment Guarantee Programme (that seeks to guarantee a minimum of 100 days of employment to at least one member of each rural-based family); the Bharat Nirman Programme (that proposes to make a thrust in infra-structure exclusively of the rural areas, for power, roads, irrigation, tele-communication, housing and drinking water), the Rural Health Mission and Jawaharlal Nehru Urban Renewal Mission, etc. All these schemes are undoubtedly ambitious and laudable. Hopefully, these may also be implemented with an element of sincerity. But the obvious roadblocks that these are bound to hit may denude them of much of the optimism with which these have been conceived and launched. Two such serious obstacles are, first the bureaucratic lethargy and, second the reckless pilferage of funds from the pipeline. The latter too is the handiwork of the *babus* (the connivance, nay the active participation of the politicians cannot be ruled out by any means). In this context, a reference may justifiably be made to the well-known lamenting remark, made by the late Prime Minister Rajiv Gandhi to the effect that hardly 15 paise out of a rupee reach the end-beneficiary of any project that the government charts out for his welfare. The position since then must have deteriorated rather than improved. It handly needs to be emphasisad that earlier too a number of governments had chalked out such ambitious plans and programmes but with little success, obviously for the same reasons. It is therefore imperative that we must fine-tune the implementation machinery. Unless we do so, there is the danger that these measures too may flop and herein lies a big challenge to the UPA Government.

Attention may also be drawn to the paradigm shift that has taken place in recent years, making knowledge the be-end and the be-all of the whole social set-up. Knowledge has so attuned every aspect of our life that it has rendered our basic living difficult without acquiring it. Conversely, those who are not suitably equipped with the proper knowledge of the field concerned, cannot seek entry into it, much less making a mark therein. In other words, there would be no room for the uneducated or even the under-educated, not to speak of the illiterate ones. We must, therefore heed the writing on the wall that only the duly qualified persons alone can hope to be suitably employed. The others will have nothing but frustration in their way.

This paradigm shift appears to have rendered the constitutional provision that every child between the age of 6 and 14 years must be given education on free and compulsory basis too inadequate, qualitatively to meet even the bare minimum requirements of the day. The world has gone far ahead. The government shall have to extend this limit to the senior secondary (10+ 2) level and make a provision for imparting that much education to every child on free and compulsory basis. Unless it does so, there is very bleak future both for our young men and young women and for the country at large. Equally urgent is that the state shall have to accomplish this goal as early as possible because we are running short of time. This constitutes another big challenge to the political system. It also needs to be borne in mind that today we do not have adequate number of schools to provide education to all our incoming generations of the children, especially in the rural areas and in still lesser number are the technical institutions so as to cater to the needs of all the aspirants that swell the ranks of the job seekers day by day. More serious, the number of the quality institutions is still far less. The situation thus appears to be too disheartening. But we are sure that we have the capability as well as the requisite degree of the political will to achieve these targets also.

VI

Another source of deep concern is the distortions that have crept into the process of democracy building. There are two aspects of democracy, conceptual and operational. At the conceptual plane, democracy postulates perfect equality among the citizens and that the whole governing apparatus of the country should function at the behest of the people, through the instrumentality of a constitutional government. At the operational plane, this form of government presupposes the existence of certain rules and regulations (for that matter this is true of every other form of government) and that every person, irrespective of the fact whether he is a functionary of the government or an ordinary citizen should be equally and uniformly amenable to these regulations. The latter postulates, what is commonly described as the rule of law, is the hallmark of this form of government. As for us, while we have owned and adopted the former so zealously, we have blatantly refused even to recognize the latter.

To elaborate, the only meaning that we, Indians could derive from democracy is that it implies an end to all types of social stratification, economic disparities and political discrimination, thereby putting all the citizens on an equal pedestal. In the flush of our enthusiasm to set up democracy we forgot to put due emphasis on one of its vital requirements that where it provides to the common man liberty and justice, it also binds him to certain rules and restraints that help others to enjoy the fruits democracy in an equal measure. (Laski, Harold.) Instead, we threw all types of norms of discipline to the winds. In the initial stages of our Independence we did, however care to give due respect to rules and regulations and conducted ourselves with an element of dignity and restraint. But unfortunately, things have deteriorated over the years, more specifically since the mid-sixties. There has taken place a serious erosion of our sense of law-abidingness that, in turn has pushed us into the presently horrible state of affairs.

Once again the villain of this show was none other than the politician and more specifically the elected members of the State Legislatures. It has been widely observed that once a person is elected to any of these coveted forums of supremacy, he takes into his head that he is above the law of the land and is not answerable to anyone. (Sunil Khilnani. pp.114-15). Whatever he may do, right or wrong, is justified and nobody can have the cheek to question his conduct. Obviously, such a headstrong attitude would make him care two hoots for rules and regulations. He would violate them him self but would also encourage others as pointed an earlier, is do so. Unfortunately, our values have so much debased that what society until recently looked down upon has acquired an element of legitimacy. Those who broke the law were hated and condemned, today they are adorned and respected.

The net result of this sad development is that not only the respect for the law has worn away but there have also emerged two different sets of rules of behaviour (if not of the law), one for the ordinary man and one for those who are either the decision-makers themselves or enjoy their patronage. That is the reason why the police personnel or even the judicial officers shirk taking cognizance of the offences of the latter. This is borne by the fact that over the years so many ministers and bureaucrats have been found involved in so many different types of scandals and scams and have also been proceeded against, yet very few have been convicted. Once some one is caught, he is proceeded against in the court, making bold headlines in the newspapers. After a few initial hearings, the case dies a natural death. On the contrary, if some poor, hapless person is involved in some offence, he is 'put to the gallows' without the loss of any time. Writing in the context of the court judgment in the well-known Jassicalal murder case, a political commentator puts it so ironically, "We are a strange country. We punish the poor. We rescue the rich." ('Justice Murdered'. *The Hindustan Times*. 23 February 2006) In other words, the rule of law, the cardinal principle of democracy has fallen victim to this rot. *When would the 'biggies' be made to obey the basic tenets of democracy and when would the rule of law is restored in this country constitutes another very big challenge to our political system?*

VII

Yet another shortcoming of our democracy-building process is that it has thus far remained confined only to the governmental structures and processes. It could not somehow percolate down to the level of the political culture with the result that while we could democratize our governmental structure we could not adopt democracy as a way of life. One of our highly cherished national goals thus failed to be achieved. The traditional, socially-ordained *jee hazuri (jholi-chuk)* culture not only remained intact but has also come to be further reinforced over the years and it is true of the old pecking order as well. Those placed junior to somebody are always on their toe to keep their superior constantly in good humour, no matter what cost they have to bear for it. Such a situation is not confined only to the lowlier placed *babus* but pervades all over the hierarchy, up and down.

Equally deploring is that this vulgar culture has gripped the realm of politics as well, perhaps in a more naked way. It has been observed on many an occasion that if the boss of a political party is not shown due respect by its members (invariably in the form of *charan saparsh*, touching one's feet) at any given point of time, the person indulging in that disrespectful behaviour might have to lose his position or even the membership of the party concerned. This is true not only of the boss at the top but also correspondingly of all others at various levels of the party hierarchy. Everyone flaunts his power ruthlessly, irrespective of the political party that one belongs to. In fact, this has become the established pattern of our political culture. This *jee hazuri* culture poses yet another danger to our political system.

It may further be emphasized that our political parties have unfortunately, remained untouched by the sweep of democracy. This is manifest in more than one feature of their functioning. In the first place, they do not maintain their primary members' register. Secondly, they do not hold periodic elections to their various organizational bodies. They have miserably failed to develop healthy democratic traditions to that effect. Of late, the Election Commission has made it obligatory for them to do so. In order to satisfy that obligation, the exercise that they go through turns out in almost all cases nothing short of a farce. For, it is the High Command of the party concerned that invariably decides as to which of their persons is to contest the elections (those dare devils who offer their candidature against their will are branded as black sheep, thus having no place in the organization). Later on, when the time comes for the 'elected' members to choose the key functionaries of the various party forums, again the same High Command or more specifically the Supreme Leader does the job. Interestingly, queer traditions have been developed to authorize the latter to take the decision in his/her discretion. The matter does not end here. It extends even to their day-to-day functioning. Whenever an occasion arises that warrants some crucial decision, again the High Command or the Supreme Leader is requested to do the needful. It hardly needs to be emphasized that the Supreme Leader cult is highly inimical to the growth and development of democratic traditions. By definition, this cult "cannot create modern democratic movements. Supreme leaders are totalitarian figures whose existence quells dissent, stamp down debate and discourages fresh talent." (Sagrika Ghosh).

VIII

To conclude, the marvelous way we have been nurturing the hitherto depressed and discriminated section of our citizenry has ensured to a very great extent that India would not end up as a typical capitalist society wherein a small segment of the population rolls in wealth and the mass of the people seethe in poverty. For, not only the interests of the latter section are not being ignored but on the contrary they are also being groomed to get politically so much articulate as to themselves ensure that nobody dares to trample their interests. As delineated above in detail, these sections have become by and large fairly well conscious of their own interests as is manifest in the manner they flaunt their rights and might, thereby developing a stake in the political class of the country. The process however is not complete. However, we must not lose sight of the fact that even after this process is consummated fully, the capitalist model of economy that we have been building up in this country will still leave some chasm between the 'haves' and the 'have-nots, of course not to the extent of the latter suffering too miserably as has been the case elsewhere. The trickle down effect would push the benefits of development down to the bottom of the society in a faster way, for they would themselves snatch the same from the former without leaving the things to take their normal course. In this way, democracy will get strengthened to the extent of not being subverted in any way. However, we need to be conscious that there are so many hurdles that still stand in our way and we should try to clear them as speedily as possible so that the cherished goal is achieved at the earliest. Some of them that pose the challenge may be referred to again, as under:

(a) The unholy coalition of the politicians, the bureaucracy and the musclemen that constitutes the main source both of corruption and the exploitation of the common man needs to be liquidated at the earliest. The hardest nut among the three is the politician. To tame him constitutes the kernel of the challenge;

(b) The administrative structures and processes still continue to lack the desired degree of transparency and zest for work;

(a) The efforts to alleviate the unhappy lot of the common man are too incommensurate. Unless efforts to that end are redoubled, the masses may lose patience, especially the newly 'enfranchised' ones and that may put the whole system to jeopardy;

(b) Democracy-building process that thus far remains suspended in the air needs to be pulled down to cover all facets of society so that not only the various political structures are democratized but also the value pattern of society is also suitably reformed so as to bring the exploitation of the common man to an end.

Unless these challenges are effectively tackled, the time ahead may not be smooth. However, we are confident that we have developed enough of capability to meet them effectively and the day is not far when we would be able to overcome them too.

Here, a reference may be made in passing to an impression that has caught hold the minds of some the well-meaning persons that we might have been a nation of basically dishonest human beings and that is why we are not able to overcome some of the highly defying problems of society, especially those relating to the degenerating standards of our day-to-day conduct. On our part we do not subscribe to any such pessimist view. By no stretch of imagination, we can believe that we have been a dishonest people. If our conduct is not very straight and forthright today, it is all because of the distortions that the British had deliberately and mischievously inducted into our behvioural pattern. Our basic Hindu culture preaches us to be honest both in word and deed and that we have always been conducting ourselves that way, seldom giving an evidence to the dichotomy between what we proclaim and what we do. This fact is borne out even by a person of the eminence/ infamy of Lord Macaulay (that 'famous' member of the Governor-General's Executive Council of the thirties of the nineteenth century, who had been the pioneer of the policy of baking the Indians into the subservient *babu* culture, thereby destroying in them the very fibre of honesty and uprightness) in one of his statements made before the British Parliament. He had averred, " I have travelled across the length and breadth of India and I have not seen one person who is a beggar, who is a thief. Such wealth I have seen in this country, such high moral values, people of such calbre . . . the very backbone of this nation which is her spiritual and cultural heritage.. ." (quoted by the *INDIA VISION 2020* The Report. p. 49). This statement provides an ample proof that we have had excellent traditions of honesty, uprightness and straightforward public conduct. There is thus no room for any pessimism. We wind up this paper on this highly optimistic note for better days ahead.

References

Sainath. P. 'The Age of Inequality'. Romila Thapar (Ed). *INDIA Another Millennium*. New Delhi. Viking. 2000;

The Tribune, Chandigarh. 13 January 2006

The Hindustan Times, Chandigarh. 23 February, 2006

Jagmohan, *Soul and Structure of Governance in India*. New Delhi. Allied Publishers. 2005

Arun Shorie, *Governance and the sclerosis that has set in.* New Delhi. ASA Rupa. Co. 2004

Mani Shankar Aiyyar, *The Tribune,* Chandigarh. 26 & 27 April 2006

Gupta, Dipankar. 'India's unmodern modernity'. Romila Thapar. *Ibid.*

Maclver, R.M.. *The Modern State*. London. Oxford University Press. 1947.

Sen, Amartya. *The Argumentative Indian: writings on Indian culture, history and identity*. Penguin Books. 2005

Navriti, Bhutalla. 'Hindustan Times-C fore survery'. *The Hindustan Times.* Chandigarh. 26 February 2006

INDIA VISION 2020. The Report -(Report of the Committee on India Vision 2020). Planning Commission, Government of India. New Delhi. 2004

Laski, Harold J. *A Grammar of Politics*. London. George Allen & Unwin. 1960

Khilnani, Sunil. 'The Balance of Democracy'. Romila Thapar. *Ibid.*

Swapan Seth, 'Justice Murdered'. *The Hindustan Times.* Chandigarh. 23 February 2006

Jagmohan.. *Op.Cit.* 2005

INDIA VISION 2020. *Op.Cit.*

Table 1 : Technical details of Rainwater Harvesting Structures

Particulars	Sukhomajri	Bunga I	Bunga II	Relmajra	Bharauli*
Year of Construction	197[illegible]	198[illegible]	198[illegible]	199[illegible]	200[illegible]
Catchment area (ha)	[illegible]	15	10	5[illegible]	[illegible]9
Height (m)	1[illegible]	15	1[illegible]	13.[illegible]	1[illegible]
Storage Capacity (ha m)	5.[illegible]	60	[illegible]	13.[illegible]	24
Command Area (ha)	1[illegible]	240	23[illegible]	32	150

* Constructed by HCFP

Note : One ha m = 10,000 cu m

2

NEW PUBLIC MANAGEMENT-INTERNATIONAL EXPERIENCE AND LESSONS FOR INDIA

B P Mathur

Quality of governance is increasingly being realized as amongst the primary factors behind most remarkable economic development of rich societies. The lack of good governance also explains the missed development opportunities of many nations. It is widely perceived that India's poor development record on economic, social and moral front is largely due to poor governance. The Planning Commission in its Tenth Plan (2002-2007) document, candidly admits, " people perceive bureaucracy as wooden, disinterested in public welfare and corrupt... Weak governance manifesting itself in poor service delivery, excessive regulation, and uncoordinated and wasteful expenditure, is seen as one of the key factors impinging on growth and development." (Vol. I. P. 22)

Public bureaucracies when they were initially constituted, more than a hundred and fifty years ago, were considered instruments of checking arbitrary exercise of power by the State. The theoretical foundation of bureaucracy was expounded by German sociologist Max Weber (1864-1926). He observed that it is the most effective organization for exercising legal authority and is capable of attaining highest degree of efficiency and has applicability in all kinds of administrative tasks. Public bureaucracy has certain characteristics: separation of office and its incumbent;

selection by merit; it constitutes a career with a system of promotion largely based on seniority; fixed remuneration for officials with right of pension; officials are organized in hierarchy; they are subject to discipline and control; and each office has a clearly defined competence.

While bureaucracies served the intended objectives very well for almost a century of their existence, they seem to be incapable of meeting the requirements of the current day New Welfare States. Some of the charges leveled against bureaucracy are, that they are unresponsive to popular demands, embroiled in red tape and formalism, and officials are power hungry and corrupt. Northcote Parkinson has graphically portrayed that officials make work for each others and believe in empire building, in what has come to be known as Parkinson's Law. The popular BBC serial *Yes Minister* and Jaspal Bhatti's TV serial in Hindi *Ulta Palta* captures the true face of bureaucracy and how people perceive it. It is obvious that old bureaucratic structures are incapable of meeting the current day aspirations of people, in an environment where developments in the field of computers, electronics and avionics have crushed time and space. Today's environment demands institutions which are extremely flexible and adaptable, capable of delivering high quality service to the people and responsive to their needs. The World Bank observes, " In a world of dizzying changes in markets, civil societies, and global forces, the state is under pressure to become effective." (World Development Report. (1997. p.15)

I

INTERNATIONAL EXPERIENCE IN REFORM

The experience of two decades of reform in UK, New Zealand and other countries shows that wherever, successful reform measures have been implemented, it has resulted in dramatic improvement in the quality of services and helped invigorating the economy.

The United Kingdom

Britain was the first country to change the scope, organization and management of public services. In this regard, the lead was given by former Prime Minister Margaret Thatcher who advocated a philosophy of rolling back the frontiers of the State. Successive Conservative governments throughout the 1980's and 1990's sought to reduce and transform the 'overloaded, inefficient and unresponsive bureaucratic state', into a 'lean, enabling, customer oriented and value for money organization'. These reform measures were continued by the Labour government of Tony Blair.

Financial Management Initiative: A major initiative at reform was the launching of the Financial Management Initiative (FMI). (Les Metcalfe & Sue Richards. Pp.1-55 and 177-238). The objective as set out in a White Paper (September 1982) was to promote in each department an organization and a system in which managers at all levels have: a) a clear view of their objectives, and means to assess and, wherever possible, measure outputs and performance in relation to those objectives; b) well-defined responsibility for making best use of their resources, including a critical scrutiny of output and value for money; and c) the information (particularly about costs), the training and access to expert advice that they need to exercise their responsibilities effectively. The FMI sought to shift responsibility for better resource utilization to line managers by increasing their discretion and instilling the motivation to improve performance.

Executive Agencies: **The Next Steps**: The next major reform of British public service was setting of the Executive Agencies. The initiative in this regard came from Sir Robert Ibbs who was drawn from the private sector and was chief executive of ICI. Ibbs in his report (1988), titled, *"Improving Management in Government: the Next Steps"* recommended three main priorities: a) The work of each department must be organized in a way which focuses on a job to be done; the systems and structures must enhance the effective delivery of policies and services. b) The management of each department must ensure that their staff have the relevant experience and the skills needed to do the tasks that are essential to effective government. c) There must be real and sustained pressure on and within each department for continuous improvement in the value for money obtained in the delivery of policies and services. In order to focus on the job to be done, the report recommended that agencies should be set up to carry on the executive functions of the government within a policy and resources framework set up by a department. The main strategic control should lie with the ministers and permanent secretaries, who set the policy objectives and budgets,- provided management operated within those strategic direction, they should be left as free as possible to manage.

Following Ibbs' recommendations, the Central government departments were restructured into Executive Agencies under a Chief Executive, with delegated responsibility to deliver services to defined output, quality and efficiency standard within a defined budget. The headquarter staff is now responsible for only policy advice, oversight, target setting, budgets and monitoring. A framework document is drawn which sets out responsibilities, authorities and annual performance targets. The agencies are required to operate along commercial lines. The Agency Chief Executive reports directly to the Minister and is personally accountable for service delivery within budget. They enjoy full freedom to manage within their framework document and annual agreements.

To implement the change, a Next Steps Unit was set up in 1988. By 1998 government departments had been restructured into 140 Agencies and they employed about 75 percent of civil servants.

Citizens Charter: In order to raise the standard of public service Citizens Charter was launched in June1991 by the then Prime Minister John Major. It is based on the premise that all public services are paid for by individual citizens, either directly or through taxes and they are therefore, entitled to high quality services, responsive to their needs, provided efficiently at reasonable cost. The six key principles of Charter programme are: setting standards, information and openness, choice and consultation, courtesy and helpfulness, putting things right and value for money. The Charter initiative embraces greater competition, independent scrutiny of public services, greater accountability and openness and a programme of management change to improve public services. Today in Britain all main public services such as health, social security, education, and higher education set out, what government promises to deliver and how citizens can make suggestions and complaints and thus empower the users.

Civil Services: As a result of reform measures, Civil Service have undergone most profound change, from the time its basic structure was laid down in Northcote-Trevelyan Report of 1854, more than a century back. The main features of the Civil Service system had been appointment by competitive examination, tenure security, payment based on uniform pay scales, restriction against dismissal and pension payment on retirement. Policies on pay, grading, pensions, recruitment, promotion and union determination was centrally determined. High employment security and promotion rooted in seniority bred both an institutional conservatism and a collegial and supportive mentality, associated with public service ethics. Senior officers were generally supportive of subordinates and their employment interests. Staff were not driven through patronage or fear of loosing their jobs rather by loyalty or the realization that by conforming they would eventually be rewarded by promotion. Personnel policies were uniformly applied and regulated by rules and procedures set down in voluminous codes relating to each public service. Over the years, public services were generally in the forefront of enlightened and progressive personnel policies and practices and came to offer secure employment, training and career development, equal opportunity and good pensions.

As a result of reform measure a new paradigm of public management began to replace the traditional bureaucratic model. Its key characteristics are: decentralization is preferred to centralization; diversity to uniformity; performance management to routinised administration and entrepreneurship to consistency in practice. In contrast to job stability, planned career pathways and the employment security of the past, the public sector is now resorting to more open recruitment and diverse mode of employment and working patterns adopting many of the practices of private sector. There is also greater flexibility in pay and benefits.

A new Senior Civil Service (SCS), covering 3000 posts was created . (Sylvia Horton. Pp.108-137). Though full-time contracts is still the norm, fixed term and temporary contracts are being introduced. Each member of SCS has a personal contract and post, which include chief executive of Next Steps Agencies which are normally recruited through open competition. This offers flexibility to attract people from the private sector and other public bodies who have specific skills and competencies. The appointment, promotion, pay and conditions of service of SCS are still centrally determined. In 1996, Agencies have been given complete pay and grading flexibility for staff below grade 5. This means that department and agencies now have full powers to recruit all staff below the SCS, decide on promotion, training and development, determine an appropriate pay and grading structure and deal with grievance and discipline. Agencies are not completely autonomous, as they have to operate within the constraints of agreed running costs and other financial requirements and the civil service management code. They have to follow rules regarding merit based recruitment and equal opportunities. In the new SCS, the old grading structure has been replaced with nine overlapping pay bands. Each pay band relates to a number of jobs, which are assigned to a pay band using a job evaluation system. Departments can decide which pay band is appropriate for each individual taking into account performance record and skill.

Faced with cuts in expenditure, enforced staff ceilings and demands for increased efficiency, public services in Britain were forced to look for ways of restructuring the service's activities, reducing staff and increasing workforce flexibility. The civil service workforce fell from 732000 in 1979 to fewer than 480000 in 1998. This was achieved through a combination of transfer of functions and staff to the private sector and contraction of staff through early retirement or redundancy. There have been many positive outcomes of decentralization and flexible strategy. There is evidence of greater efficiency, overstaffing has been eliminated and costs are closely controlled. Services are more responsive to customer needs and there is more variation and innovation as employees are encouraged to be entrepreneurial.

Public Service Agreements: In 1998, the government of Tony Blair has introduced Fiscal Responsibility Code, whose main feature is comprehensive public spending review with expenditure planned firmly for three years and public service contracts which are quasi-contracts between treasury and each departments about what they would deliver in return for budget funding. Public Service Agreements (PSA's) require departments to give measurable targets in terms of end results that the taxpayer's money is intended to deliver. They cover such areas as improvement in health, educational achievements and reduction in crime and include service standards such as reduction in waiting list of patients, smaller class sizes, and swifter justice. The idea is to set Specific, Measurable, Achievable, Relevant and Timed targets related to outcomes, in what is called SMART.

New Zealand

New Zealand a small country has seen some of the most far-reaching changes in management of public services and is cited as a model for public administration reform. New Zealand's economy was in bad shape in early 80's when the government was subsidizing agriculture, protected industry, maintained a plethora of income support schemes and was generally following a protectionist and interventionist policy resulting in huge fiscal deficits and foreign exchange crisis. The government fell in a snap poll in 1984, and in its place a Labour government came. Having been already committed to reforms, it changed the direction of the economic policy. The new policy viewed the public sector, with its traditional focus on wealth resource distribution, regulation and control, and with little transparency in its process and activities, not so much as a tool for reform, but as a significant part of the problem.

The key guiding principles for reforms in New Zealand have been: a) withdraw the State from the activities that can be more efficiently and effectively performed by the community or private enterprise; b) establish strategic directions and clear organizational objectives; c) provide incentives for higher performance; d) delegate authority to managers to empower them to manage; e) increase transparency of government through improved accountability and monitoring processes. (The Reformed Economy. 1999. New Zealand.)

Civil Service Reform: The core public service which was formerly characterized by large multifunctional institutions with entrenched cultures and identities now comprise smaller, more sharply focused organizations, uncluttered by mixed objectives and functions. Its overall size was reduced to half. Almost all central control imposed by the core public services has been removed and replaced with incentive to improve managerial performance.

The State Sector Act of 1988 has brought about changes in the method of appointment and employment of heads of government departments as well as their authority, responsibility and functions. Each department came under the management of a Chief Executive Officer appointed for a limited term, usually five years, with renewal subject to satisfactory performance. The State Service Commission obtained greater discretion over the procedure it adopts for appointing chief- executives. Under the new act the chief- executives are required to act as agents of their ministries. They are to follow the objectives laid out by minister in an annual performance agreement, and they are responsible for satisfactorily meeting those objectives. The ministries are expected to set policy agenda, determine departmental priorities, and specify policy outcomes and departmental output and monitor performance. Chief Executives are expected to carry out the functions and duties of the department, tender advice, engage in general conduct of the department and ensure effective and economical management of the activities of the department. The State Sector Act also provides for establishment of a Senior Executive Service made up of senior managers in each department- those immediately below the chief executive officers. While the State Service Commission has a general oversight over these appointments, the individual executive officers themselves have most say over who is appointed and under what conditions.

Fiscal Responsibility Act (1994): The objective of the Act is to promote consistent good quality fiscal management. The Act requires Governments to follow a legislated set of principles of responsible fiscal management, and publicly assess their fiscal policies against these principles and publish a Budget Policy statement well before the annual budget containing their strategic priorities for the upcoming budget, their short term fiscal intentions, and long term objectives. The Act establishes a set of principles for use as a benchmark against which the fiscal policies of the government can be judged and enjoins the government to limit its borrowing by stipulating that, 'the total operating expenses of the government should not exceed its total operating revenues'.

New Zealand reform has three key features. First, civil servants accountability was clarified by law. The Chief executive in-charge of a department is directly accountable to the minister through the annual performance agreement. In return the Chief Executive was given autonomy in personnel, finance and other matters to manage his department. Two, fiscal prudence was followed by strict control on public expenditure and borrowing Three, the new model envisaged output or results as a basic indicator to evaluate public service performance. The emphasis on output and outcome was used to improve efficiency and accountability of public services. These reforms have helped New Zealand becoming a highly competitive and open economy. New Zealand's public services are considered one of the most efficient and responsive in the world. The World Competitiveness Yearbook (1998), ranked New Zealand fourth in the overall quality of government and New Zealand's public services were ranked first.

The United State of America (USA)

National Performance Review ((NPR). In order to improve the working of US Government, President Clinton appointed a high-powered task force headed by Vice President Al Gore (1993). The NPR noted that Federal agencies are large, top down central bureaucracies in which tasks were broken into simple parts, each defining the responsibility of different layers of employees, and specific rules and regulations which need to be applied. With their rigid preoccupation with standard operating procedure, their vertical chain of command, and their standardized services, these bureaucracies were steady, but slow and cumbersome. Many federal organizations were monopolies, with few incentives to innovate and improve. Employees have virtual lifetime tenure, regardless of their performance. Success offers few rewards; failure few penalties.

The NPR laid down four key principles of reform; 1) *Cutting Red Tape*: Need to shift from systems in which people are accountable for following rules, to systems in which they are accountable for achieving results. They should reorient their control systems to prevent problems rather than simply punish those who make mistakes. They should strip away unnecessary layers of regulation that stifle innovation. 2) *Putting Customers First*: Effective entrepreneurial government insist on customer satisfaction, use market dynamics as competition and customer choice and create incentives that drives their employees to put customer first. 3) *Empowering Employees to Get Results:* Need to transform culture by decentralizing authority- empowering those who work on the frontline to make more of their own decisions and solve more of their own problems. This embraces labour management cooperation, provision of training and other tools employees need to be effective, and humanize the work place. 4) *Producing Better government for Less:* There is constant need to do re-engineering, abandon the obsolete, eliminate duplication and end special interest privileges. There is need to invest in greater productivity through long-term capital investment and embrace advanced technologies to cut costs.

NPR observed that its object is to invent a government that puts people first by: Cutting unnecessary spending; Serving customers; Empowering employees; Helping communities solve their problems; and Fostering excellence. The objective is: a) Create a clear sense of mission; b) Steer more, row less; c) Delegate authority and responsibility; d) Replace regulations with incentives; d) Develop budgets based on outcomes; e) Expose federal operations to competition; f) Search for market not administrative solutions; g) Measure success by customer satisfaction.

The Review suggested six steps to change the culture of federal employees who by habit resist change and do some thing new. First, decision-making power be given to those who do the work, pruning layer upon layer of managerial overgrowth. Second, every organization and individual should be made accountable for clearly understood feasible outcomes. Accountability for results will replace command and control as the way to manage government. Third, employees be given better tools for the job-training to handle their own work and to take advantage of modern computer and telecommunication technologies. Fourth, federal offices be made a better place to work. Rules and conditions should convey that employees are trusted. Fifth, labour and management should forge a new partnership. Change will never happen unless unions and employees work together. Sixth, top down support for bottom up decision-making is required. There is need for full backing of top management to bring change.

NPR's proposals for major reform related to decentralization of personnel policy, streamlining the budget and procurement system and elimination of thousands of regulations which hamstring the federal employees. (Report. US. September, 1993)

Government Performance and Results Act 1993 (GPRA): With a view to improve efficiency and effectiveness of governmental operations a legislation known as Government Performance and Results Act (GPRA) was enacted. Its objectives are: (a) to improve the confidence of people in government by holding agencies accountable for achieving programme results, (b) to stimulate reform with a series of pilot projects that could be used as examples for others, (c) to promote a focus on results, service quality and public satisfaction, (d) to help managers improve service delivery by requiring them to plan for meeting programme objectives and providing them with information about programme results, e) to improve congressional decision making by providing information on achieving statutory objectives and relative effectiveness of various programmes, (f) to improve internal management of federal government.

GPRA inherits the legacy of Programme, Planning and Budgeting system (PPBS), Management by Objective (MBO) and Zero Base Budgeting (ZBB). The act required agencies to focus on programme results, service quality and customer satisfaction by requiring strategic planning and performance measurement. The GPRA required drawing of a strategic plan which should include a comprehensive mission statement for the agency, a specification of general goal and objective and how they will be achieved. The second set of requirement focused around specifications of annual performance plans that could include each programme activity set in the budget. The third set of requirement calls for annual performance reports that would compare the actual performance of each programme activity to the performance goals in the plan for that fiscal year. GPRA gives time to designated agencies to prepare for shifting to the new system of performance measurement. The objectives laid down by GPRA have also been adopted by most of the states of the US.

In March 1996, Vice President Al Gore announced a plan to change the federal bureaucracy by converting them into Performance Based Organizations (PBO). The PBO's would be given more freedom in operations and held accountable for the achievement of specified results. An initial experimentation was done with ten organizations (such as Patent and Trademark office, US Mint), accounting for 2 percent of federal civilian workforce.

President's Management Agenda (PMA). The reform measures which were initiated during the Presidency of Bill Clinton have been continued by President Bush II. A new initiative known as President Management Agenda, has been launched, which contains five specific goals to improve federal management and deliver results: (a) Strategic management of human capital; (b) Competitive sourcing; (c) Improved financial performance; (d) Expanded electronic government; (e) Budget and Performance integration. To implement PMA, a President's Management Council has been constituted with officers from every department designated as Chief Operating Officer (who will take responsibility for day today operations) to take leadership, solve problems and innovate. The Office of Management and Budget (OMB) assesses performance of each department/ agency relating to five goals set in PMA through a score card/ grading system. Green, shows that implementation is progressing satisfactorily; Yellow, shows some slippage or other issues requiring adjustment by the agency; Red, shows initiative in serious jeopardy and unlikely to realise objective. The main focus of the initiative is to deliver results that matter to American people.

The World Bank Model

The World Bank has been taking a leading role in reform of civil services in developing countries as part of its structural adjustment programme. According to the World Bank there are five fundamentals that lie at the core of every government, without which sustained poverty reduction is not possible. They are: establishing a foundation of law; maintaining a non-discriminatory policy environment; investing in basic social services and infrastructure; protecting the vulnerable; and protecting the environment. Markets and governments are complementary and therefore the state is essential for putting in place the appropriate institutional foundation for market. There is need for well-designed regulatory framework which can help influence market outcomes for public ends.

World Bank suggests a two-part strategy for reform – first, matching the state's role to capacity and second to raise state capability by reinvigorating public institutions. States with weak institutional capabilities should focus on providing the public goods and services that markets cannot provide as well as goods and services with large positive externalities, such as property rights, safe drinking water, roads and basic education. The state should respect, nurture and take advantage of private and voluntary initiative and competitive markets. The notion of state's capability encompasses the administrative or technical capacity of state officials, but it is a much broader term. It includes institutional mechanism that gives politicians and civil servants to act in collective interest. These mechanisms aim to enforce rules and restraints in society; promote competitive pressure from outside; facilitate citizens' voice and partnership with them.

A key task of reform is to provide incentive to public officials to perform better while keeping arbitrary action in check. Civil servants need to be motivated to perform better through a combination of mechanisms to encourage internal competition such as, a recruitment system based on merit not favoritism; a merit based internal promotion system and adequate compensation.

Reinventing Government

The Ideas of Osborne and Gaebler

One of the most path breaking study for reforming bureaucracy has been done by two Americans, David Osborne and Ted Gaebler in a book titled *Reinventing Government*. They have advocated ten principles for redefining the role of government.

1.*Catalytic Government*: *Steering rather than Rowing*: Entrepreneurial governments should separate policy decisions (steering) from service delivery (rowing) so as to allow policy makers to concentrate on decision-making and direction. Steering requires people who see the entire universe of issues and possibilities and can balance competing demand for resources. It allows them to use competition between services. Rowing requires people who focus intently on one mission and perform it well.

2. *Community Owned government: Empowering Rather than Serving*: Communities understand their problems better than service professionals. Professional and bureaucracies deliver services while communities solve problems, communities are more flexible and creative and offer cheaper services than professionals.

3. *Competitive Government*: When service providers compete they keep their costs down, respond quickly to changing demands and strive to satisfy their customers. An obvious example is garbage collection by town municipal bodies.

4. *Mission Driven Government*: As compared to rule driven organizations, mission driven organizations are more efficient, they produce better results, are more innovative, more flexible and have higher morale. Government rules are aggregated into systems-budget systems, purchase systems, personnel systems. Governments need to deregulate these systems, because they create the basic incentives that drive the employees. A personnel system built around civil service is destructive. Civil services are characterized by elaborate rules relating to hiring, classification of jobs, graded scales and pay, promotion, firing, lay-offs, all of which create problems.

5. *Results Oriented Government: Funding Outcomes, not Inputs:* Organizations that measure results perform better. The advantage is what gets measured gets done, if you can't measure results you can't tell success from failure. The techniques like TQM developed by W Edwards Deming for managing performance need to be used. In government the most important lever that drives behaviour is budget. There is need to develop budget systems that fund outcomes rather than inputs.

6. *Customer Driven Government: Meeting the Needs of Customer not Bureaucracy:* Public agencies get most of their funding from legislatures, city councils and elected boards and therefore public managers try to please them and not their customers. This marks a contrast with the business world where enormous attention is paid to the interests of the customers. Traditional public service still offer one size fits all, services.

7. *Earning rather than Spending*: In government few people outside revenue and finance department ever think of revenue.

Hardly any one thinks of profit. One of the ways to raise non-tax revenue is to charge fees from those who use public services. User-fees have become more popular as resistance to tax increases. An enterprising government should have an investment perspective- a habit of gauging return on investment.

8. *Anticipatory Government: Prevention rather than Cure*: Traditional bureaucratic governments focus on supplying services to combat problems. To deal with illness they fund health care services, to combat fire they buy more fire trucks, to deal with crime they fund more police. Governments need to focus more on prevention and a have a long- term point of view. There is need for doing strategic planning and anticipate the future.

9. *Decentralised Government, from hierarchy to participation and teamwork:* In today's information age things will work better if those working in public organisations have authority to take more decisions. Decentralised institutions have a number of advantages: they are more flexible and can respond quickly to changing circumstances, they are more effective, more innovative, they generate more commitment and greater productivity. Public institutions should be decentralised with greater labour management co-operation.

10. *Market Oriented Government*: Administrative programmes have a series of flaws, when compared to market. Programmes are driven by constituencies not customers, they are driven by politics not policy, programmes tend to create fragmented service delivery systems, programmes are not self correcting and rarely die and programmes use commands not incentives. There are market-oriented alternatives to most administrative programmes. Government can restructure the market to achieve this, using techniques such as: setting the rules for market place, providing information to consumers, catalyzing private sector suppliers, changing public investment policy, pricing activities through tax incentives and managing demand through user fees.

New Governance Paradigm

The new paradigm of governance successfully practised by many countries, as discussed above, can be said to have five main components as summarized below:

(i) Emphasis on providing high quality services that citizens value.

(ii) Increased autonomy, particularly from central agency control, so that they can use their expertise and creativity.

(iii) The organizations and individuals are being measured and rewarded on the basis of their meeting demanding performance targets. Senior public servants are signing performance agreements with their political masters. They have been making greater use of performance pay at senior levels and are moving from a tenure system towards fixed term contract and permitting competition from outside the public services for senior positions.

(iv) Making provision for human and technological resources that the managers need to meet the performance targets. This means recruiting the most talented people and improving their skill through constant training. The public sector is coming to recognize the importance of leading edge information technology.

(v) Receptiveness to competition and an open-minded attitude about which public services should be performed by public sector: The public sector should steer (set policy) and seek private sector involvement in rowing (implementation).

II
THE INDIAN SCENARIO

Some of the reasons for poor performance of public administration in India are:

(1) Special Service conditions with high emphasis on job security;

(2) Out-dated rules and regulations;

(3) High degree of centralization;

(4) Lack of professionalism and the IAS domination;

(5) Politicization of services.

Service Conditions: In government there is no incentive for good work and disincentive for poor performance. Once appointed, it is almost impossible to remove an employee. The provisions of discipline rule are so cumbersome and tortuous that it is almost impossible to take action against a delinquent employee for indiscipline and misbehavior. The rules relating to promotion with excessive reliance on Confidential Reports are so framed that everyone gets his promotion when his turn comes and encourages mediocrity.

Outdated Rules and Procedures: One pervasive feature of Indian bureaucratic machine is the large number of rules relating to service conditions as well as operational matters such as Fundamental Rule (FR), General Financial Rule (GFR), Treasury Rules, Conduct Rules, Public Works Account Code. They were framed during British rule and bear a heavy imprint of colonial philosophy of check and balance, lack of trust and suspicion. Over years numerous clarifications, administrative instructions and guidelines have been issued making them bulky, confusing and often incomprehensible. These rules stand in the way of introducing modern management practices and speedy decision-making.

High Degree of Centralization: The functioning of Government of India is highly centralized with very little delegation to field outfits. The most centralized working is of the Department of Personnel and the Ministry of Finance who act as super–ministries, completely throttling the initiative of other ministries and departments for innovation and change. The Appointments Committee of the Cabinet (ACC), with Prime Minister as chairman and the Home Minister and the concerned minister under whose jurisdiction the appointment falls as members, approves all senior appointments of the rank of Joint Secretary and above in Central Secretariat and Group A Services, besides Board level appointments in PSU's and autonomous organization. Such appointments run into hundreds every year. As it is simply not possible for Prime Minister, to have an application of mind and judge merit of each case, it leads to abuse with the PMO becoming a new center of power.

Lack of Professionalism and Specialization: The task of policy making in government is complex and needs specialist knowledge of the subject. Under the existing system all senior appointments in the government are monopolized by Indian Administrative Service (IAS) who are generalists. The hold on policy-making by a group of people who have no expertise in the area where they are working, is regarded as the single biggest reason for the poor administration of the country by most expert committees and knowledgeable persons. The Administrative Reforms Commission (1969) had called for the IAS to be converted into functional service and its sphere of activities confined.

Politicization of Services: The civil services have been politicized, particularly in the states. As soon as a new government comes in power after the elections, hundreds of transfers of IAS, IPS and other senior officers are effected, with a view to have 'chosen men' in key administrative posts. Merit and continuity becomes the last consideration. This completely demoralizes the civil services and has a telling effect on efficiency.

Restructuring Government

A large part of the problem of poor performance of public services in our country is attitudinal. Due to colonial legacy, the people in public administration have a ruler mind-set and feel no obligation to serve the public. We need to change this psychology. The philosophy of New Public Management has valuable lessons for us.

1. **Make Senior Appointments open to Competition and Contractual**: All appointments to the senior posts of the level of Joint secretary and above in the Central Secretariat, as well as field, be done with the approval of Union Public Service Commission on the basis of merit and individual's qualification for the post. The field of selection should be thrown open to candidates outside the civil services, to persons in academics, business and industry. The appointment should be contractual for three to five years with a provision for annual review. The proposal will meet several objectives: it will help in getting the best men for each job as recruitment will be job specific, it will introduce the much needed specialization in services and it will take away power of appointment of top posts from the hands of politicians and depoliticize the services.

2. **Bring Discipline in Government Service:** The provisions of Civil Service Conduct and Discipline Rules are so complicated and tortuous that it becomes very difficult to take action against an employee for indiscipline and misbehaviour. The

Commission to review the Working of the Constitution headed by Justice Venkatachaliha has pointed out that constitutional safeguards under Article 311, have in practice acted to shield the guilty against punishment for abuse of public office for private gain and has suggested its review with a view to rationalize and simplify the procedure of administrative and legal action so that dishonest are not allowed to prosper in office. There is need to frame new Civil Service Code, so that honest and efficient officers are given protection and dishonest are given quick and summary punishment. Civil service code of UK, Australia and US can act as valuable guide. (Report. Vol. I. P. 186)

3. **Downsize the Bureaucracy**: India has a vast bureaucracy. The organized sector employment in India is of the order of 272 lakhs, out of which 205 lakhs persons are paid wages out of government coffers, if we take into account employment both by Central government and State government, and institutions funded or controlled by them such as municipal corporations, autonomous bodies and schools etc. The salary payment to these employees account for 10 percent of India's GDP. If we also add pensionary liability, the wages bill works out to 12 percent of GDP, a staggering sum considering the pressure on resources in the country. In several States the wages and pension bill of the employees is more than its revenue, if we exclude the Central share of taxes and grant. The burgeoning expenditure on the wages of employees is the primary cause of the huge fiscal deficit of most states. Cutting the size of bureaucracy will not only reduce the expenditure but also bring greater efficiency in the working of the government.

4. **Improve Productivity:** The Fifth Pay Commission (1997) and Expenditure Reforms Committee (2000-01) headed by K P Geethakrishnan came out with wide array of proposals for improving the efficiency of public services and need to be implemented. Some of their important recommendations are: (a) Government offices have hierarchical structure due to which decisions get delayed causing harassment to the public. There is need to introduce officer oriented system with level jumping to speed up decision making. (b) The existing nine levels in which government hierarchies are organized should be reduced to six:

Top Executive, Senior Executive, Executive, Supervisory Staff, Supporting Staff and Auxiliary Staff. The ministerial staff divided in numerous categories be abolished and replaced by a multi-skilled position called Executive Assistant who should be computer savvy. (c) Government offices should be modernized with provision of computer and other gadgets and a conducive work environment should be created.

5. **Privatization and Deregulation**: Government has to initiate a general policy of economic reform such as deregulation, liberalization and privatization, so that government reduces its role in directly running the economy. Government should privatize the loss-making public enterprises or those which fall in secondary or tertiary sectors of the economy and where private sector has already established its presence. In order to improve efficiency and cut costs a large part of services used by government department can be contracted out to private parties and NGO's. Thus activities such as maintenance of office building and cleaning, office security, catering, staff cars etc. can be contracted out. Municipal Corporations can contract out activities such as solid waste disposal, street cleaning etc.

6. **Create Performance Based-Organizations (PBO's):** There is need to create performance based autonomous organizations with full delegation of powers in administrative, financial and operational matters on the UK pattern. This includes greater autonomy to managers at lower levels, general delegation of authority to cost and profit centers, with flexibility to achieve agreed goals within a framework of accountability. PBO provides an organizational structure to a government agency to be entrepreneurial and innovative.

Concluding Remarks

The new philosophy of public administration, popularly known as New Public Management (NPM) has dramatically transformed the performance of governments in developed countries. The main elements of sea changes which are taking place in managing public services as summarized in an OECD document are:

1. Decentralization of authority within governmental units and devolution of responsibilities to lower levels of government.

2. Downsizing the public services and privatization and corporatization of activities.
3. Re-examination of what government should both pay for and do, what it should pay for but not do, and what it should neither pay for nor do.
4. Consideration of more cost-effective ways of delivering services, such as contracting out, market-type mechanism and user charges.
5. Customer orientation including explicit quality standards for public services.
6. Benchmarking and measuring performance and
7. Reforms designed to simplify regulations and reduce its cost.

There are three main components of public services reforms: *(a) Devolution of Authority*- This is based on the premise that decisions made closer to their actual point of impact, are with greater knowledge of likely results and therefore better decisions. A significant feature of devolution is removal of unnecessarily prescriptive rules and regulations. This implies substantial freeing up of centrally imposed rules on budgetary and staffing matters. Creation of autonomous agencies or units is part of the devolution package. *(b) Client or Customer focus* -A major theme associated with improving performance of public services is the development of a customer or a client focus or service quality initiatives in the public sector. The U K Citizens Charter is the best known example. *(c) Performance Contracting*- increased emphasis on performance. This helps imposing accountability on public officials for delivering results.

The new model of governance philosophy recognizes that the task of promoting public purpose has changed. How to design new systems, which will meet the changed realities is a challenge which the government should accept, if the country is to move forward as an economically powerful nation.

REFERENCES

Government of India. Planning Commission. New Delhi. *Five-Year Plan. 2002-07*. Vol. I.

Government of India. New Delhi. Report of the Commission for the Review of the Working of the Constitution. Vol. I. March, 2002.

Government of New Zealand, Ministry of Foreign Affairs and Trade. *The Reformed Economy*. 1999.

World Bank. *World Development Report. The State in a Changing World*. Vol. I.

Government of USA Report of the National Performance Review. Creating a Government that Works Better and Costs Less. September, 1993.

Les Metcalfe and Sue Richards. *Improving Public Management*. London – New Delhi. Sage Publications. 1990.

Moshe Maor. The Paradox of Managerialism. *Public Administration Review*. January-February. 1999.

William D. Eggers. Reinventing Government. *The Wonder Down Under*. March,1997. on Website.

Sylvia Horton. Human Resource Flexibilities in UK Public Services in Davis Farnham and Sylvia Horton. (Eds). *Human Resource Flexibilities in Public Services International Perspective*. London. Macmilan. 2000.

Beryl A. Radin. The Government Performance and Results Act: Hydra Header Monster or Flexible Management Tool. *Public Administration Review*. July-August, 1998.

Jeffery L.Brudney. et all. Reinventing Government in American States. *Public Administration Review*. January-February, 1999.

Alasdair Roberts. Performance-Based Orgaanization, Assessing the Gore Plan. *Public Administration Review. November-December*. 1997.

US Government *website. Results.gov/agenda. September, 2004*

David Osborne and Ted Gaebler. *Reinventing Government*. London. Addison Wesley. 1992.

3

CHALLENGES BEFORE THE INDIAN ECONOMY IN THE TWENTY-FIRST CENTURY :

(Grow the Rate Development Strategies, Poverty and Unemployment)

D.D. Narula

Introduction

I believe that "growth is the best antidote to poverty.......... Growth will be our mount; equity will be our destination". So stated Union Finance Minister, P. Chidambaram, while presenting the Union Budget, 2006-07. How far is this belief justified, on the basis of international experience and our own experience? How far has the development strategy of 'liberalization, privatization and globalization' (LPG), adopted under economic reforms launched in 1991, stepped up the growth rate of GDP and with what results in terms of poverty alleviation and generation of employment? How far has the growth process been inclusive? We seek to answer some of these challenging questions. The study is divided in three chapters. The first chapter (i.e. chapter No. 3) examines the growth rate of the GDP, its structure and its use-value composition. It makes a broad comparison of development strategies of India and China, and looks at the impact of growth on poverty and on employment / unemployment. The second chapter (i.e. Chapter

No. 4) attempts to appraise critically some aspects of development strategy— foreign trade, foreign direct and portfolio investment, capital account convertibility, external debt and assistance, WTO, saving and investment, infrastructure, SEZs, real estate, financial institutions, public-private partnership, rural non-farm growth and rural industrialization, use of labour intensive techniques etc. The last of the series (i.e. Chapter No. 5) takes up the problems of hunger, starvation and under-nutrition, question of food security, recommendations of the National Farmers Commission in this regard; problem of housing of migrant workers, slum-prevention and slum-upliftment. Social Security for unorganized sector workers etc. It presents the grim contrast of the affluence of upper and middle class, their expensive and imitative western life styles and the degrading poverty, hunger and disease-prone majority of the population. It attempts to delineate the dilemmas of the development process in a democratic polity, and steps needed to meet the challenges ahead. It builds on the analysis in earlier sections and presents the concluding remarks.

Section 1
Growth Rate and its Structure

1.11 Growth rate of Indian economy continues to be subject to the vicissitudes of nature, especially rainfall, with droughts occurring almost in every decade[2] since independence. The average annual growth rate was 3.5 percent: - the so-called "Hindu" growth rate, during the first 3 decades of Independent India. Growth rate rose to 5.6 percent and 6.0 percent respectively during the

Table 1.1 Growth rate of GDP, during the five decades, 1951/52 to 2000/01

Annual Average Percent Change				
1951/52 to 1960/61	*1961/62 to 1970/71*	*1971/72 to 1980/81*	*1981/82 to 1990/91*	*1991/92 to 2000/01*
3.94	3.74	3.14	5.64	6.0

Source: Central Statistical Organization, **National Accounts Statistics** (Various years) & author's estimates.

next two decades, (Table 1.1) Thus, a significant stepping up of growth rate occurred in the 1980s, due to wide ranging industrial policy reforms in early 80s. Growth rate of GDP continues to depend heavily on the growth rate of GDP in agriculture even, in the 21st century as is evident from Table 1.2. Thus, with the drought of 2002-03, agriculture suffered a decline of 6.9 percent and overall growth rate declined from 5.8 percent in 2001-02 to 3.8 percent in 2002-03. Similarly, with the annual percentage change rising to 10.0 percent in agriculture, total GDP annual percentage change shot up to 8.5 percent in 2003-04. Projections for 2006-07 are 8.0[3] percent, for the economy.

1.12 The Mid-term appraisal (MTA) of the 10th five year plan had postulated a growth rate of 3.8 percent for agriculture. However, the realized average growth rate in the first three years of the Plan was about 1.3 percent, at best. This failure is an important factor underlying rural distress in recent years and also for the slower growth of the economy as a whole. MTA was worried that this pattern of growth was unsustainable, in the longer term. Reddy and Galab, 2006 have presented a grimmer picture. They find that growth in per worker income in agriculture has declined from 1.16 percent (1988-89 to 1993-94) to 0.28 percent (1998-89 to 2003-04), whereas income per worker in non-agricultural sector has gone up from 3.31 percent to 4.30 percent, during the same period. They find that "agriculture is becoming increasingly an unviable proposition irrespective of rainfall pattern". They further find that "the returns to investment in agriculture from rain-fed regions are substantially higher than from irrigated region". Incidentally a majority of the poor live in the rain-fed regions. "In the absence of appropriate technologies to boost land productivity of rain-fed agriculture, provision of irrigation and moisture conservation have become critical for improvement or stabilization of crop production in these regions". They very rightly argue that there has been a policy bias against agriculture in general and rain-fed agriculture in particular. This is evident from the decline of public investment in agriculture "from 4 percent of agricultural GDP (Rs. 70 billion) at in early 1990s to 1.5 percent recently (Rs. 46 billion both at 1993-94 prices). Further "price policy is biased in favour of wheat and paddy to the neglect of other cereals and

Table 1.2 Sectoral real growth rates in GDP at factor cost (at 1999 – 2000 prices)

Sector	Percentage change over the previous year					
	2000-01	*2001-02*	*2002-03 (P)*	*2003-04 (Q)*	*2004-05 (A)*	*2005-06 (P)*
I. **Agriculture**	0.0	6.2	(-) 6.9	10.0	0.7	2.3
II. **Industry**	6.3	2.7	7.0	7.8	8.6	9.0
Mining & quarrying	2.5	1.8	8.7	5.3	5.8	1.0
Manufacturing	7.7	2.5	6.8	7.1	8.1	9.4
Electricity, gas & water supply	2.0	1.7	4.8	4.8	4.3	5.4
Construction	6.1	4.0	7.7	10.9	12.5	12.1
III. **Services**	5.6	7.1	7.3	8.2	9.9	9.8
Trade, hotels, transport & communication	7.1	9.2	9.1	12.0	10.6	11.7
Financial services	4.1	7.3	8.0	4.5	9.2	9.5
Community, social & personal services	4.7	3.9	3.8	5.4	9.2	7.9
IV. Total GDP at factor cost	4.4	5.8	3.8	8.5	7.5	8.1

P: Provisional, Q: Quick estimates, A: Advance estimates.

Source: **Central Statistical Organization** (as quoted in Economic Survey, & RBI Annual Report 2005-06)

dryland crops like groundnut. Also, "extension services in agriculture are neglected resulting in poor coverage and ill-qualified services......... leaving farmers in the dark regarding quality of inputs, soil quality, availability of ground water etc." Thus the growth rate of GDP for the 10th five-year plan period, 2001-02 to 2006-07, might work out at about 7.0 percent.

1.2 Indian economy has witnessed major structural shifts in the sources of domestic output, as a consequence of varying rates of growth of output of agriculture, industry and services sectors, since Independence as shown in Table 1.2. Agricultural sector (including forestry and fishing) which accounted for average of 55 percent share in GDP in the 50s declined to 28 percent in the 90's and is currently around 22 percent. This has reduced the vulnerability of the economy to monsoons. (Table 1.3) Industry's contribution to GDP has moved up only marginally, from an average of 21 percent in the 60s to 27 percent in 1990's. It is the services sector whose contribution has moved up significantly from around 28 percent in the 1950s to 54 percent in 2005-06. "Its size and growth have helped in maintaining the overall resiliency of India's economy, most importantly by creating employment opportunities for skilled people, as evidenced by massive gains in the field of information technology (IT) in recent years." (Singh & Bery, 2005). Unluckily, however, services neither provide wage-goods nor employment to the poor and under-privileged. Social services could have been an important source of education and health services to the poor. But here also one is dismayed at the outcome.

1.3 In contrast to developed economies, where most production sub-sectors are organized in corporate and other forms of business organization, it is the unorganized/informal sub-sectors, defined as production units without power and having less than seven workers, which continue to dominate India's GDP, as shown in Table 1.4. Looking at Tables 1.2 and 1.4 together, one finds that output of sub-sectors 'construction' and 'manufacturing' in 'Industry' sector continues to grow at a pace higher than that of the economy as a whole. It is the organized/corporate sector, which has gained primacy 'in manufacturing' but not yet in 'construction', where the 'unorganized' continues to hold its own. This is, perhaps, because a

Table 1.3 Sectoral shares in GDP at factor cost in Indian Economy 1951/52-2000/03(at 1993/94 prices)

Period	*Agriculture & allied sectors*	*Industry*	*Services*
1951/52-1960/61	55.4	16.3	28.1
1961/62-1970/71	47.0	21.4	31.6
1971/72-1980/81	42.1	23.0	34.9
1981/82-1990/91	35.7	25.4	39.0
1991/92-2000/01	28.2	27.1	44.7
2001/02	23.9	26.7	49.5
2002/03	22.1	27.1	50.8

Source: Reserve Bank of India, **Handbook of Statistics on the Indian Economy** (various years)

Table 1.4 Share of Unorganized Sub-sectors in India's Net Domestic Product (NDP) (as percent of Sub-sectorTotals)

	Sector / Sub-Sector	*Period*			
		1971/72 to 1980/81	*1981/82 to 1990/91*	*1991/92 To 1995/96*	*1996/97 to 2000/01*
	Agriculture & allied sectors	97.7	95.4	96.4	96.6
Industry	Mining and Quarrying	7.9	6.5	8.2	7.3
	Manufacturing	37.5	37.3	36.9	37.6
	Electricity, gas and water supply	0.9	5.6	5.0	5.8
	Construction	54.3	48.2	52.4	55.6
	Trade, hotels and restaurants	90.7	90.2	88.0	82.6

(Contd.)

(Contd. Table 1.4)

Services

Sector / Sub-Sector	***Period***			
	1971/72 to 1980/81	*1981/82 to 1990/91*	*1991/92 To 1995/96*	*1996/97 to 2000/01*
Transport, storage and communications	38.4	48.8	47.9	49.8
Finance, insurance, real estate and business services	51.5	50.5	43.0	42.2
Community, social and personal services	18.4	21.6	19.6	17.7
Total NDP at factor cost	68.4	65.1	62.5	60.3

Source: Central Statistical Organization, **National Accounts Statistics** (various years).

substantial share of construction activity takes place in rural areas. Trade, hotels and restaurants' sub-sector still continues to be dominated by the unorganized, as in 'agriculture'.

However, the share of the organized sector has almost doubled from 9.3 percent during 70s to 17.4 percent during the 9th Five Year Plan period (1996/97 to 2000/01). Similarly sub-sector 'transport, storage and communications' had registered double digit growth. There has been impressive progress in the expansion of railway passenger network, production of commercial vehicles and runaway expansion of telecommunications. Growth in financial services, including banking, insurance and real estate services reflects the maturing of Indian financial markets. However, 'Community, social and personal services, which includes public administration, defence, education, health etc are estimated to have suffered a growth deceleration of 1.3 percent in 2005/06. Of these, it is the 'social and personal services', which have suffered growth deceleration of a much higher order.

1.4 The unorganized sector suffers from poor economies of scale, lack of research and development, low productivity and quality, and problems of marketing and finance but has the benefit of higher adaptability to changing market conditions, because of decentralized production process. It can be a powerful tool for rural industrialization, relieving agriculture of its surplus labour force. With economic reforms, the composition of the organized sector has been changing in favour of the private sector, though public sector still continues to hold a dominant position in terms of contribution to NDP, with its share being around 25% as against private sector (organized) having around 15 percent share. However, with privatization and no further expansion of the public sector, the roles might get reversed soon. Further, public enterprises are increasingly entering into agreements/ arrangements with private sector, outsourcing some of their functions/activities and operations to them. Private sector is even taking over several of the traditional roles of government such as power through captive power plants, handling of cargo at major ports development of minor ports (as in Gujarat), airports, telecom etc. Further the State is increasingly resorting to divesting part of its holdings of public enterprise equity in favour of the private sector.

Table 1.5 Growth rates of Industrial production by User-based classification (Base: 1993-94 = 100) (Average annual percentage change)

Period	*Basic goods*	*Capital goods*	*Intermediate goods*	*Consumer goods*		
				All	*Durable*	*Non durable*
1981/82-1990/91	7.9	11.5	5.9	6.7	13.9	5.5
1991/92-1995/96	7.8	0.3	7.4	6.3	9.3	5.8
1996/97-2000/01	4.2	7.7	7.1	5.5	9.4	4.3
2000/01	3.7	1.8	4.7	8.0	14.5	5.8
2001/02	2.6	-3.4	51.5	6.0	11.5	4.1
2002/03	4.7	10.5	3.9	7.1	-6.3	12.0
2003/04	5.4	13.6	6.4	7.1	11.6	5.8
2004/05	5.5	13.9	6.1	11.7	14.3	10.8
2005/06§	6.0	15.7	2.2	12.2	13.6	11.7

§ : for 9 months, April-December 2005

Source: for 1st three rows, **Singh & Bery** and for 2000/01 to 2005/06, **Economic Survey**, 2005/06.

1.5 Manufacturing and construction have been the leading sectors in industry with 'mining and quarrying' and 'electricity', being laggards since 2000-01 as seen in Table 1.2. When we examine user-based classification of industrial output, we find that it is the capital goods and consumer goods which have recorded the highest annual increases in output during the 4 years, 2002-03 to 2005-06. One finds that the growth rate of output of basic goods (Table 1.5) had suffered deceleration during 2000/01 and 2001/02 but has been picking up since 2002/03. Growth rate of output of capital goods too, suffered a decline in 2000/01 & 2002/03 (actually recording a negative growth rate in 2002/03), but its growth rate has been rising sharply (in 2 digits) since then. Growth rate of 'intermediate goods' output has been rather erratic. The growth rate of consumer goods output declined to 6.0 percent in 2001/02 as against 8.0 per cent in 2000/01; it has been on an upswing since then, reaching 12.2 per cent in 2005/06. 'Consumer durables' have been outpacing the 'non-durable' except in 2002/03, when it recorded a negative growth rate of 6.3 percent. Among the durables, it is the automotive industry which recorded a very high rate of growth of 16 per cent during 1999-2000 to 2005-06, with the manufacturing sub-sector recording a growth rate of about 6.9 per cent over the same period. Within the automotive industry, it is the two-wheelers (motor bikes & scooters) and personal cars which are calling the tune and not the commercial vehicles. The Draft Auto Mission Plan (AMP), 2006-2016 (released by the Government of India Sept., 2006) in projects over four-fold increase in turnover, from $34 billion in 2006 to $ 145 billion in 2016. Here again, the two-wheelers and passenger cars are calling the shots.

Information Technology (IT) and IT-enabled business-process outsourcing services have been on a robust growth path. While electronics production rose from Rs. 28,100 crores in 1999-2000 to Rs. 50,500 crores in 2004-05 – a rise of 80% over the period, computer software production rose from Rs. 24,350 crores in 1999-2000 to Rs. 97,860 crores- - quadrupling, with exports rising from Rs. 17,150 crores to Rs. 78,230 crores over the period (an increase of 356 percent).

1.6.11 We have already commented upon the high volatility from which growth rate of output of Indian agriculture had been

Table 1.6 International comparison of yield Selected commodities -2002

Rice/Paddy		*Wheat*		*Maize*	
Bangladesh	3448	Bangladesh	2164	China	5022
Egypt	9135	China	3885	Egypt	7789
India	2915	France	7449	France	8813
Japan	6582	India	2770	India	1705
Myanmar	3532	Iran	1905	Italy	9560
Pakistan	2882	Pakistan	2262	Pakistan	1769
Thailand	2597	U.K	8043	Philippines	1803
USA	7372				
World	3916	World	2720	World	4343
Sugarcane		*Tobacco Leaves*		*Ground nut (in shell)*	
Bangladesh	39890	Bangladesh	1233	Argentina	2329
China	66353	Canada	2600	Brazil	2043
Columbia	94789	France	2778	China	2986
Egypt	119893	India	1353	India	794
Guatemala	94032	Indonesia	829	Sudan	630
India	68049	Italy	3333	USA	2864
Pakistan	48042	Pakistan	1848	Uganda	701
World	65802	World	1589	World	1381

Secondary Source: **Economic Survey 2005-06**, Table 8.4

suffering. It is afflicted by low productivity. However, productivity has increased considerably, especially after the mid-60s, with the green revolution. For example, the average yield of cereals rose from 977 kilograms per hectare in the 1960s to 2318 kg. per hectare in 2001/02. However, it still remains lower than that in some of the neighbouring countries. Thus, even though India accounted for 21.8 percent of global paddy output, the yield per hectare in 2002, at 2915 kg, was lower than that of Bangladesh and Myanmar at 3448 kg and 3532 kg. respectively (Table 1.6) and only one third of that of Egypt. Almost similar situation prevails in wheat, maize, sugarcane, tobacco and groundnut. Further, growth rate of agricultural output has slowed down over the past decade, with real value-added in agriculture increasing by an average rate of 2.6 percent in the 1990s as against 3.5 percent during the 1980s " (Singh & Bery). Further, while there is some scope for wasteland reclamation, there are obvious limitations to extension of acreage. It may also be noted that the total output of foodgrains in Rabi (winter) season is almost approaching that of the Kharif (autumn) season

1.6.12 Foodgrains output since the 1990s has been less than the growth rate of population; the average growth rate of foodgrains output works out to about 1.1 per cent during 1990-91 to 2005-06. Further the growth rate of output of coarse cereals, which has been an important source of nutrition for the poor and of pulses, chief source of protein, for majority of India's poor has been lower still. This has resulted in lower net availability of foodgrains per capita, taking account of exports and changes in stocks, has fallen by 14.5 kgs during 1990-91 to 2000-01, to less than 160 kgs per year. Per capita net availability of pulses declined from 15.2 kg per year in 1990-91 to 10.6 kg in 2003, rising somewhat to 13.1 kg in 2004

1.62 Horticulture, which includes fruits, vegetables, spices, floriculture and coconut, increased its gross cropped area by about 10 percent in 2004/05 at 17.8 million hectares, from 16.3 million hectares in 2002/03. Its output at 164 million tonnes (MT) in 2004/05, contributed 28 percent of GDP from agriculture. India was the second largest producer of fruits and vegetables in the world, at 49 million tonnes and 85 million tonnes respectively in 2003/04.

Realizing its importance, "for improving the productively of land, generating employment, improving economic condition of farmers and entrepreneurs, enhancing exports and above all, providing nutritional security to the people "(ES), Government of India, has launched the National Horticulture Mission (NHM) in May 2005, to double horticultural production by 2011. However if horticultural output is expanded at the cost of foodgrains output, it would seriously compromise food security and real wages of the poor.

1.63. Livestock, Poultry & fisheries: Dairying, poultry farming and fisheries, not only provide employment and income to millions of people in both rural and urban areas, but also provide nutritional security to people. Milk output has risen more than five times since independence from 17.0 million tonnes in 1950-51 to 90.7 million tonnes in 2004/05, thereby nearly doubling the per capita milk availability from 124 grams to 232 gms per day, for the respective years. According to the 17th Livestock Census (reference date: mid-Oct.2003), India owns one of the largest livestock population in the world—accounting for 57 percent of the world's buffalo population and 16 percent of the world's cattle population. It stands first in terms of world's cattle & buffalo population, second in goat population and third in world's sheep population. With output of 45 million eggs and 1.65 MT of chicken-meat in 2004/05, it is the 5th largest producer of poultry, one of the fastest growing segments of the economy.

1.64 Being the third largest producer of fish and the second largest for inland fish, it provided livelihood to over 11 million people, engaged fully, partially or in subsidiary activities related to the sector. It produced 3.0 MT of marine fish and 3.4 MT of inland fish in 2003/04 and exported 474,000 tonnes of fish and earned Rs.6086 crores as foreign exchange.

1.63 Plantation Sector – Tea, Coffee & Rubber India is the largest producer and consumer of tea in the world, with the output being 850.5 million kg. in 2003/04 and exporting about a quarter of this output, earning foreign exchange worth Rs. 1637crores in 2003/04. To help tea industry, additional excise duty of Rs. 1 per kg on tea was withdrawn in the Union Budget, 2005-06 and two schemes of subsidy for production of orthodox teas and assistance to two R&D Institutions - Tea Research at Tocklai

(Assam) and United Planters Association in Southern India- have been sanctioned. Although India produces only 4 percent of world output of coffee, over 80 percent of its output of 2.75 lakh tonnes in 2004-05, was exported, earning foreign exchange worth Rs. 1224 crores. India produced (anticipated) 780 thousand tonnes of natural rubber, with consumption being estimated at 799 thousand tonnes in 2005/06 (ES).

Section 2
Development Strategies – India and China

2.1. Before we dwell on the development strategies of India and China, it would be appropriate to, briefly, dwell on their respective political history and legacies. China was, by and large, a stable centrally-run state throughout its history, with limited periods of instability and lack of a single authority". (Desai, 2005) India, on the other hand, had, very rarely, a single king or political authority, controlling even a major part of its territory. China being a unitary state conferred certain advantages which have not been often recognized. In a recent survey of Chinese economic history, Deng (2000) pointed out "a basic structural factor – namely that most of the time, most of China, had a nation-wide market, a single government (which was active in maintaining food supply, famine relief, and price control), a standardized written language, a uniform calendar and a system of weights and measures, a dominant Confucian code of conduct, a nationwide transport network, and the mechanisms for social mobility and inter-regional migration..........China could claim to have been a proto-industrialized country by the 13th century and indeed has been considered by many scholars to have been a prime candidate for a capitalist revolution which it missed". In contrast, the Indian system of royal power, as Meghnad Desai observes, was "like a multi-tiered cake. It was flatter and while there was a top and a bottom, the power of the top king over his vassals was not absolute, loyalty, though owed by the lower tiers to the top, was always negotiable and there had to be some give and take. The British were perhaps the first rulers to try a more absolute and hierarchal structure of power, under the limitation of oversight by a democratic

Parliament back in London". Further, it was British rule that gave India its definitive territory, fixed its boundaries and gave it a structure of provinces and central government with an administrative 'steel frame'. They introduced English language to brainwash us into western mores and subservience but which is now an asset for accessing the global market. Railways and cotton textile mills i.e. modern industry commenced in India in the 1850s, a quarter century earlier than in China. "China's attitude to foreigners was and is much more hostile than India's" (Desai).

2.2 Both India and China were highly urban civilizations by the 18th century, though bulk of the population lived in rural areas. Needham's (1954) work showed that China was much advanced in science and technology, with gunpowder, printing, paper and paper currency as its inventions. India was known for its mathematics and philosophy. The Chinese gave the world wheelbarrow and bureaucracy. India contributed with zero, decimals, and Buddhism. Both were major exporters of textiles, silks and muslins; their ships sailed round the world and really dominated seas till 1500. The Moghuls did not need a navy. It was the kingdoms in South India which were maritime adventurers. As their power declined, Indian shipping began to be conducted on a private basis and control of seas increasingly passed to a series of West European countries. The Chinese withdrew from the seas from 16th century onward.

Table 2.1 Share of World Output and Population (in Per cent)

Year	*Share of gross world product*		*Share of world population*	
	China	*India*	*China*	*India*
1913	0.89	7.5	26.4	17.0
1950	4.5	4.2	21.3	14.2
1998	11.5	7.7	21.0	16.5

Source: **Maddison** (2001), as quoted by Desai.

Chinese agricultural productivity has been traditionally much higher than that of India. Their irrigation systems were bigger and better than any in India. Maddison estimates Chinese per capita income at M$ 600[(4)] and that of India, at M$ 533 in 1820. He further estimates that India made up during the next 130 years, with output per employed at $ 1377 in India, as against $ 1297 in China and per capita income of both declined in the first half of 20th century[(5)]: India's from M$ 673 in 1913 to M$ 619 in 1950 and China's from M$ 552 in 1913 to M$ 439 in 1950. Maddison points out that while population of both China and India rose during the first half of the 20th century, the per capita income of both declined, as shown in Table 2.1, but India was somewhat better off than China.

However, in the second half of the 20th century, the relative positions got reversed. By 1998, China's per capita income rose to M$ 3117 (a seven fold increase) as against India's M$ 1760 (a near trebling)

2.3 Indian national movement had been deeply affected by Soviet growth strategy of fast pace of industrialization, of concentrating on building up of basic goods industry such as steel and machinery— "Department I goods" in Marxian terminology – rather than consumer and other low-tech goods. China had only the Soviet model of industrialization for adoption, to start with. Further, the hostility against foreigners impelled both towards import substitution, independence from foreign capital and self-sufficiency.

However, the contrast between the two was most glaring in agriculture. With their sub-continental size territories and a similar diversity in eco-agricultural structure of regions in both countries, China had a uniform revenue collection system and land ownership pattern; India, by contrast, had different systems of land tenures and land revenue collection in different regions, depending upon whether they were Ryotwari, Mahalwari or Zamindari type land tenures, Land reforms in China involved expropriation of large land holders and distribution of land among peasants equitably. Agriculture being a state/provincial subject, rather than in the union/central list, land reform legislation has varied across states, in India. Further the landlords received some compensation for the land taken over. Also, landlords were able to retain considerable chunks of land which was shown as Khud Kasht (under personal cultivation). How much surplus land and how much of this surplus was barren/cultivable land, with Land Ceiling legislations, does not need recounting[(6)]. The only state, where effective land reforms took place was West Bengal, when the Left Front Government came to power in 1977 and perhaps, this is one of the reasons, that they have continued to be re-elected. The role of effective land reforms in creating a level playing field in China's rural areas, in eradication of poverty and generating self-respect among the peasantry, needs to be under-scored. Despite many convulsions and misadventures - the Great leap Forward, the Cultural Revolution, China was able to develop the internal market and bring about rural industrialization under the Great Helmsman. However, it was only after the passing away of Mao, and the elimination of the hold of the Gang of Four, that Deng Xiao Ping was able to launch China on the high growth path of liberalization, controlled privatization and globalization, boosting exports, competitiveness and foreign investment.

India took the first steps to liberalization in December 1977, with the Janata Government introducing a new Industrial Policy by ushering in the concept of District Industry Centre, giving a greater priority to small scale industries (SSIs). Further, the export-import policy for 1977/78 widened the scope of Open General License imports by SSIs and end-users. Further, instead of 'permissible' items, it introduced the concept of absolutely prohibited items. Coming back to power in 1980, Prime Minister Indira Gandhi discarded the doctrine of self-sufficiency and accepted a loan from the International Monetary Fund (IMF). However, this loan was used "to ease the consumption constraint in the public sector and to cushion loss making public enterprises" (Desai, 2005). Prime Minister, Rajiv Gandhi further eased industry capacity limits, simplified licensing procedure and adopted further export-promoting measures. However, the basic paradigm of Industrial Policy Resolution of 1956, continued to rule. The balance of payments crisis of 1991 forced rethinking on the earlier development paradigm and the economic reforms were announced in June 1991, opening up the economy to liberalization, privatization and globalization. Rupee was devalued and exchange control regime was relaxed, fiscal deficit was cut and the external sector was liberalized. These measures led to raising the growth rate to 7 percent in 1994-95, but a slide back started from May 1996, with political instability for almost two years and with the East Asian crisis from mid-1997. The National Democratic Alliance (NDA) Government with Shri Atal Behari Bajpai as Prime Minister, undertook a number of measures to carry forward reforms- "accelerating privatization, rationalizing the regulatory framework and further liberalizing the trade and financial sectors" (Singh & Bery). The United Progressive Alliance (UPA) Government, taking over in May, 2004, has adopted a Common Minimum Programme (CMP). Both the NDA and the UPA Governments have been coalition governments of national and regional political parties, with some of these parties supporting the government from outside. The Left has serious reservations on disinvestment in public enterprises, on labour sector reforms, on foreign direct investment, on privatization and certain financial sector reforms. However, since the West Bengal Government, with Chief Minister, Buddhadev Bhattacharya, is implementing some of the reform measures, one may expect their resistance to these measures e.g. acquisition of agricultural land for Special Economic Zones[(7)] (SEZs), FDI in retail, financial sector reforms etc, may get somewhat modified. Besides the land reforms, "China's lead in agricultural productivity remained to the end of the first phase and indeed increased when in the second phase, China moved to a more private initiative system". (Desai, 2005). China's emphasis on education and health-care for all[(8)] from early on, has paid rich dividends; neglect of education and health for all, in India has cost her dearly. However, the setting up of a chain of national laboratories for R&D in India, starting from 1948, has been a boon, which is paying rich dividends now. However, despite these changes in the human development and agrarian transformation in China, and green revolution in India, the relative position of per capita income changed somewhat in favour of China, with M$979 and India's M$ 966, in 1978. Since 1978, China has followed the path of export led-growth. It introduced the family responsibility system in agriculture, a sort of privatization. It invited foreign capital in industry. Chinese from Hong Kong and Taiwan have responded with billions of dollars in foreign direct investment (FDI). It set up the Special Economic/Export Zones (SEZs) on the Eastern coast, where the foreign investors were given highly favourable terms in taxation, labour laws etc, to make Chinese exports highly competitive. It simultaneously took steps for the growth of rural and local enterprises. However, state enterprises continue to exist. China has since, been having a high annual growth rate of 9-11 percent. China's growth rates, based on revised data were 10.1 percent and 9.9 percent respectively in 2004 and 2005 and projected rates for 2006 and 2007 are 9.1 percent and 8.5 percent respectively (World Bank, 2006). Srinivasan (2006) finds that China and India "accounted for two fifths of global growth during 1989-95 and a third during 1985-2003, once adjustment for purchasing power parity (PPP) is made". He further finds that "the relative share of China's growth in global growth compared to India's seems to have decreased over time when adjustment for PPP is made. This suggests that relative to India, prices in China seem to be moving closer over time to world prices, confirming once again the findings that China is integrating with the world economy faster than India". China's integration with the world economy is evident from the share of its international trade in its GDP at 65 percent in 2004 and 70 percent in 2006, which was very high for an economy of China's continental size and level of per capita income. An important feature of Chinese exports has been their high labor intensity. In contrast, Indian exports are highly capital intensive, with the exception of textiles and garments, gems and jewellery and leather products. However, it may be noted that the share of textiles and garments in the aggregate exports has declined from 13.7 percent and 11.6 percent in 1995-96 to 7.45 percent and 8.2 percent respectively in 2005-06 (Economic Times, 2006).

Section 3
Poverty and Employment

3.1 Incidence of poverty is estimated on the basis of large scale quinquennial and annual sample surveys on household consumer expenditure conducted by the National Sample Survey Organization (NSSO). The last two quinquennial surveys were conducted in 1999-2000 and 2004-05 corresponding to 55th round and 61st round whose results have been recently reported by the media. The 55th round had indicated that poverty ratio had come down from 36 percent in 1993-94 to 26 percent in 1999-2000, a sharp decline in just 6 years. These estimates created a serious controversy regarding the reference period. Since 1950s, NSSO had been collecting consumer expenditure data on the basis of a uniform 30-days recall period. It was contended that 30-day recall period was too long especially for the expenditure on food which it was claimed, was under-reported. The NSSO responded by modifying the reference period for the 55th round; consumer expenditure on food, pan, tobacco etc. was recorded for two reference periods: one-week recall and one-month recall. The reference period for clothes, consumer durables etc. was 365 days and for other items, it was 30 days. The changed reference period increased the expenditure estimates and reduced poverty figures. This stirred up controversy. It was also contended that the headcount poverty ratio of 26.7 percent was at variance with the rising poverty trends indicated by annual surveys and supplementary evidence culled from other poverty-related variables. It was, therefore, agreed that the 1999-2000 estimates were not comparable with 1993-94 estimates. Hence, no inference could be drawn, regarding the impact of economic reforms on poverty.

3.2 The Alternative Survey Group (Mehta, 2004) had contended that "the rural poverty line of Rs. 327 in 1999-2000" corresponds not to 2400 K-cal but to 1868 K-cal." The rural poverty line corresponding to 2400 K-cal would be Rs. 567 and corresponding poverty ratio would be 74.9 percent. The intention of the scholar was to bring home the wide divergence between the two sets of figures and thus point at the absurdity of official estimates." Less than US 1 dollar per day's is considered absolute poverty and India, had surprisingly the highest proportion of 44.2 percent among the 5 Asian countries listed as compared to 18.5 percent in China. An important measure of poverty (relative) is defined in terms of bottom 10,20 or 30 percent of the population which cannot sustain the desirable patterns of life that exist in a given society at a given time: Defining poverty in terms of calory intake and hence, only in terms of expenditure on food is obviously inadequate and needs to be supplemented by expenditure on non-food items clothing, shelter, education, health etc.

World Development Report 2000-01 gave data on the percentage of population living on less than US $ 1 and $2 as given below:-

3.3 The 61st round sample survey of consumer expenditure conducted by the NSSO has confirmed the misgivings expressed by the Alternative Survey Group, referred to earlier. It has estimated that poverty declined by a mere 0.74 per cent per annum during the 11-year period, 1993/94-2004/05, although the rate of poverty decline was a little higher at 0.79 percent between 1999/2000-2004/05. It found that the number of people living below the poverty line (BPL) had come down from 26.09 percent in 1999/2000 to 22.15 percent in 2004/05.

Table 3.1 Poverty Population in select Asian Countries[a]) (in percent of total population)

Region	*GDP per Capita (1998) in $[b]*	*Share of population living on*	
		Less than 1 $ per day	*Less then $ 2 per day*
Bangladesh	1423	29.1 (1996)	77.8 (1996)
China	3356	18.5 (1998)	50.7 (1998)
India	2101	44.2 (1997)	86.2 (1997)
Indonesia	2806	7.7 (1999)	55.3 (1999)
Pakistan	1794	31.0 (1996)	84.7 (1996)

(a) Figures in parenthesis represent year of observation.

(b) In US dollars on a purchasing power parity basis.

Source: World Bank, **World Development Report**, 2000-01.

The survey also found that poverty declined the sharpest in the poorer states – Assam & North Eastern states: nearly 4 per cent annually, Jharkhand: 2.51 per cent p.a.; Chhatisgarh: 2.15 per cent p.a. and Bihar: 1.69 per cent p.a. Further, the survey found that BPL population declined by only 2.12 per cent during the quinquenniam 1999/2000 – 2004/05 in the urban areas as against 4.68 per cent decline in rural areas. This could be due to rural-urban migration. If, however rural-urban migration is the culprit, then the rate of actual decline in poverty in rural areas, has been over-estimated. The survey also found an increase in BPL population in Haryana, Maharashtra, Delhi, Rajasthan and Goa, possibly due to labour moving out of Bihar, U.P. and Jharkhand. It is also surmised that the decline in the growth rate of state domestic product of Maharashtra, may have added to the increase in the BPL population. The decline in the BPL population in the three poorest states over the 5 years period are expected to be:

Orissa: 1999/2000: 47.15 per cent, 2004/05: nearly 40 per cent (a decline of 8.36 per cent in rural areas and 1.2 per cent in urban areas).

Jharkhand: 1999-2000: 47.40 per cent, 2004/05: 34.83 per cent

Bihar: 2004/2005: 32.57 per cent

3.4 The National Human Rights Commission in its report submitted to the Supreme Court, on starvation deaths in KBK tribal districts of Orissa, stated that there was under-estimation of the BPL families by 18 lakhs; the actual number of BPL families was 50.19 lakhs. It further stated that BPL families were not getting adequate quantity of food grains every month under the Antyodaya Anna Yojana. It recommended that the Centre raise the allocation of rice to 35 Kg per month instead of the current 25 kg. per month so that family members were assured of two square meals a day. It noted from the reports of its investigation team that there was a huge pendency of unsettled claims under the National Family Benefit Scheme (NFBS) in every district of the KBK region.

Prime Minister, Manmohan Singh, in his speech at the Economic Times Awards for Corporate Excellence, accepted this grim reality in the following words. "Millions of our fellow citizens are still deprived of the benefits of a fast growing economy. While the belief in a market economy is certainly justified, it must be remembered that markets serve those who are part of it. They have no relevance to those who exist on the margins of subsistence and who have neither the physical nor the human resources to participate in them." He further emphasized this point while presiding over the meeting of the full planning commission to discuss the approach to the Draft 11th five year plan (2007-12) and setting the target of 9 per cent growth for the 11th plan, with the following words. "While there are pluses to the economy, I must emphasise that there are also serious weaknesses, poverty is falling but not fast enough. The current consumption poverty rates of over 20 per cent are simply not acceptable in this high growth scenario. It is our collective responsibility to ensure that they become stake-holders in the growth process under way. This is essential not only from an equity perspective but also for maintaining social and political harmony". The question arises why a growth rate of about 6 percent over the period 1993/94-2004/05 had so little effect on consumption poverty and on employment? We may better understand the issue if we simultaneously examine the question of employment / unemployment.

3.5 Employment

3.51 The Planning Commission Special Group on Employment Generating Growth had noted, that "even if the organized sector grew at 20 percent per annum and the private sector, at 30 percent per annum, their contribution to total employment would increase by 1.5 to 2.0 percent over the 10th plan" (2002). Obviously, it follows that the unorganized sector has to be specially targetted for increasing employment. However before discussing the nature of growth and employment we need to have a glimpse of the total picture.

3.52 The organised sector has been experiencing disparate growth rates for different groups. For example, A-1 group(9), consisting of cotton ginning, textiles, food products, leather products, chemical products, rubber products, other non-metallic minerals, fabricated metals, precision equipment, motor vehicles and other manufacturing had a growth rate of value-added at 7.90 per cent during 1984-90, it rose to 8.63 per cent during 1994-2000, after declining to 7.50 per cent during 1989-95. Employment grew by 0.67per cent in period I (i.e. 1984-90), by 1.73per cent in period II and by 1.92per cent in period III. Labour productivity rose by 7.23per cent, 5.77per cent and 6.71per cent in periods I, II, III respectively. Within this A-1 group, the highest growth rate of employment during 1994-2000, was for motor vehicles at 4.31per cent, followed by fabricated metals at 3.74 per cent. All industries in group A-2, consisting of tobacco products, publishing, printing, other transport equipments, electrical machinery, machinery and equipments, communication equipment and basic metals recorded employment growth rate of (–) 2.07 percent during 1994-2000, while the growth rate of value- added, and productivity was 6.22 percent and 8.29 percent respectively (Unni, 2006).

3.53 Within the unorganised sector, 67per cent of the workers were in own-account enterprises in 2000-01, with their proportion being still higher in rural areas at 79per cent compared to urban, 43 percent. "There was a slow shift of workers in the unorganised manufacturing to the urban areas, from 26 percent share of employment in 1983 to nearly 35 percent in 2001. This shift was marginally greater among smaller enterprises". Most of the industry groups in the unorganised sector recorded relatively high wage growth. The average growth rate per annum of wage earnings in the unorganised sector, 12 per cent, was much higher than in the organised sector, 1 percent.

A shift towards skilled workers was observed in both regular and casual workers. The skill premium, (in terms of wages) however, was much higher among the regular workers than among the casual workers. "While an increase in the skilled work force and in the skill wage-premium was a positive feature, the flip side was that the inequality between the skilled and unskilled and regular and casual worker increased".

"Labour market linkages between various segments were established through attempts at increasing labour flexibility in the organised or formal sector firms........ This basically involves adjustment of labour, using mechanisms such as turnover, temporary lay-off and recall, temporary workers, part-time workers, subcontracting and home working or through flexible working time (that is, work shifts and overtime practices) without modifying the number of employees". An increase in the proportion of contract workers to total workers, was observed in wearing apparel, leather, wood, paper, chemical, rubber products, basic metals and machinery industry.

The impact of these policy changes and consequent changes in the organisation of production had both positive and negative implications:

On the positive side, the expansion of markets meant growth of employment opportunities and growth of real wages almost across for all segments of the workforce. There was also growth of a skilled workforce with increasing wage premiums. Inter-linkages of the firms in the organised and unorganised sector through subcontracting and through technology transfers, led to upgradation of workers' skills.

On the negative side, there was greater inequality between various segments of workers – benefitting male skilled workers in regular employment. Urban workers did better than their rural counterparts. The policy challenges for strengthening the prospect of enterprises and workers in the unorganised sector are: i) Improving the technology of production processes, to raise productivity ii) Launching a massive skill training programme to create market skills among the workers. This would involve upgrading ITIs, polytechnics and private sector institutions in tune with market needs. The whole process of informal skills, training and learning on-job should be recognised and arithmetic and communication skills has to be the base on which any other form of technical skills can be built up. iii) A comprehensive social security policy to all the workers in the informal sector.

3.54 One of the nagging but important question is: Why has a growth rate of 6 percent or more failed to reduce poverty and to provide adequate employment? The explanation lies in:

(i) **Failure of land reforms:** As already mentioned, land reforms in India, have failed to unshackle the oppressive feudal agrarian structure, which coupled with the caste systems [10)], did not permit the high growth rate reaching the *Aam Aadmi*- the bonded labourer, the landless labour, the small peasants, the artisan, scheduled castes and scheduled tribes.

(ii) **Slow growth of agricultural, especially foodgrains output:** We have shown in para 1.612 that foodgrains output grew only at 1.1 percent during 1990-91 to 2005-06 as against about 4 percent stipulated in the 10th five year plan.

Table 3.2: Public investment in Indian agriculture and as percentage of agricultural GDP and of total public investment (at 1993-94 prices)

Year	*Public investment (in Rs. ten crores)*	*Agricultural GDP %*	*Total Public Sector Investment %*
1960-61	2270	2.09	12.22
1970-71	2990	2.19	6.55
1980-81	6990	4.39	17.27
1990-91	4320	1.94	6.23
1999-00	3870	1.27	0.34

Source: National Account Statistics.

(a) The crisis in Indian agriculture can be explained primarily by the decline in public investment in rural infrastructure, public works, minor irrigation and soil conservation works as is clear from table 3.2. Public investment rose from 2.09 percent of agricultural GDP in 1960-61 to 4.39 percent in 1980-81, but declined to 1.27 percent in 1999-2000.

(b) **Price rise:** With almost stagnant foodgrains output for the last decade and a half, and the procurement price of wheat and rise, being raised every year, foodgrains prices have reached levels, which impose a severe burden on the common man. The deficiencies and in adequacies of Index of Wholesale Prices, and of the Cost of Living Indices are too well known to need recounting. Prices of pulses have more than doubled during the last six months, putting them out of the consumption basket of even the lower middle class and thus accentuating the problem of malnutrition and poverty.

(c) **PDS:** The public distribution system (PDS) had been designed to insulate the poor against rising prices of essential consumption goods. With the introduction of Targetted PDS in 1997, two sets of prices of foodgrains for the 'below poverty line' (BPL) and 'above poverty line' (APL) households, are being announced and these prices have been revised upwards several times since then. Consequently, the difference between the APL and market prices has narrowed down; some times the market prices were lower. The Programme Evaluation Organization (PEO) of the planning commission in one of its evaluations of the Food Corporation of India, commented upon the bureaucratic functioning and inefficiency of the FCI's operations thus; the FCI's economic cost (incurred for its procurement, storage and transportation) was more then the open market prices. The study noted: "Taking into account all the inefficiencies of PDS, it is found that GOI spends Rs. 3.65 to transfer Rupee 1 to the poor".

All these factors have made the poor in India more insecure and vulnerable.

(iii) **Inadequate and tardy rural non-farm growth, especially of rural industrialization:** The proportion of male workers in the primary sector (Table 3.3) declined from 77.5 percent in 1983 to 70.4 percent in 2003 however, their proportion in secondary, tertiary and total non-farm sectors has steadily increased. Their employment in non-farm sectors rose from 22.5 percent in 1983 to 29.6 percent in 2003.

However, "the employment base of rural female workers remains heavily tagged with agriculture, even as late as 2003; not more than 15-16 percent of them, could get absorbed in the network of non-farm activities" (Chaddha 2005). Chaddha also underlines halting pace of inter-sectoral shift during 1987 – 1993-94 period, both for male and female workers, except for the manufacturing and the community-social-personal sectors. However during the post-reform period (1993-94 onwards), the annual compound growth rate (Table 3.4) has declined in manufacturing, both for rural and urban workers, in trade for rural workers, in 'finance insurance and real estate' for rural workers and a very steep decline in community 'social and personal services' for both rural workers (from 3.13 per cent to 0.32 per cent) and urban workers (from 4.16 per cent to 0.13 per cent). Within the community 'social and personal services' sanitary service workers (mostly scheduled caste) suffered a decline from 4.92 per cent to (-)15.60 per cent, for rural workers and from 2.35 per cent to (-) 6.35 per cent for urban sanitary workers. Similarly recreational and cultural workers in rural areas suffered a decline in employment from 7.72 per cent

Table 3.3: Sectoral distribution of Usual Status Workers in India by Sex 1983 to 2003 (in percentage)

Year	*Public investment (in Rs. ten crores)*	*Agricultural GDP %*	*Total Public Sector Investment %*
1960-61	2270	2.09	12.22
1970-71	2990	2.19	6.55
1980-81	6990	4.39	17.27
1990-91	4320	1.94	6.23
1999-00	3870	1.27	0.34

Source: Part of Chaddha's Table No. 3.

in pre-reform period to (-) 10.07per cent in the post-reform period. Sectors which recorded the higher growth rate in the post-reform period were 'construction', 'transport storage and communications' and 'education' for both rural and urban workers and 'retail trade', and 'banking, insurance and real estate' and 'medical, health' for urban workers.The only exception to this trend is increase in employment in 'trade hotels and restaurants' in rural areas and a decline in urban areas, possibly because of higher capital and technology intensity in this sector in urban areas.

Chaddha has noted a few important differences in the mode of employment between agricultural and non-agricultural sectors both for male and female workers. First, self-employment dominates in both agriculture and non-farm sectors. Second 'while regular salary jobs are almost conspicuous by their absence in agriculture, again for both categories of workers, they are available to a fairly sizeable proportion of workers in non-agricultural activities, especial to rural males'. This implies that casual wage labour is not that significant in non-farm segment as it does in the farm sector, for both male and female workers. Third the index of casualisation has been increasing for non-farm employment as well, most markedly for rural males. Finally the tertiary sector jobs, within the rural non-farm economy have been more favourable to rural male and female workers than the secondary sector jobs, because a higher proportion of rural male and female workers are employed in regular salaried jobs, but also because a very low proportion of them are engaged as casual labourers. A significant observation made by Chaddha is that "rural economy stands well enmeshed with the rest of the economy, or the rural job aspirants can no more operate outside the precincts of the national labour market is authenticated, *albiet indirectly and meekly*, by a pattern of employment growth commonly shared by rural and urban workers". This is confirmed by the simultaneous improvement and decline of growth rates of employment in the rural and urban sectors in the post-reform years. As shown by Table 3.4.

The programme of rural industrialization in India has been undertaken principally through the Khadi and Village Industries Commission (KVIC), set up in 1955, and the state level Khadi &

Table 3.4: Annual compound growth rate of employment for Usual Status (Principal + Subsidiary) workers by residence & production sectors: 1983/1999-2000

Sector Code	*Description*	*Rural*		*Urban*		*Total*	
		1988	1999-00	1983	1999-00	1983	1999-00
1	2	3	4	5	6	7	8
	All Sectors	1.75	0.66	3.27	2.27	2.06	1.02
0	Agriculture	1.38	0.13	1.54	-3.40	1.39	0.05
2 & 3	Manufacturing	2.14	1.78	2.21	1.83	2.17	1.80
5	Construction	5.18	6.43	6.20	6.26	5.60	6.36
6	Trade	3.72	1.81	3.94	5.54	3.84	3.99
60-64	Wholesale	9.14	0.88	5.91	-1.84	6.91	-0.86
65-68	Retail	3.39	1.60	3.69	6.96	3.55	4.66
7	Transport etc.	4.58	7.29	2.90	3.91	3.53	5.31
8	Finance etc.	5.99	2.51	5.63	7.05	5.71	6.07
9	Community etc. Services	3.13	0.32	4.16	0.13	3.69	0.21
91	Sanitary	4.92	-15.60	2.36	-6.35	3.47	-10.10
92	Education Science	2.90	3.01	4.04	4.65	3.44	3.82
93	Medical & Health	2.27	0.73	1.58	5.88	1.85	4.00
94	Community	3.74	-4.62	1.63	0.42	2.82	2.42
95	Recreational & Cultural	7.72	-10.07	4.65	0.11	5.84	-3.60
	Non-Agriculture	3.23	2.31	3.54	2.95	3.40	2.65

Source: Secondary source Part of Chaddha's Table 6.

Village Industries Boards (KVIBs). The KVIC had, over the last 50 years, "created around 19 lakh rural enterprises and generated cumulative employment for 23 million persons "(Parthasarathi, 2005) by March 2004 i.e. approximately 7 percent of the rural labour force. In contrast the number of employees in the village and township enterprises in China, rose" from 28.3 million in 1978 to 130.9 million in 2001 (9.2 percent and 26.7 percent of the total rural work force respectively). In addition 38.2 million people worked in private rural enterprises or were self employed in 2001, accounting for 7.7 percent of the total rural work force." (Hu Angong et al, 2005). Thus 34.4 per cent of the rural work force was absorbed by village and town industries in China.

(iv) **Jobless economic growth:** The Economic Survey noted the following salient features of trend of employment/ unemployment rates in the country, based on 60th round annual survey:

(a) The unemployment rate went up between 1993/94 and 2004. On the basis of current daily status (CDS)[(11)], the unemployment rate for males increased from 5.6 percent to 9.0 percent in rural areas, and from 6.7 percent to 8.1 per cent in urban areas. (Table 3.5)

(b) Similarly, unemployment rate for females rose from 5.6 percent in 1993/94 to 9.3 percent in rural areas and from 10.5 percent to 11.7 percent in urban areas, over the period.

(c) Unemployment rates on the CDS basis were much higher than on the usual status basis, implying a high degree of intermittent unemployment which could be mainly due to absence of regular employment for many workers.

(d) Urban unemployment rates (CDS) were higher than rural unemployment rates for both males and females in 1993/ 94. However, in 2004, rural unemployment rates for males were higher at 9.0 per cent than that of urban males at 8.1 per cent; and

(e) Unemployment rates varied sharply across states. States where wages were higher than in neighbouring ones because of strong bargains or social security provisions, had high incidence of unemployment in general.

Table 3.5 Employment and its growth rates by Industrial Sectors a during 1993-94 to 2004-05.

	Employment (in millions)				*Growth Rates %*			
	1983	1993-94	1999-00	2004-05	1993-94/ 1983	1999-00/ 1993-94	2004-05/ 1999-00	2004-05/ 1993-94
Primary	207.02	239.5	240.1	262.5	1.39	0.05	1.80	0.84
Secondary	44.3	59.8	69.3	86.9	2.90	2.51	4.61	3.46
Tertiary	50.7	75.0	88.4	115.0	3.81	2.77	5.41	8.96
Total	302.1	374.3	397.9	464.4	2.06	1.02	3.14	1.98

Source: NSSO, 61st Round.

The economic survey also noted that while the orgnised sector had highly protective labour legislation, labour in the unorganized sector was completely unprotected Labour legislation had, therefore, restricted labour mobility and which, in turn, had led to capital intensive methods in the organized sector.

The 61st quinquennial survey on employment / unemployment on UPSS (Principal + Subsidiary) basis reveals a growth rate of employment of 1.98 per cent per annum for the economy as a whole, in the post-reform period, 1993-94 to 2004-05 with the primary sector growing sluggishly at 0.84 per cent per annum, with most of the growth occurring during the five years period 1999-00 to 2004-05. In fact agriculture has reached a plateau in output and employment. The tertiary sector employment grew at 3.96 per cent per annum with the secondary sector growing at 3.46 percent p.a. during the eleven-year post-reform period. The 60th round of NSSO sample survey (annual) on employment / unemployment thus presents us a scenario of high growth – stagnant poverty and lower employment (on current daily status basis). However, the 61st round quinquennial survey presents a somewhat different picture on employment / unemployment on usual principal and subsidiary status (UPPSS) basis, (Table 3.6)

The salient features to be noted regarding the employment situation, revealed by Table 3.6 over the 5 year period are: -

(a) The share of the manufacturing sector in total urban employment has increased from 22.7 percent to 24.6 percent over the 5-year period. The share of manufacturing in rural areas has also moved up from 7.4 per cent to 8.1 per cent over the period. Three states Gujarat, Haryana and Himachal Pradesh registered sharper rise in the relative share of manufacturing in urban employment. In Gujarat, 372. urban workers, out of 1000, are now employed in manufacturing sector against 246 in 1999-2000

(b) While the share of construction in rural employment has increased from 3.3 per cent to 4.9 per cent over the period, its share in urban employment has remained stationery at 8.0 percent, probably due to capital-intensive technology in construction, in urban projects.

Table 3.6 Employment Situation by Rural-Urban as Shown by 61st Round (2004-05) and in 1999-2000.

Industry	*Rural*		*Urban*	
	2004-05	*1999-2000*	*2004-05*	*1999-2000*
Agriculture	727	763	88	88
Mining & Quarrying	5	5	8	8
Manufacturing	81	74	246	227
Electricity, water supply	2	2	7	7
Construction	49	33	80	80
Trade, hotels & restaurants	61	51	246	269
Transport & Communications	25	21	86	87
Finance, Banking, Business services	5	3	53	41
Public Admn. & Social & personal services	45	49	187	195
Total	1000	1000	1000	1000

Secondary Source : Economic Times 23-10-2006.

(c) The share of trade, hotels & restaurants in urban employment has risen from 24.6 to 28.9 percent, their share in rural employment has also risen from 5.1 percent to 6.1 percent.

(d) The share of financial & business service rose from 4.1 per cent to 5.3 per cent in urban employment and also in the rural sector employment, from 0.3 per cent to 0.5 per cent.

(e) An important trend shown by the data is the decline in the share of agriculture in rural employment from 76.3 percent in 1999-2000 to 72.7 percent in 2004-05. And this decline has occurred across the country with 29 out of 32 states and union territories sharing the trend. The contradictory trends shown by the 60th and 61st rounds of employment surveys need to be examined carefully, besides the smaller sample size for the annual surveys. Organised sector manufacturing as already noted is highly capital-intensive. The planning commission has yet to devise and announce measures to increase the employment potential of growth.

Further, anti-poverty measures need to address themselves for banishing hunger and malnutrition. The employment position revealed by 61st round of NSSO on employment situation is as under:

Table 3. 7 shows that the growth rate of the economy during the 11-year period 1993-94 to 2004-05 was 1.98 per cent, with the primary sector which mainly consists of agriculture and allied sectors growing only by 0.84 per cent. Services sector grew at 3.96 per cent whereas the secondary sector by 3.46 per cent. Further preliminary examination of 61st round data for rural – urban and male – female classification seems to suggest that employment growth has been very rapid during the 5 year period, 1999-2000 to 2004-05 (partly due to the fact that 1999-2000 was a bad agricultural year) and also much higher for urban than rural areas. A definitive comment should await further analysis of data.

3.6 National Rural Employment Guarantee Scheme (NREGS) 2006

3.61 An important step towards addressing the problem of rural unemployment and under-employment has been the passing of the NREG Act in 2005 and the launching of the scheme initially

Table 3.7 Employment Situation & Growth Rate by Industrial Classification

Sector	*Employment (millions)*				*Growth Rate 1993 / 2004-05 (%)*			
	1983	1993-94	1999-2000	2004-05	1993-94/ 1983	1999-00/ 1993-94	2004-05/ 1999-00	2004-05/ 1993-94
Primary	207.2	239.5	240.1	262.5	1.39	0.05	1.80	0.84
Secondary	44.3	59.8	69.3	86.9	2.90	2.51	4.61	3.46
Tertiary	50.7	75.0	88.4	115.0	3.86	2.77	5.41	3.96
Total	302.1	374.3	397.9	464.4	2.06	1.02	3.14	1.98

Source: NSSO 61st round, Survey of Employment and Unemployment.

in 200 districts in Feb., 2006. All the districts in the country are to be covered within five years.

The objective of the scheme is "to enhance the livelihood of the people in rural areas by generating wage employment through works that develop the infrastructure base of that area" The choice of works suggested should address the causes of chronic poverty, like drought, deforestation and soil erosion. The proposed work should be able " to rejuvenate the natural resources of the area, to stimulate the local economy enabling those who work for wage employment in creating an asset to take advantage of it, to engage in productive ways of self-employment and augment their income". (ES)

3.62 Every state government was expected to make a scheme for providing not less than 100 days of guaranteed employment in a financial year to every household in the rural areas covered under the scheme and whose adult members volunteer to do unskilled manual work subject to the conditions laid down in the Act. The Act lays down a number of provisions, the more important being:

(a) The household has to apply to get employment under NREGS. After the job card is issued, the household has to apply for work either on prescribed form or on plain paper. The administering authority – the gram panchyat – is required to issue a receipt giving the date of receipt of application duly signed.

(b) Payment of wages is to be made weekly, but not later than a fortnight.

(c) The job card should carry on the back side of the job card, entitlements under the NREGS, duly printed.

(d) A separate job card is to be issued to each nuclear household.

(e) Labourers working under NREGS are entitled to basic work-site facilities such as shade for periods of rest, safe drinking water and first aid. Further if more than 5 children under the age of six are present, one of the woman labourers is supposed to be deputed to look after them, as a sort of crèche attendant.

(f) The project should be able to create assets of permanent value to the community such as rain water harvesting systems, excavation of tanks construction of Kaccha roads, regeneration of wasteland etc, decided in a gram sabha (GS), meeting specifically convened for this purpose. The work is to be executed by the gram panchayat (GP).

(g) If no work is assigned to the household within a fortnight of the application he/she will be entitled to unemployment allowance.

(h) Pucca muster rolls should be available at the work-site and should be open for inspection by the households.

3.631 A survey in two districts of Jharkhand, conducted in May 2006, found many serious flaws in the implementation of NREGS, some of which could be deemed as teething problems. The NREG Act had stipulated that every state government was to launch the scheme within six months of the Act coming into force. In Jharkhand, the scheme was still in the process of being drafted and it was initiated within the framework of the earlier National Food for Work Programme (NFWP) and Sampoorna Grameen Rozgar Yojana (SGRY) based on the operational guidelines issued by the ministry of rural development in Jan. 2006. The survey found that the promise of 100 days of employment for every rural household, had become a matter of great public interest. However, there was very little awareness of the basic features of the Act in the survey area. The survey team was surprised to find that the Hindi version of the guidelines, was not available in the two sample districts, not even in the office of the district collector. Also the training programme for key officials had barely started.

3.632 Under the guidelines, registration of applications and issuing job cards is the responsibility of the Gram Panchayat (GP). However, since no panchayat elections had been held in Jharkhand since 1978, implementation of NREGA is a major problem there. Therefore, the responsibility of preparing, distributing job cards has been assigned to gram sevak, adding to his other multifarious duties. Further, general lack of staff at all levels, and especially at the crucial level of programme officers at the block level, gram rozgar sewaks at the panchyat level, supervisors, engineers etc acts as a stumbling block in implementation of the scheme. Cases were reported of applicants being charged money to get the application forms and for the photographs for the purpose. Nuclear families living together as a joint household, were not issued separate cards. Similarly, households missed in the BPL (below poverty level) list during BPL census 2002, were denied registration, Further the design of the job card was defective, with no space for recording wage payments and the quantum of work done. The BDO could not furnish figures for current employment under NREGA, but the survey estimated the number to be only a few hundred of a total population of 64,000.

3.633 The survey found a number of irregularities and problems in relation to wage payments. They found muster rolls being fudged, work measurement to be flawed, non-payment of minimum wages and delay in wage payment. Pucca muster rolls were nowhere to be found.

The survey team did not find any of the work site facilities to be available at any of the sample work sites.

The survey team found that most of the work had not been completed and ran the risk of being washed away in the next monsoon. They further found that the technical standard of Kaccha roads built under NREGA was very low.

There was no evidence of NREGA related gram sabhas being held in the survey area. Instead, "contractors and other local vested interests were using the sanction of a fictitious or cosmetic gram sabha to further their own ends".

3.634 Bhatia and Breze conclude their paper thus "All said and done, NREGA has created a sense of hope amongst the rural poor". (which) "can be further strengthened if people understand that the Act gives them employment as a matter of right and that claiming this right is within the realm of possibility. Translating this latent energy into public pressure is the best way to ensure that implementation problems reviewed in this article are addressed without delay". (emphasis mine)

3.635 The implementation of NREGS in Bihar has yet to start, even though funds for the scheme (Rs. 405 crores) were released on April 25, 2006 for the 23 districts out of 38 chosen for its operation. The State EG Council has not yet been formed nor district programme officers appointed. "Like its predecessor this government seems to be strong on rhetoric and weak on implementation." (Louis, 2006)

3.636 A survey by the Economic Research Group of St. Stephen's College, Delhi, in Oct., 2006 of the implementation of the scheme in 91 panchayats of Palakkad district (Kerala), under 13 Block Panchayats found: -

(i) Since the scheme does not offer white-collar jobs, the educated unemployed youth, kept away.

(ii) Women constituted 90% of the total work force employed under the scheme.

(iii) Women workers were paid wage that ranged between Rs. 60-80 per day while their male counterparts received Rs. 120-150 per day; the minimum wage in the district was Rs. 125 per day. Lower payment to women was justified on the plea, that their work output was less.

(iv) Wage payments were some time delayed more then 20 days.

"The state has done its homework and is doing fairly well in implementing the Act in select districts, if not in absolute terms, then surely in relative terms" (Jacob & Verghese, 2006).

3.641 NREG Act has been commented upon widely. The more important comments and suggestions are:

Since no evaluation was done of the National Food for Work (NFFW) programme launched last year in 150 districts and since the FFW was to serve as a pilot to the NREG Act, all the negative elements of FFW have found their way into EGA. Maharashtra EGS has been functioning for over two decades. Has any evaluation of its functioning been done? What are the lessons to be learnt?

NREGS is being implemented by panchayati raj institutions (PRIs). What has been the track record of panchyats in implementing the Sampoorna Grameen Rozgar Yojna ?

A massive publicity campaign explaining the scheme and its operational details and responsibilities must be launched. Voluntary agencies and independent bodies must be involved to send out the message and independent bodies with activists should monitor the implementation process.

Food security must occupy centre stage in the NREGS. The household seeking employment must be listed and the grain they prefer be supplied in the first week of the month on the lines of PDS.

- "The power to select workers must be taken away from bureaucrats, engineers and sarpanches. The villagers, especially those offering to work must plan and create assets that they see as enhancing their quality of life." There is urgent need "to develop a cadre of village-based barefoot engineers who can assist the community." (Gopal 2006)

3.642 Aiyar and Samji (2006) have offered a number of valuable suggestions to make NREG Act more effective through strengthening accountability relationships. They have argued for a clear separation of functions across tiers of government, with the Gram Panchayat GP responsible for all operational activities, and the state government responsible for overall monitoring and regulation of the process, with Zila Parishads (ZPs) & Panchayat Samities (PSs) also having a role in monitoring.

- They have also emphasised the central role that citizens must play in monitoring the provision of public services. Here regular flow of information and the enhanced ability of citizens to exercise enforceability, through tools such as social audits and community scorecards, is emphasised.

3.643 Kannan (2005) has pleaded for linking Employment Guarantee (EG) Act to human development, which implies that the wage rate fixed under the Act should help poor households to cross the poverty line. Further EG should not be viewed and designed as a stand alone one but as part of a larger package, linked to the objective of human development especially of the poor"

- It should widen the range of employment-generating activities beyond manual field work of a particular type. This would prove to be much more gender-friendly.
- Conscious efforts should be made to widen the linkage of EG at the local level, as an additionality to the existing schemes/projects.

3.644 The foregoing discussion, comments, suggestions and experience of the functioning of NREG Scheme in three states, clearly bring out the following:

- The scheme has aroused great public interest and expectation, but there is very little awareness of the basic features and guidelines.

An evaluation and review of the earlier employment and other public works programmes should have alerted concerned authorities regarding problems in measurement of work done by labourers, fudging of muster rolls, non-payment of minimum wages and delays in their payment, irregularities by contractors in collaboration with bureaucracy, politicians and technical staff.

Public works selection and execution must involve the concerned community and should not be technically deficient.

Absence or inadequacy of monitoring of work being executed.

Lack of accountability

Financial irregularities, leakages and corruption. However, Dungarpur district in Rajasthan has demonstrated that mass mobilization, Jan Sunwai (Public hearing) along with effective use of right to information (RTI), can create assets beneficial to the community. This was made possible by effective functioning of a peoples's organisation - the Mazdoor Kisan Sangharsh Samiti (MKSS), along with other people's groups.

3.645 We have been asking in this section, the question of impact of high growth rates on poverty and employment. Development as distinguished from growth "is a multi-dimensional construct: its aims are always social and ethical (synchronic solidarity). It contains an explicit environmental conditionality (diachronic solidarity with the future generations); economic growth, though necessary, has only an instrumental value; development cannot happen without growth, yet growth by itself does not warrant development; it can equally sustain maldevelopment, in which growth of GNP goes hand in hand with increasing social inequalities, unemployment and poverty. Instead, why should we not ask for *employment-led growth?*

Sachs (2004) has distinguished four categories of employment-led opportunities of growth; these are: (i) production of non-tradables which offer far greater choice of labour intensive techniques. A reorientation of policies on infrastructure investment, which is likely to be a significant component of the 11th five-year plan "could ensure that technically viable and cost-effective employment-intensive options are used and this could speed the reaction of poverty by generating productive and dignified employment." (ILO, 2003). This could reduce the cost of investment by 10 to 30 percent, as witnessed in a number of other countries. Further it could reduce the foreign exchange requirements by about 50 to 60 percent and create between 3 to 5 times as much employment for the same investment.

"Construction is another sector where labour intensive techniques could be deployed. But the bulk of new opportunities for decent work in the production of non-tradables is likely to a emerge in the services sector. India has an advantage in this respect since services sector constitutes over 50 percent of its GDP. These opportunities are likely to be far greater in social services such as education, health, and sanitation as well as in communications, post and public administration. There is great scope for greatly expanding technical services, repair and maintenance as well as transportation of merchandise and people. Similarly trade and personal services could create many occupations, other than poorly paid and over exploited domestic servants" in information technology (IT). Of course India is already a leading provider of software & computer-based services which are being outsourced to it.

Expansion of services should figure prominently in rural development, providing with rural industries, many openings for off-farm employment.

(ii) The second category which could offer scope for large employment is what "might be called 'quasi non-tradables' such as perishable food stuffs and bulky agricultural products which cannot stand the cost of long distance transportation." "Wherever possible preference is to be given to labour-intensive cultures, fruits, vegetables and flowers." Labour-intensive production of biomass has also a bright prospect for achieving food security and ensuring elastic supply of wage goods (mainly food). Field, forest and aquatic biomass would also be an important candidate for this purpose. Danger of piracy of traditional knowledge though patents by developed countries as happened in the case of Neem, turmeric etc. exists and should be guarded against.

(iii) The third component of the employment-led growth is constituted by naturally labour intensive industries and crafts producing non-agricultural wage goods, and a variety of products for local, national and international markets. These industries would face competition from other developing countries. The danger of some of these industries transforming themselves into sweat-shops on the basis of spurious competitiveness, are likely to be self-defeating in the long run. "Niches of genuine competitiveness may arise in artistic crafts with solid traditions of uniquely qualified labour" such as weaving, carving, production of software and CIT-based services deserve special attention.

(iv) The fourth category of labour intensive activities, that help in releasing additional resources for development are the so-called non-investment sources of growth. (Kalecki, 1993, Sachs 1999). All activates directed to saving natural resources (e.g. energy & water conservation), recycling of waste, result in a better utilization of existing productive capacities and thus result in a higher rate of growth. Additionally, these measures also lead to a better sustainability of growth. Further better maintenance of the existing infrastructure, equipment and buildings, help extend their life cycle and thus reduce their actual (physical) depreciation, and thus leading to a reduced demand for fresh capital. Incidentally, both resource saving and maintenance are fairly labour intensive activities. The main problems here might be in providing financial and organizational schemes and incentives for small enterprises.

In the same genre of ideas, we should explore the potentialities of non-monetary investment, a fairly common practice in our villages and peasant farms (although not accounted for in GDP), is of mutual self-help groups, constructing houses, community centres, schools, hospitals, health centres etc. A vast potential exists for programmes of assisted self-help housing construction, upgrading of slums and shantytowns, water-addition and storage (cisterns), sanitation, building of schools and cultural outfits, partly funded by unpaid, voluntary work. Traditions of such self-help community groups, e.g. among Sikhs, need to be strengthened for secular purposes. The case of Kali Bein, a rivulet in Punjab, cleaning recently by a dedicated saint, along with the community, is a shining example.

It is important to remind ourselves that the aim of employment-led growth is not just to perpetuate survival strategies (which are important in the short-run) but also to provide growing numbers of decent jobs.

While the starting point is characterized by very low labour productivity, a steady process of improvement, at all levels of activity, must be built into the development strategy, involving the upgrading of all informal activities, which loom so large on the employment and output fronts in India.

Petty producers in the informal sector would not be able to survive in the competitive game. Hence, development strategies, aimed at transforming them, should be an integral part of the future scenario. This should be possible through a bunch of complementary public policies "based on the principle of unequal treatment of unequals" in this case, affirmative actions in favour of petty producers.

A Brazilian study conducted for UNDP and SABRAE (Sachs 2003) identified a set of six policies, which could stimulate a gradual planned transformation. These policies are: - (i) Reduction of red tape and administrative costs associated with the opening of a formal micro-enterprise; (ii) Fiscal exemptions and rebates; (iii) Access to non-expensive and plentiful credits; (iv) Access to appropriate technologies, training and technical assistance; (v) Access to markets, in particular preferential treatment of petty producers in public procurement.

The combined effect of these may induce some of informal micro-entrepreneurs and self-employed own account enterprises and workers to formalise their business, or else set up cooperatives.

3.646 Since market forces are short-sighted, socially and ecologically insensitive, sustainable and sustained development cannot be achieved, by relying on pro-market reforms proposed by IMF and World Bank. We need to evolve new patterns of planned mixed economy[16] in India; planning would be needed here, not only for accelerating economic growth, but also for making it socially responsive; planning should be able to identify bottlenecks, mobilize latent resources, human and natural, put to use suppressed and idle capacities, for implementing "of a long term strategy whose exploitation and implementation requires a proactive attitude on part of a lean and clean developmental state.

4

CHALLENGES BEFRORE THE INDIAN ECONOMY IN THE TWENTY-FIRST CENTURY (CONTD:)

(Foreign Trade, F.D.I. Capital Account, Convertability, W.T.O. Development Strategy)

(D.D. Narula)

Section - 4
Foreign Trade, Foreign Direct Investment, Capital Account, Convertability, WTO

4.11 As stated earlier, both India and China adopted the export-led growth strategy with their economic reforms. China had only 1.5 percent share of the World trade in 1953, whereas India's share was higher at 2.2 percent in 1948; China's share fell to 0.7 percent in 1977 as a result of convulsions caused by the Cultural Revolution. With Economic reforms in 1978, its share in world trade had grown to 4.8 percent in 2002 (Lardy, 2005). India adopted almost the whole panoply of measures - devaluation of the rupee, tax rebate on exports, duty drawback on imports used as inputs for exports, convertibility of the rupee on current account and the passing of the Special Economic Zone (SEZ) Act in 2005 and yet, its share in world trade has declined to 0.8 percent in 2003. The plausible reasons for the low share in world trade of India are:

(i) Inadequately high growth rate of GDP – China, S. Korea, Hong Kong, Taiwan had very high rates of growth of GDP, exceeding 9 percent over a decade or more, whereas India is hoping to reach a growth rate of 9 percent over the 11th five year plan (2007-2012).

(ii) Industry and manufacturing were the dominant components of this growth process in China, with industry and manufacturing constituting 50.9 per cent and 34.5 percent respectively of the GDP in 2000. Their share in India's GDP were 26.9 percent and 15.8 percent respectively. Industry and manufacturing have much stronger linkages, both backward and forward, than 'services' which accounted for 50.8 percent of India's GDP in 2002-03. It is disquieting to note that the share of manufactured products in total exports declined from 74.7 percent in 1995-96 to 69.9 percent in 2005-06, and this despite a 9% rise in output of manufactures in 2005-06 (Economic Times).

(iii) India is just beginning the setting up of SEZs, whereas China established them over a decade back. Even now, there are problems to be sorted out, in consultation with the states.

4.12. Foreign Direct Investment (FDI) received by India reached its highest level at $7.75 billion in 2005-06 rising from $ 5.65 billion in 2004-05, as shown in Table 4.1 below: Outward FDI during 2004-05 was $ 2.4 billion. Outward FDI during 2005-06 and 2006-07 exceeds/likely to exceed inward FDI, so that net FDI would be negative, due to acquisitions by Indian MNCs and corporates abroad. Foreign investment flows into India, comprising FDI and FPI (foreign portfolio investment) have risen sharply from 1990s reflecting the policies to attract non-debt creating flows. These flows rose from negligible levels during 1980s to $ 20 billion in 2005-06. FDI exceeded FPI for 5 years, 1993-94 onwards; FPI flows have exceeded FDI since then.

Recognizing the macro-economic implications of volatility associated with capital flows, India has adopted a policy of managing the capital account with a preference for non-debt flows. Consistent with the principle of hierarchy of capital flows, India has been enhancing the quality of portfolio flows by strict adherence to "Know your Investor' principle." (RBI, 2006). Further, the government has taken steps to raise the FDI sectoral caps upto

Table 4.1 Foreign Investment Flows[1] to India

Items	*2003-04*	*2004-05*	*2005-06 P*
A. Direct Investment	4.32	5.65	7.75
i. Equity	2.23	3.78	5.82
a) Government (SIA/FIPB)	0.93	1.06	1.13
b) RBI	0.53	1.26	2.23
c) NRI	N	N	N
d) Acquisition of shares	0.74	0.93	2.18
e) Equity capital of	0.03	0.53	0.28
unincorporated bodies	1.46	1.51	1.68
ii. Reinvested earnings[2]	0.63	0.37	0.26
iii. Other capital[3]			

(Contd.)

Items	*2003-04*	*2004-05*	*2005-06* *P*
B. Portfolio Investment	11.38	9.32	12.49
a) GDRs/ADRs	0.46	0.61	2.55
b) FIIs	10.92	8.69	9.93
c) Off-shore funds & others	-	0.02	0.01
Total (A+B)	**15.70**	**14.97**	**20.24**

P : Provisional: N: Negligible.

Note:

1. Data on reinvested earnings for 2004-05 & 2005-06 are estimates.
2. Data on foreign investments represent inflows in the country and may not tally with the data in other tables and may also differ from net investment data in stock exchanges by FIIs 1990-91 have cumulated to $ 49 billion and total FPI reached $ 57 billion by 2005-06 (RBI
3. Inter-company debt transaction of FDI entities
4. Net inflow of funds by FIIs

Secondary source: *Reserve Bank of India, Annual Report 2005-06.*

100 percent through the Reserve Bank's automatic route for a number of new sectors in 2005-06, for coal and lignite mining for captive consumption and setting up infrastructure relating to marketing of petroleum and natural gas sector, telecom and civil aviation. Though the FDI flows into India are small as compared to other emerging markets, their size is growing, with a number of world's leading MNCs evincing keen interest in India. A T Kearney's FDI Confidence Index Survey (2005) finds that India has greatly improved its rank from 15th in 2002 to 2nd in 2005, as the most desired FDI destination. The Reserve Bank has emphasized the need to examine the likely implications of excessive inflows and outflows on macro economic management as also the need to take appropriate steps to address the growing international concerns regarding origin & source of investment funds flowing into the country.

4.13 Remittances from overseas workers to India have surged, in response to the oil boom in the Middle East during 1970s and 1980s and the information technology revolution in 1990s and have put India as the highest remittance receiving country in the world. These remittances were $ 24.6 billion, constituting 12.5 percent of current receipts and 3.1 percent of GDP in 2005-06. (RBI)

4.14 Impressive growth in receipts from business services continued during 2005-06. Earnings from exports of software and IT-enabled services, at $ 23.60 billion, recorded a growth of 33 percent in 2005-06, over 2004-05.

4.15 Tourism earnings have been bouyant since 2003-04, reflecting both business and leisure travel; these earnings totalled $ 7.82 billion in 2005-06, with 3.9 million tourist arrivals. Outbound tourist traffic from India reached 7.2 million recording a growth of 16.1 percent in 2005 over that in 2004, with an outgo of $ 6.4 billion, reflecting rising business and leisure travel, due to rising merchandise and services trade and growing disposable income of residents.

4.16 India had a trade balance of $ 51.56 billion in 2005-06 with invisibles (net) bringing in $ 40.94 billion, leaving a current account balance of (-) $ 10.61 billion, which constituted (–) 1.3 percent of GDP. On capital account, there was a surplus of $ 24.69 billion. The overall balance of payments was a surplus of $ 15.05

billion. India's merchandise exports rose by 23.0 percent in 2005-06 . These require higher POL, machinery and equipment for automotive industry cars and durable consumer goods. Similarly increased tourism by Indians would be both for business and pleasure.

4.181 India received external assistance (net) to the tune of $ 3.87 billion in 2005-06, as against $ 3.92 billion in 2004-05. Of the total external assistance (net) of $1.5 billion, $ 595 million was as grants and the rest as loans. Repayments made amounted to $ 1.57 billion and interest payments were $ 706 million, thus leaving a net external assistance of $ 1.594 billion with India. India extended assistance of $ 489 million to other developing countries of which $ 102 million was as grants and the rest as loans.

4.182 India's external debt (as at March 2006) was $ 125.18 billion (Rs 558,372 crores) of which $ 116.39 billion was long term and $ 8.79 billion short term. 31.5 percent of the total debt was concessional. The debt-service ratio for 2005-06 was 10.2 percent of current receipts.

4.183 India's foreign exchange reserves had cumulated to $ 151.62 billion (Rs. 676,387 crores) at the end of March 2006, of which $ 145.11 billion (i.e. 95.3% of total) was in foreign currency assets, 3.8% in gold and the balance in the IMF. These reserves constituted 26.07 percent of India's GDP and were equivalent to 12.77 months of imports.

4.191 Capital Account Convertibility The Tarapore Committee in its second report had laid out a five-year road map for fuller capital account convertibility. It has suggested a ban on participatory notes (PNs) and imposition of an unremunerated reserve requirement on fresh FII inflows. The committee has called for fiscal consolidation, strengthening of the banking system and greater autonomy for monetary policy, before going further on the road to fuller convertibility. Premature capital account convertibility can impose huge costs on the economy, in case of large scale capital inflows and outflows, as some of the Asian and Latin American countries found to their cost. Keeping in view these concerns, the committee recommended a progressive easing of capital controls for various categories of Indian individuals and corporates, so as to reduce the discrimination existing between foreign investors (who more or less enjoy full convertibility, subject to some sectoral caps) and Indian companies and residents. It has recommended easing of capital controls on external commercial borrowing (ECB) by Indian companies and banks, overseas investments by Indian companies and mutual funds and the amount that individuals can remit abroad. The committee also recommended that FIIs may be provided with the facility of cancelling and rebooking forward contracts and other derivatives booked to hedge rupee exposures to minimize the influence of NDFs (non-deliverable forwards) market off-shore in Singapore.

4.192 The government has taken a number of policy initiatives to further liberalise cross-border capital flows in the field of foreign investment and external commercial borrowing (ECB) such as limit of investment overseas under the automatic route from 100 percent of net worth of the investing Indian entity to 200 percent of its net worth. FDI in petroleum sector, air transport services (domestic airlines) sector, print media sector and construction development sector, has been further liberalized. Persons/entities eligible under the FDI route have been allowed to invest in the equity capital of asset reconstruction companies (ARCs) registered with the RBI. FIIs have been allowed to invest upto 49% in security receipts issued by ARCs under the government approval route. Authorised Dealer Banks have been allowed to make prepayment of ECBs upto US$ 200 million, instead of the earlier limit of $ 100 million.

4.193 Economic and Politically Weekly devoted a special section to debate on the pros and cons of capital account convertability (CAC) after the government of India and RBI decided to revisit the subject. Willianson, John (2006) argued that at this stage full CAC offers no large benefits, while it increases the risk of things going badly wrong. Dutt, Amitava Krishna (2006) argued that while India may miraculously avoid the boom-bust cycles associated with CAC, but the costs of failure are terribly high. And the country has very little slack with which to gamble. Sen, Partha (2006) was of the view that a strong financial sector is a must, if a nation has to reap the potential gains from trade in assets, which CAC assumes. Wray, L. Randall (2006) argued that CAC has inflicted more damage than provided benefits in many large developing and middle-income countries as shown by the recent experience of Argentina, Brazil, Mexico, Poland and Russia. Others who have supported India adopting CAC, counsel a moderate acceleration.

Further current account transactions procedures have been further simplified in order to improve customer services. The Reserve Bank has brought detailed Anti-Money Laundering guidelines to enable Authorised Money Changers (AMCs), to put in place the policy framework and systems for prevention of money laundering, in their money changing transactions.

4.2 World Trade Organization (WTO) – Issues

4.21 The Doha Round of Negotiations are still in a stalemate and one is not sure that negotiations would be fruitful. Agriculture continued to occupy centre–stage under the Doha Work Programme. The issue of methodology of converting non-*ad valorum* duties to their *ad valorum* equivalents in order to establish an agreed and transparent basis for applying the tariff reduction formula, reflected the deep divergencies in the position of WTO members. However, a broad understanding on the conversion methodology was reached in May 2005, clearing the way for substantive negotiations. The G-20 has become a credible negotiating entity. The Hong Kong Ministerial Declaration did address some of the concerns of developing countries related to agriculture. It had recommended elimination of export subsidies in agriculture by 2013, with a substantial reduction in the first half of the implementation period. Developing countries without Aggregate Measurement of Support (AMS) such as India would be exempt from reductions. It also provided for duty-free market access to all LDCs products to all developed countries. It had provided elimination of cotton subsidies by developed countries in 2006.

The declaration also reaffirmed the need for amendment to TRIPS agreement to address public health concerns of developing countries. The General Council amended the TRIPS agreement accordingly. This amendment enables manufacture and export of pharmaceutical products under compulsory licence to countries with limited or no manufacturing capacities in pharmaceutical industry. US and EU have shown great resistance to the Hong Kong Declaration plea for reduction of subsidies for agricultural exports and have, it seems, almost wrecked the Doha Round of negotiations.

4.22 The US government and the EU Commission have been the key figures in agenda setting during the Doha round. "Arenas were switched at the multilateral and from the multilateral to the plurilateral[12] and the bilateral levels" (Blaas, 2006). Forum switching at the multilateral levels is usually motivated by the hope that switching to a new arena might increase the chances of pushing through the preferred set of norms. Thus this strategy was solely linked to norm-making. However, the switching from multilateral to plurilateral or bilateral arenas by US and EU, has been motivated by a more complex set of considerations. On the one hand, it has been aimed at increasing the spread of specific norms to geographically more circumscribed areas, when the chance of getting them adopted globally was low. On the other hand, plurilateral and bilateral agreements have been aimed at gaining specific trading privileges.

However, neither the U.S. nor the EU, been completely successful in pushing through their agenda, because they have encountered determined opposition from groups of Third World countries on a number of occasions, especially on the issue of agricultural trade and on attempts at an enlargement of negotiation agenda. The stand of the Third world countries received support from the NGOs. When US and EU faced such strong resistance, they attempted to coopt specific key players more closely in the negotiation process, in order to soften their stand. The other tactics were to switch to other arenas of negotiations or to bilateral negotiations, where the asymmetry was far more pronounced.

In bilateral negotiations, they have been attempting to push through for concessions beyond the WTO agenda e.g. on subjects like equal treatment of foreign and domestic investors, government procurement, opening up of the service sector and property rights. The aim was to use the results of these negotiations, as a kind of *fait accomplie* to be included in multilateral negotiations. Further, promoting bilateral agreements were also aimed at seeking to gain privileged access to specific markets for their capital, thus gaining a competitive edge.

However, multilateral negotiations may be seen as advantageous for promoting business, as in the case of Multilateral Agreement on Investment (MAI) in the OECD. Here, a single national government, viz. of France, had to give in to strong protests against MAI and had the MAI project to be shifted from WTO to OECD and then to the European Commission. Thus, here, switching the arena also implied switching the negotiating institution, potentially opening the way to over-riding resistances at the national level.

4.23 China, India, Brazil and South Africa – all emerging powers, the G4 – preferred to negotiate on the multilateral level, where the power asymmetries are not as large as in bilateral negotiations. Both China and India have intensified efforts at South – South Cooperation. Chinese government has recently struck a number of plurilateral and bilateral trade and cooperation agreements and has developed close links with ASEAN and African countries, aimed at creating privileged economic relations, in order, it seems, for securing access to raw materials and energy. India, too, has entered into a number of plurilateral and bilateral agreements with Asian countries.

4.24 The WTO grew out from a proactive tariff reduction regime under GATT to a full bodied trade governance forum over the previous decade. However, the general perception is that trade liberalization is still driven by developed countries. But the growth of its membership has significantly changed its liberalization dynamics. "WTO law is rooted in the American system of common law and corporate regulation, but its institutional trajectory is increasingly influenced by emerging economies" (Drache & Froese, 2006) China, India and Brazil with their industrial capacity and burgeoning middle class are registering such high growth rates which are challenging the superiority of US and Europe. This is leading to the emergence of a new balance of power within the WTO.

4.25 "Dispute settlement is the most significant deliverable of WTO governance and embodies all that is both problematic and progressive about the trade institution" (Drache & Froese). Anti-dumping trade – a retaliatory dynamic of dispute settlement and the continuing dominance of developed countries at the Dispute settlement mechanism (DSM) has contributed greatly to the current negotiating deadlock.

4.26 Dumping – The practice of exporting a product for less than the cost of producing it, or for less than the 'normal value' of the product on the firm's home market – is a common practice to reduce a glut in one's own market. It is also one of the methods to gain access to a foreign market dominated by other firms. Chinese exports are often hit by anti-dumping duties for this reason. On the domestic market, producers sometimes sell their goods below cost in order to clear inventories or to break into a market dominated by rival producers. However, in international trade, where countries have very different factor endowments, dumping is considered by the WTO to be an unfair form of competition. Anti-dumping measures are frequently abused and reforming the rules that regulate them is key to creating a fairer trading system.

China has been slapped with 338 anti – dumping measures since its entry into WTO in Dec. 2001, with the most frequent complainants being the EU, US and India, who applied measures against Chinese chemicals, base metals and electronics. India, U.S.A. and Europe have been the top three anti-dumping remedy initiators with 399, 354 and 303 cases respectively. The WTO's non-performance in this area has had corrosive effect on other areas of trade regulation, such as dispute settlement.

4.27 Dispute Settlement Mechanism (DSM): It is a sad commentary on the WTO that DSM is used largely by the developed countries. Of the 148 members, 81 have never used the DSM. Further, 278 out of 329 cases taken to the DSM to date involve developed countries as complainants or respondents. Dispute settlement has not been democratised in the least. Of the 329 cases, 203 cases (62 percent) have been launched against developed countries. In fact, the current dispute settlement dynamics is such, that the developing countries are enlisted as proxies for the hard power interests of the global north, as happened in the Banana Dispute between the EU and U.S.

The original goals of WTO were to raise standards of living for the poorest nations and to develop trade strategies for sustainable development. WTO has failed miserably to rise to the challenges posed__Anti-dumping procedures, dispute settlement and its representational crisis. These suggest that the trading system is due for a major overhaul.

Section 5
Development strategy – some other aspects

5.11 Saving and investment: As stated earlier, the development strategy of import substitution and self-reliance followed from the 1950s through the 1980s was mostly aimed at increasing domestic savings and investing it in public enterprises; investment by private big business houses was regulated and prices for most of their products were administrated. Prices for most of the public sector products were fixed on cost-plus formula, with hardly any incentive for efficiency. The new development strategy of export-led growth, as noted earlier, emphasized liberalization, privatization and globalization, and competition, Raising the rate of growth, under any development strategy, requires stepping up the rate of savings and capital formation.

5.12 The Economic Survey had noted that investment had increased from 23 percent of GDP in 2001-02 to 30.1 percent in 2004-05. It attributed this to a virtuous cycle of growth and savings. The survey argued that since most of the investment had been financed by domestic saving and that with higher income growth, savings would rise and make possible a higher investment rate. The higher savings rate was largely due to a rise in the public saving rate, which reversed from negative 0.7%. This public savings increase arose from the implementation of the Fiscal Responsibility Budget Management (FRBM) Act and higher savings of non-departmental enterprises.

5.2 Infrastructure

5.21 The Economic Survey also takes note of the demographic dividend in terms of a larger and younger labour force gainfully employed in production, and generating a larger national income. According to it "the multi-pronged challenge lies in providing an appropriate policy framework to harness the dormant latent pool of Indian work-force and entrepreneurs to position the economy on a sustained high-growth trajectory"

Table 5.1 Saving & Investment in the Indian Economy (New series, Base: 1999-2000)

	1999-00	*2000-01*	*2001-02*	*2002-03*	*2003-04 P*	*2004-05 Q*
					(as per cent of GD Pat current market prices)	
Gross Domestic Savings	24.9	23.5	23.6	26.5	28.9	29.1
a) Public	-0.9	-1.8	-2.0	-0.7	1.0	2.2
b) Private	25.7	25.3	25.6	27.2	27.9	26.8
i) Household	21.3	21.2	22.0	23.1	23.5	22.0
Financial	10.5	10.2	10.8	10.3	11.5	10.3
Physical	10.7	11.0	11.2	12.7	12.0	11.7
ii) Corporate	4.5	4.1	3.6	4.1	4.4	4.8
Gross Domestic Capital Formation (GDCF)	26.0	24.2	23.0	25.3	27.2	30.1
a) Public	7.5	6.9	6.9	6.2	6.5	7.2
b) Private	17.9	16.7	16.8	18.5	18.9	20.0
c) Valuables	0.8	0.7	0.6	0.6	0.9	1.3
Gross fixed capital Formation (GFCF)	23.3	22.7	23.1	24.1	24.7	25.9
Change in stocks	2.0	0.9	0.6	0.6	0.7	1.4
Errors & Omissions	-0.1	-0.1	-1.3	-0.1	1.0	1.6

GDFC denotes gross domestic fixed capital formation

P: Provisional, Q: Quick estimates

Secondary Source: **Economic Survey, 2005-06 Table 1.3**

It adds "speedy provision of *quality infrastructure* through appropriate policy stimulus constitutes the first and foremost component of this challenge. India's growth prospects are intricately intertwined with the rapid development of physical infrastructure such as power, roads, ports, airports, and efficient delivery of such services, " (emphases mine)

5.22 Besides physical infrastructure, it is equally important to create the social infrastructure — education, health, safe drinking water etc. While Sarv Shiksha Abhiyan proposes to reach out to all children in the age-group of 6-14 years, with special attention being given to education of the girl child and to S.C. & S.T. children. With the imposition of Education Cess of 12 per cent on all direct and indirect central taxes, resources for elementary education have been augmented and budgetary provision for it, got more than doubled from Rs. 6000 crore in 2004-05 to Rs. 12,532 crores in 2005-06. The Economic Survey rightly points to the need for shifting emphasis and focus attention on the quality of education being imparted at the elementary level. This may require changes in teaching methods, so that children enjoy being in school.

5.23 The National Rural Health Mission (NRHM) has been launched to bring about a qualitative improvement in the health-care delivery in the rural areas. It emphasises the provision of increased access to decentralized public health system, of increased public health investment, with focus on primary health care and increased investment in programmes to control communicable diseases.

5.24 The Tenth Five Year Plan had projected an investment of Rs. 1,089,400 crores at 2001-02 prices in infrastructure. The Mid-term Appraisal of the 10th plan revised it to Rs. 1,108,800 crores. The Economic Survey mentions that " India has the potential to absorb US$ 150 billion of FDI in the next five years." Investment in infrastructure - both physical and social infrastructure have a long gestation period and are therefore, likely to raise the ICOR-Incremental capital output ratio - in the economy. The Tenth Five Year Plan had stipulated an ICOR of 3.58, even though the ICOR realized for the 9th Plan was 4.53. Since, however, most of the infrastructure projects are bunched together during the Eleventh five year plan, period, the ICOR is likely to exceed 4, since the

11th plan projects a growth rate of 9 percent, the required rate of investment would exceed 36 percent, of which domestic savings needed, would depend on the FDI during the plan.

5.3. Financial Sector

5.3.11 RBI Governor, Y.V. Reddy, in his annual policy review on Sept., 30, 2006 raised the repo-rate[13]. It is, thereby prodding banks to rebalance their portfolio and strike a balance between deposit and credit growth. This decision is, at variance with international trends, with easing of crude oil prices and has been dictated by domestic factors such as rising inflation and credit growth. RBI has projected that inflation would be contained in the range of 5-5.50 per cent. The RBI, however, appeared to be more optimistic on the growth projection for the current fiscal, raising the forecast from 7.5-8 per cent to 8 per cent. The move is to ensure that the banking system maintains sound asset quality by being more prudent in its lending decisions. Over-heated housing market continues to be cause of concern. The RBI is obviously, worried about growing indication of demand pressures and potential risks from rapid credit expansion, strains on credit quality and elevated asset prices. RBI was also unhappy with the steep growth of bank credit to households which could make them over-extended as reflected in credit card busts in several emerging economies. Further RBI thinks that large accumulation of debt could leave households prone to future interest rate and exchange rate shocks, since banks have in effect transferred a large part of their market risks to households. Further, excessive reliance on debt-financed consumption could pose serious problems if refinancing options dry up.

Bank loans for real estate — company townships, malls, cooperative housing societies, group-housing and individuals — to land mafia and builders' lobbies could pose serious risks for the economy.

5.3.12 The RBI Annual Report, 2005-06, stated the overall stance of monetary policy as follows: -

(i) Providing "appropriate liquidity to meet credit growth and support investment and export demand in the economy while placing equal emphasis on price stability."

(ii) "Consistent with the above, to pursue an interest rate environment that is conducive to macro-economic and price stability, and maintaining the momentum of growth".

(iii) "To consider measures in a calibrated manner in response to evolving circumstances with a view to stabilizing inflationary expectations". It has been raising the repo-rate and the reverse repo-rate according to global outlook for growth and inflationary risks. It took various supervisory and regulatory measures to further strengthen the financial sector, covering the scheduled commercial banks, urban cooperative banks and non-banking finance companies (NBFCs).

5.3.13 Following a higher fiscal devolution to the states as recommended by the Twelfth Finance Commission, the central government sought a pause in the final correction in terms of targets prescribed under the Fiscal Responsibility and Budget Management (FRBM) Rules, 2004. For the first time an 'outcomes' budget was presented in August 2005, providing monitorable performance indicators for the plan programmes.

5.3.14 The Planning Commission in its Approach Paper (AP) to the 11th plan has proposed a re-definition of the revenue deficit. It has suggested that government grants for building tangible assets should not be treated as revenue in the current accounting practice, but as capital expenditure. It has pleaded for treating the fiscal deficit and the primary deficit as the relevant control variables. Second, it has recommended modification of the FRBMA rules so that targets for fiscal deficit are adjusted for cyclical variations in the GDP. Three, it has suggested that FRBMA targets for fiscal deficits may be shifted "further out by say two years" to have an improved time profile of the 11th plan expenditure. This issue has been discussed by a number of distinguished economists in a special issue of the Economic & Political Weekly (EPW). The finance ministry and the RBI have not reacted favorably to the Planning Commission's suggestions, which seem reasonable. It is good that the issue has now come up for wider public informed debate.

5.321 The RBI annual report mentions that "It continued to take measures to increase depth and liquidity in the money, government securities and foreign exchange markets in the year to improve the price discovery mechanism," The provision in the FRBM, prohibiting RBI from participating in the primary market for central govt. securities w.e.f. April 2006 onwards, impelled a review of RBI's market operations, including introduction of new instruments and refining existing instruments. A financial markets department was set up and started functioning, within the Bank.

The policy initiatives in the capital market were directed towards further broadening and deepening of the capital markets, so as to make Indian primary market more efficient and transparent. Securities and Exchange Board of India (SEBI) amended its Disclosure and Investor Protection guidelines for rationalizing disclosure requirements for Listed companies. SEBI also permitted Mutual Funds, to participate in the derivatives market at par with FIIs. The legal framework for regulation of banks and the securities markets was strengthened through appropriate law by Parliament.

5.3.22 The Sensex has been rising almost continuously since May 2005, from about 6200, except for short breaks and intermediate corrections and had overshot the 14000 mark in the first week of December 2006. Many reasons have been attributed for this performance, which include. "increased investments by FIIs, entry of new investors from countries like Japan, good performance of the economy and the corporates, a market-friendly government not withstanding the occasional pulls and pressures by the Left, the efforts to improve corporate governance, low interest rates in developed countries, falling interest rates in India, and favourable fiscal measures" (Rao & Ranganathan, 2006). Such a dizzying surge, occasionally causes fears "about the nature of foreign funds, especially with regard to money laundering, round tripping by resident Indians, hot money, increased volatility etc., especially in the context of Ketan Parekh scam and the East Asian financial crisis."(Ras et al)

5.3.23 There has been a spurt in the registrations of FIIs after mid-May 2004, with the Central Government, the number rising from 499 in mid-May 2004 to 915 at the end of May 2006. Also, of the 2647 FII sub-accounts, 1237 were registered after 2003. Cumulative investments of FIIs rose from $ 26.43 billion at end-May 2004 to $ 59 billion in mid-September 2006.

5.3.24 It, however, needs to be emphasized that the surge on the Indian stock (equity) market since the beginning of 2005, is shared by a number of other developing countries such as China, Thailand, Brazil, Mexico, Turkey and South Africa. Interesting, however, is the point of departure for the share price movement in India in early February 2006, when the Sensex crossed 10,000 mark; it, then, started surging ahead of other markets.

5.3.25 The Alternative Survey Group (Rao and Ranganthan) hold that the quality and quantity of information provided on FII sub-accounts raises, further doubts about the monitoring mechanism. In its note of dissent on the expert group report, the RBI had opposed the issuance of participatory notes (PNs), since it was concerned that the nature of the beneficial ownership or the identity of the investor would not be known. It was concerned that the trading of these PNs would lead to multi-layering, making it difficult to identify the ultimate holders of PNs. Recent press reports indicate that nearly half of FII investments are held through PNs, and 60 to 80 percent of such investments are made by hedge funds. The expert group listed a number of arguments in favour of foreign portfolio investments to the Indian economy like reduced cost of equity capital and balance of payments support. The group also underlined that enlarging the demand side of Indian securities was beneficial for Indian investors.

In the context of turmoil in May 2006, it is being claimed that Mutual Funds (MFs) and Indian institutions were emerging as counter-vailing forces. It needs to be noted, however, that while MFs have come to control a sizeable amount only a fraction of it is invested in the equity market. Even though, the position changed somewhat in 2005-06, equity accounted for only about 28 percent of net purchases of MFs. The overall market capitalization, controlled by MFs is far below that owned by FIIs. The share of FIIs in market capitalization of 2837 companies rose from 13.85% to 15.62% from end-March 05 to end-March 2006, MF's share rose from 2.87% to 3.69% and that of Indian public declined from 11.62% to 10.85 over the same period.

5.3.26 The Demat / IPO Scam: During the late 1950s, the Vivian Commission which looked into allegations against the Dalmia-Jain House observed that out of the first 121 names in the register of subscribers (of D-J Airways), not less that 114, to whom share certificates were issued, were fictitious. About a decade back, hundreds of companies duped the investors as they virtually disappeared after collecting huge amounts of money through the primary market. By contrast, the recent scam is characterized, to unduly benefit from the primary market and had been going on silently for the past few years. Further "According to SEBI, certain entities had cornered IPO shares reserved for retail applicants by making multiple applications in the names of fictitious / benami applicants. Once they got the allotments, the shares were transferred to their principals, who in turn transferred them to the financiers. The financiers sold most of these shares on the first day of listing, making windfall gains." (Rao & Ranganathan). Further, according to SEBI's investigations, certain depository participants master-minded the opening of thousands of demat accounts by falsifying documents to facilitate the application process.

The scam brought into focus the malfunctioning of many intermediaries: banks, depositories, depository participants, brokers, sub-brokers and the internal auditors. Stock brokers seem to have played a key role in creating networks for these scams. Multiple company registration have also been used for cornering large chunks of IPOs. Why should financing of IPOs be allowed? The main purpose of stock markets is to directly mobilize household savings for investment purposes and avoid intermediation. It is more likely that a larger proportion of those who avail of outside finance, would be exiting the market at the first available opportunity so that they can square off with the lenders and pocket whatever net gain they could make. If the financiers are bankers, there is no additional resource mobilization. The Alternative survey group has suggested that to increase small investors participation, IPOs/ fresh issues of capital could be made a two-tier affair. At the first stage, the entire issue could be reserved for retail investors, and after a pre-determined period of 3-4 days, the issue could be opened for all. They found in a study of 20 public issues that retail investors' subscription fully met the entire offer. The scheme needs a careful examination by SEBI. "The real challenges for the regulator is to rein in unscrupulous promoters by designing more relevant disclosures, tightening the monitoring system and to minimize frivolous listing and price discovering mechanisms."

5.3.27 Banking sector reforms in India have been unique in the world, according to RBI Governor, Y.V. Reddy, in that they combine a comprehensive reorientation of competition, regulation and ownership in a non-disruptive and cost-effective manner. "Indeed our banking reform is a good illustration of the dynamism of the public sector in managing the over-hang problems and the pragmatism of public policy in enabling the domestic and foreign private sectors to compete and expand." He further claimed that the Indian financial system as a whole had exhibited vibrancy and resilience. The government securities, money and forex markets had developed over the last one and a half decade with impressive diversification of participants and instruments. The institutional, technical and micro structural aspects of Indian financial sector were in alignment with the best global standards. There has been healthy evolution of the sector through mutual cooperation amongst government, monetary authority, regulators and diverse market participants, domestic and foreign in the public and private sector. He listed the following for immediate focus for the future:-

(i) Cleaning up the remnants of under-capitalized banks; (ii) Concentrating on improvements in the rural cooperative credit system and improvement in their governance and financial management and (iii) Creating a healthy credit culture encompassing appropriate pricing, quality of service, financial inclusion and contract enforcement. He correctly listed the small and medium enterprises, agricultural sector, artisans and the informal sector as a whole, which "remain to be demonstrably benefitted."

5.3.281. Micro-Finance : By bestowing the Nobel peace prize on Prof. Mohd. Yunus and the Grameen Bank of Bangladesh for their war against poverty, the Nobel Peace committee has shown imagination. Micro credit and micro finance have now come to be recognized as important elements of what the poor require, to bootstrap themselves out of poverty. The poor, it was believed, were beyond the pale of the organized financial sector, since they had no assets to offer as security risk. Prof. Yunus and his Grameen Bank exploded this myth. The poor honour their debt obligation and micro finance typically sees loan recovery rates upward of 97 percent.

The two main functions of micro finance institutions (MFIs) are savings and credit. The system of group guarantee combined with individual responsibility is the innovation that has enabled credit to be extended to hundreds of millions of poor, assetless men and women around the world. While credit is the major function of MFIs from which they earn an interest income or service charges, they begin with the promotion of savings. MFIs promote regular savings as a habit and it is only after the Self-Help Groups (SHGs) have been saving regularly for six months or so, that the groups / individuals are eligible for credit. Repayment of loans necessarily requires that the loan be invested in some form of money-earning enterprise. NABARD in 1992, had started a programme of linking SHGs of the rural poor with banks. The SHG-Bank linkage programme has emerged as the major micro-finance programme in the country over the years. According to Economic Survey, 554 banks (47 commercial banks, 177 RRBs and 330 cooperative banks) were involved actively in the operation of this programme. As on 31st March 2005, a total of 16.18 lakh. SHGs[14] credit-linked by banks covered an estimated 242 lakh poor families, with average loan disbursement per family of Rs. 3.044". About 90 percent of SHGs were exclusively women's groups.

5.3.282. The SHG-bank linkage programme promoted by NABARD and proven profitability of operations, has led to mushrooming of micro finance NGOs (mfNGOs) and later, a number of new actors such as political parties and big corporates have also joined in. Andhra Pradesh boasts of the largest number of SHGs-36 percent of SHGs in India, including states sponsored SHGs. There has been keen competition among state and non-state micro finance institutions, as also among mfNGOs, leading each of them to, aggressively, market their products. The micro finance sector still constitutes a miniscule proportion of total credit disbursed through the formal system. Micro finance institutions and their lobbies have been urging RBI and the Government to devise a proper regulatory mechanism for micro-finance sub-sector, so that it does not have to face problems as in Andhra Pardesh. Micro credit cannot solve the problem of poverty of the rural poor; it may only provide temporary relief. A draft Micro finance Bill is under consideration of the finance ministry.

5.4 Public-Private Partnership (PPP): PPPs have emerged as a preferred mode of public procurement of infrastructure services in India in recent years. At the core of a PPP programme is a shift from the procurement of physical infrastructure assets, to the procurement of infrastructure services. Under the PPP mode, we directly specify the infrastructure outcomes, sought to be achieved and procure high quality infrastructure services – say airport services – through facilities developed and maintained by private parties at tariffs which are either contractually predetermined or determined by a competent regulator. Here the emphasis is on delivery of services rather than on physical assets, by inviting private capital to build, develop and own assets as long as they are able to deliver high quality infrastructure in relatively short periods of time. Krishna Swamy[15] (2006) rightly observes." A well-structured PPP arrangement which allots risks and rewards appropriately, allows the government to rapidly scale up infrastructure delivery by optimizing public investment and simultaneously directing private sector capital investment and operating efficiencies to secure public sector outcomes". PPP projects are finalized through various stages by the public sector agency or government: (i) defining the service sought to be procured by specifying output-based parameters; (ii) Selecting a technically competent private partner through a competitive bidding process; (iii) devising a long term contracting framework, which distributes risks and rewards suitably and (iv) managing the contracts successfully to secure specified outcomes. It is obvious from the whole process outlined above that PPPs require a central and critical role for the relevant government/public sector entity. However, the terms at which the PPP proceeds, need to be critically reviewed periodically, for safeguarding public interest.

The Supreme Court by upholding the selection of joint venture partners for Delhi and Mumbai airports has provided valuable support to this new public management technique to harness the efficiencies of the private sector to deliver public infrastructure services.

5.5. Rural Industrialisation and small scale Industry (SSI)

5.51 We had adduced "tardy rural industrialization" to be one of the reasons for the little impact of high growth rate of 6 percent on poverty eradication and employment generation in rural areas in sub-section 3.54. As stated earlier, the KVIC and KVIBs have proved unequal to the task.

KVIC is the sole promoter of the crucial input of technology. It had prepared rather elementary "profiles" of about 150 product groups and products in the 1960s. This list has neither been expanded nor updated despite many new rural-relevant technologies having been developed by laboratories of ICAR, CSIR, the National Research Development Corporation (NRDC), the Council for Peoples' Action and Rural Technologies (CAPART), the National Institutes of Industrial Technology, IITs and by several NGOs. According to Parthasarathy (2005), these institutions had about 2000 rural technologies with them, ready for commercialization by rural entrepreneurs. Instead of inducting these proven technologies into its technology portfolio, the KVIC had taken the easier route of abolishing in 2002, the original list of 150 technologies, referred to earlier and informing all the actors in the rural industrialization programme — the entrepreneurs, banks, the KVIBs etc. that all technologies except a negative list of six technologies and one product group would hereafter be accepted in the RI programme. The KVIC has recently entered into a MOU with CSIR for commercializing 420 well-identified and fully identified rural technologies. The KVIC's RI programme generated only 2.3 million jobs during five years ending 2004-05, partly because limited financial resources were invested in the programme - only Rs. 280 crore during 2004-05.

A key problem in promoting the RI programme is the designing and putting in place an effective and widespread programme of extension and demonstration of improved rural technologies for use by rural entrepreneurs. Unluckily the KVIC is incapable of performing this task, since it is highly bureaucratised and many of its "engineering and scientific" personnel have become so stale that "they themselves are badly in need of being trained in modern rural technologies and the promotion and management thereof." They should, therefore, be divested of these functions and these services be located and performed by vibrant institutions such as "Krishi Vigyan Kendras (KVKs) of ICAR located all over the country, the 12 polytechnology clinics of CSIR and 60 Rural Technology Demonstration and Transfer (RTDT) centres of NRDC." The whole effort, however, would be too small, for a country of our size and diversity and for the number of rural entrepreneurs to be covered according to Parthasarathy. And he cites for this purpose the Chinese 'Spark' programme of the 1980s and their Town and Village enterprises (TVE) programme.

5.52 The Spark programme involved a close and deep participation of provincial R&D Council, both as generators of technology and techniques relevant to commercially utilize a wide variety of natural resources - plant, animal or mineral. Party cadres were trained to demonstrate these technologies to the villagers of the province or commune concerned and to convince villagers of the commercial viability of those technologies. The programme has raised the farmers' awareness of science and technology and has encouraged and supported rural enterprises to compete in both domestic and international markets.

"Township enterprises are enterprises run by farmers in the countryside. Rural reforms and scientific and technological progress in agriculture, the efficiency of agricultural production has improved to such an extent that a large number of rural labourers have been emancipated from the land, providing the basis for the development of township enterprises, whose products sell throughout the country at competitive prices. These enterprises are involved in, besides industry, agro-processing, transportation and communications, commerce, construction and catering. China had 21 million township enterprises, employing 127 million employees generating $302 billion added value. In 2000, the added value increased to $328 billion i.e. 9.1 percent increase over that in 1999. These enterprises have become an important source for raising farmers' income and promoting rural economic development." (Parthasarathy).

According to Parthasarathy, "CSIR rural technology list also covers a number of simple information technology-based end systems and equipment which are basically tools for providing IT-based/derived services at the village/small town level. Again the problem is one of massive extension and training." He has given instances of biotech-based technologies and alternative sources of energy technologies which not only supplement farmers' income, but also create new products. It is, however, regrettable that KVIC is not even in touch with R&D institutions and technology suppliers involved. He has recommended the creation of a large network of promotional agencies coordinated by the Departments of Small Scale Industries (SSI) and Agro and Rural Industries (ARI) and guided by a high level Rural Industrialization Development Board (RIDB) with representation of all concerned agencies. RIDB should empanel a larger number of "NGOs from all parts of the country to undertake extension, demonstration and training functions on rural technology-based projects, an "escort service" to rural entrepreneurs in regard to securing funding from banks, ensure proper packaging of end-products and the technologies used, links to customers and the market more generally etc". He has further suggested an interest subsidy (besides the grant of 25 percent of capital cost), on both fixed and working capital, so as not to exceed 5 percent. Further, the need for a massive increase in Government of India outlay an RI programme, so as to reach Rs. 3000 crores in next five years, has been emphasized.

5.53 Besides application of improved / new technology for RI, another major area of concern, is that of marketing of rural industry products. Each industrial product would have its specific marketing problems – competition from domestic and foreign firms, small and large for reaping economies of scale, a certain degree of standardization of the product becomes essential besides cooperativization or other viable organization form. The fact that the Economic Survey does not make even a cursory mention of rural industrialization, shows how serious Government of India is on this subject.

5.54 Small Scale Industry (SSI) - The small enterprise sector recorded a growth of 4.1 percent per annum between 2000-01 to 2004-05, with the registered sector growing by 26.5 percent, with 16.57 lakh units at the end of the period and the unregistered sector, growing 14 percent, with 102.02 lakh units. The average annual growth rate of employment during the period was 4.3%

reaching 282.91 lakhs at the end of the period. The average annual growth rate of output was 8.1 percent at constant prices (of 1993-94) reaching Rs. 2,51,511 crores at the end of the period. Exports constituted 26.7 percent of the output (ES). The sector plays a vital role in the Indian economy contributing 40 percent of the gross industrial value-added in the Indian economy and 44 percent of the total manufactured exports (RBI). With increasing competition due to globalization of the Indian economy, size of the enterprises and the level of technology used by them, have assumed critical significance in the context of global competition. Several policy initiatives have been taken by the Government of India for promoting small enterprises. The more important of these initiatives were: -

(i) Dereservation of 193 items in 2004-05, earlier reserved exclusively for SSI sector, bringing the number of reserved items to 506. More items were to be de-reserved in 2005-06.

(ii) The turnover eligibility limit under the General SSI exemption scheme was raised from Rs. 3 crores to Rs. 4 crores.

(iii) Credit-linked capital subsidy rate for technology upgradation raised from 12 to 15 per cent and the ceiling on loans raised from Rs. 40 lakhs to Rs. 1 crore.

(iv) Investment limit in plant and machinery for technology upgradation in 69 items on reserve list for SSI and for all items in the drugs and pharmaceutical sector raised from Rs. 1 crore to Rs. 5 crore.

Recognizing "the advantages of public-private partnership (PPP) in terms of cost saving, access to specialized expertise and proprietary technology, sharing of risks with the private sector, and the ability to take up a large shelf of infrastructure investment, the Government of India is actively encouraging them" (ES)

The enterprises in the unorganized sector are subdivided into Own Account Manufacturing Enterprises (OAME) consisting of enterprises based primarily on family labour, formed nearly 85 percent of all manufacturing enterprises and 49 per cent of all workers in 2000-01. Non-directory Manufacturing Enterprises (NDME) i.e. enterprises, with at least one hired worker and less

Table 5.2 – Distribution of enterprises and workers in organized & unorganized manufacturing in India, 2000-01 (percentage)

	Organized			*Unorganized*			
				(a)	*(b)*	*(c)*	
No. of workers per enterprise	*> 100 workers*	*10-100 workers*	*Total*	*DME 6-9 workers*	*NDME 1-5 workers*	*OAME*	*Total*
Enterprises	0.1	0.8	0.9	4.4	9.7	85.1	99.2
Workers	10.2	16.3	26.5	14.1	10.4	49.0	73.5

Source : Table 1 of (Unni – 2006)

Notes: (i) Directory Manufacturing Enterprises (DME) (ii) Non-Directory Manufacturing Enterprises (NDME) (iii) Own Account Manufacturing Enterprises (OAME) than 6 total workers, formed about 10 per cent of all enterprises and workers. Directory Manufacturing Enterprises (DMEs) with at least one hired worker and 6-9 total workers, constituted about 4 per cent of all enterprises and 14 per cent of all workers (Table 5.2)

5.6. Real Estate

5.61 Economic Times (Oct 30, 2006) blazons' "Realty hots up as funds mop up big money" and writes – The Fund action in India is booming real estate. TSI Ventures, has mopped up over $1 billion in just 15 months. This comes even as more mega funds are in the pipeline. Actis is looking at an India-specific reality fund. Newspapers daily offer residential heavens, company towns, malls, residential-cum-commercial plazas for the well-to-do upper class and middle class, alluring accommodation, with various facilities at fabulous prices, creating the boom in real estate. SEZS also have residential accommodation facilities. Land prices have sky rocketed in the last two years in metropolitan cities as well as in non-metro towns.

5.62 Simultaneously, the Reserve Bank of India (RBI) has cautioned the banks' exposure to real estate sector, citing the volatile nature of real estate prices and saying that central banks across the world treat exposures to real estate as a sensitive sector. The concern stems from the adverse consequences on banks balance sheets in the event of a meltdown in the prices of such assets. Large flow of bank funds to the real estate sector runs the risk of fuelling prices further (RBI Annual Report, 2005-06). It has, therefore, counselled banks/financial institutions to develop risk management systems, as part of the overall strategy, before any exposure to this sector.

5.63 According to data provided in Basic Statistical Returns of Scheduled Commercial Banks (SCBs), commercial banks exposure to home loans had increased steadily over the years. In 2005-06, SBI's advances on this account increased by 28.1% over the previous year. Dena Bank's advances on this account doubled during this period from Rs. 541 crores to Rs. 1,075 crores. Aggregate advances of all Scheduled Commercial Banks (SCBs) on this account have gone up five times during last four years from Rs. 25,421 crores in 2000-01 to Rs. 126,797 crores in 2004-05. The outstanding credit of banks during this period rose 114%, leading to a sharp rise in the share of home loans in total credit, which rose from 4.7% in 2000-01 to 11% in 2004-05. The outstanding credit of private sector banks on home loans went up from 2.7% in 2000-01 to 15% in 2004-05.

5.64 Special Economic Zones (SEZs)

5.641 An important institutional mechanism used by the Chinese for boosting exports and attracting foreign investment has been the SEZs. The Government of India passed the SEZ Act in 2005 and about 200 SEZs have been approved. However, considerable controversy has arisen regarding the terms and conditions for their setting up and operation, causing delay. The issues needing attention are:

a) Acquisition of large tracts of fertile agricultural land for setting them up and terms and conditions of their acquisition. Displaced farmers and their organizations are resorting to demonstrations, and other direct action measures. It is understood that certain guidelines for land acquisition have been formulated and circulated to the state governments. These are presumed to be:-

   i) Rehabilitate families before taking over land (ii) go for options involving minimum displacement (iii) farmers should have stake in development through their employment and training in skills for employment (iv) standard of living of displaced families should not go down.

b) Labour reforms demanded by corporate sector in terms of hire and fire freedom are likely to be resisted by the Left.

c) Mr. Sharad Yadav (2006) former Union Food Minister, has contended that (i) since large tracts of fertile agricultural land in the Doabs in Punjab, Haryana and West Uttar Pradesh are proposed to be given to SEZs and this region contributes 67 percent of total wheat procurement and 56 percent of total rice procurement of the Food Corporation of India, this might endanger food security. (ii) It is further contended that SEZs are likely to encourage large scale migration of people from backward to advanced regions and thus cause social tensions through regional imbalances. China, too, faced this problem. (iii) The policy of SEZs will cause huge revenue losses estimated at Rs. 90,000 crores and thus impair action on social sector. (iv) The danger of SEZs units diverting a large part of their output to the domestic market, and thus causing closure of units working outside the SEZs has also been pointed out. (v) A considerable part of the SEZs area is likely to be used for building fancy residential townships by corporate land mafia and builders' lobbies and (vi) Lease-holders of small farms and labourers working on the farm also need to be considered for sum compensation when the land is acquired.

If some of the doubts and misgivings of the farmers are redressed, the SEZs may become less attractive to investors. Further some form of insurance needs to be worked out, to ensure an adequate future income and social security for the farmer and his family. It is hoped that ground rules for setting up and operation of SEZs would be finalized by the Union and State Governments soon, Hopefully, Indian diaspora would respond enthusiastically.

5.642 I have in earlier paras pointed out the danger of SEZs becoming real estate-developers' paradise. It is heartening to note that the Ministry of Commerce is stipulating certain conditions to be satisfied for building houses, hotels, hospital etc. in SEZs. According media reports, Special Secretary to Ministry of Commerce, in a statement, made the following points: (i) The number of houses and size of schools, hotels and hospitals will be linked to the employment generated in the designated SEZ. (ii) Any breach of norms will make the developers ineligible for tax benefits.

The Board of Approvals (BDA) has stipulated a minimum investment of Rs. 1000 crores or a net worth of Rs. 250 crores for multi-product zones. For setting up SEZs for specific projects say IT or textiles, an investment of at least Rs. 250 crores or having net worth of Rs. 250 crores is stipulated. The finance ministry had insisted on clear-cut guidelines to ensure that corporates did not enter the arena and buy duty-free cement, steel and electrical fittings to make a quick buck by selling houses to those not associated with the zones or set up hotels that catered to people not connected with the SEZs.

Though the processing and non-processing area ratio has been left at 50:50, all product SEZs can set up a maximum of 7500 houses, build a hotel with 100 rooms at the most, 25-bed hospitals, earmark not more than 25,000 square meters for schools and educational institutions, besides allocating 50,000 sq. metres for office space, shopping centres and multiplexes. In case of multi-product zones, 25000 houses can be built, 250-room hotels and 100-bed hospitals can be set up and 250,000 sq meters can be earmarked for building office space, malls and multiplexes.

Further, BOA will permit in phases and only 20 percent houses can be built initially and more dwellings can be built after units start operating. Each developer is required to keep 40 percent area for water & sewage treatment.

5.643 Since employment generation is an important objective of the SEZs, it is important that manufacturing units located in the zones adopt labour-intensive techniques; similarly construction of real estate need to adopt labour intensive methods of construction. This may however, require some modification in labour laws. With lower capital intensity on these projects, the return on capital should increase.

5.644 The setting up of SEZs will lead to creation of oases of development amid vast deserts of undeveloped rural and under-developed urban centres. We have already stated that the problem of uneven growth across various states and promotion of regional disparities are likely to encourage fissiparous tendencies, which are dangerous for our democratic polity.

5.7. Hunger, Starvation and Malnutrition

5.71. A U.N. report on hunger states that 854 million out of the world's 6.55 billion people are hungry, under-nourished, malnourished or starving. 95.9 percent i.e. 820 million of the hungry—, a population exceeding the combined total of U.S., Canada and European Union—, live in developing countries. With more than 221 million of India's population under-nourished, we beat sub-saharan Africa's 203.5 million and China comes third with 142.1 million.

National Nutrition Monitoring Bureau estimated that about half of rural children aged five years suffered from malnutrition and 40 percent of adults suffered from chronic deficiency in 2000-01. While the number of children suffering from severe malnutrition declined significantly in the 1990s, the prevalence of mild and moderate under-nutrition especially among those in the lower three deciles (i.e. 30%) income groups was still high. The nutritional status of tribals was still worse. The National Family Health Survey (1998-99) had the following findings: "47 percent of children are malnourished and 74 percent are anaemic; 36 percent of ever-married women aged 15-49, have chronic energy deficiency; 54 percent of women aged 15-49 have no education; about half the pregnant women suffer from iron deficiency; 71 percent of rural households do not have any toilet facility; 19 percent villages do not have any health facility and 51 per cent villages do not have any drainage system either under-ground or open."

The Food & Agriculture Organization (FAO) echoes Amartya Sen's thesis when it says that hunger can be overcome only if necessary resources, political will and correct policies are applied. Millions remain hungry, not because of shortage of food, but because of poverty and distribution and consumption patterns, conditions aggravated by politics.

5.72 Since the geography of hunger has a direct bearing on the geography of disease, it is important to take into account the fact that availability of nutritious food has a dramatic effect on incidence of disease. And the hungry are not just those who experience famine and starvation. And just because we have fewer famine-like situations, does not imply that we have solved the hunger problem, for endemic under-nourishment and malnutrition render people weak and susceptible to not only disease but also to conditions that stunt mental and physical growth. According to the World Health Organisation (WHO), hunger and malnutrition are the Number One risk to global health and kill more people than AIDS, malaria and TB combined. Silent hunger – in the form of under-nourishment and malnutrition is a covert cause of death that remains virtually understated and unaddressed as attention is appropriated by diseases that are symptoms of a deeper malaise.

The question arises: can we make hunger a history?

5.73 The National Commission on Farmers (NCF), under the chairmanship of Dr. M.S. Swamination, has proposed a six point action plan, in its final report to the Government of India, to this effect. The plan recognizes that the problems of hunger and poverty are multi-dimensional and cut across various ministries and departments of government. Hence, a pan-government of India approach both in planning and implementation is needed. Various components of the plan are as under:-

(i) "Reorganize delivery of nutrition-support programme on a life cycle basis, starting with pregnant women and extending to old and infirm persons, with the participation of panchayats and local bodies. Maternal and foetal under-nutrition to be prevented in order to avoid incidence of babies with low birth weight."

(ii) "Eliminate micronutrient deficiencies like iron, iodine, vitamin A and zinc through an integrated food-cum-fortification approach."

(iii) "Promote establishment of community food and water banks, operated by women self-help groups (SHGs) based on the principle of 'store grain and water every where".

(iv) "Help small and marginal farmers to improve the productivity, quality and profitability of farm enterprises and organize an integrated rural non-farm livelihood initiative."

(v) "Introduce support systems to SHGs to make them economically and organizationally sustainable. Establish for this purpose SHGs' capacity- building and mentoring centres and focus on converting micro-credit banks into sustainable livelihood banks."

(vi) "Introduce a national food guarantee Act combining the useful features of food for work' and 'employment guarantee programmes', on August 15, 2007, which marks the 60th anniversary of our independence. The food guarantee Act will be a powerful tool in achieving the goal of a hunger-free India. By increasing demand for foodgrains as a result of increased consumption by the poor; the economic conditions essential for further agricultural progress can be improved."

5.74 In order to motivate farmers to produce more foodgrains, horticultural and animal products, a three pronged strategy has been suggested: -

(a) Announce minimum support price (MSP) for a wide range of crops of importance to the public distribution system (PDS), taking into consideration, the recommendation of the Commission of Agricultural Costs and Prices (CACP).

(b) Fix the procurement price at the time of harvest taking into account cost-escalation in inputs, since the announcement of MSP.

(c) Issue a smart card or coupon for entitling those farmers who sell their produce to purchase inputs like seeds, fertilizers, veterinary pharmaceuticals and implements at concessional prices (say 10 percent less than the market price).

This three pronged strategy would ensure national food security as also freedom to farmers to get the best possible price. Further, the PDS should become universal and include local grains like Bajra, Jawar, Ragi and other millets, which are rich in nutritive value. Eradicating hunger arising from deprivation must be a national priority.

NFL has also suggested that union and state government should seriously consider the question of including agriculture in the concurrent list, since several pieces of legislation such as protection of plant varieties and Farmers' Rights Act, the Biodiversity Act and the Food Bill are administered by the Centre.

5

CHALLENGES BEFORE THE INDIAN ECONOMY IN THE TWENTY-FIRST CENTURY (CONTD)

(Widening inequalities and Development dilemas)

(D.D. Narula)

Section - 6

Widening Socio-Economic Inequalities – Conspicuous Consumption and Demonstration Effects

6.11 Growth theory and experience clearly suggest widening of income and wealth disparities during early phase of economic growth; these disparities get somewhat reduced at later stage of development, through trade union and state action. Though no definitive studies on the extent of income and wealth disparities generated by the high growth rate of Indian economy since the economic reforms are available, there are studies on impact of high growth rate on socio-economic inequalities for newly industrializing countries such as South Korea, Taiwan, Hong Kong, Malaysia, Singapore and recently, China, Further, studies on growth of different sectors of the Indian economy such as agriculture, corporate sector, unorganized/ informal sector in manufacturing/ services etc are pointers to the widening of the gulf between the affluent and depressed classes / regions / groups. Globalization and global competition in most sectors of the economy is creating both opportunities and challenges.

6.12 An important reason for the persistence of food insecurity in India is the demand deflation that has been caused by declining agrarian incomes over the past decade "Our economy traditionally has had a significant amount of private ownership of assets by a small section of the economic elite. The high disparity in wealth between this small elite class and considerable-sized poor section of the society has always given our economy a dualist nature where growth-led policies adopted by the government have co-existed with support-led measures" (Golait & Pradhan, 2006). Further, a reduction in the state intervention — PDS, food for work, direct aid programmes — coupled with a rapid opening up of the agrarian sector to foreign competition from vastly subsidised foodgrains from developed countries (which leads to a change in the composition of output and a lowering of agricultural prices) had led to a rise in rural poverty and a lowering of food security (Patnaik, 2001, 2003, 2004). Also income distribution within the population in India is more skewed today than it was a decade back. Sen and Himanshu (2004) find that 80 percent of rural population, numbering 600 million, have been experiencing declining per capita consumption since 1989-90 which is in stark contrast to the top 20 percent of the population whose per capita consumption (and income) has gone up by about 40 percent in the 1990s. Thus while the averages of parameters of wealth ownership may look impressive, they obscure the serious problem of the rising numbers that go hungry everyday.

6.13 A study conducted by the National Buildings Organization (NBO) on Housing says that the upper echelons have been buying houses at a heady pace and that 9 per cent of houses owned by them, have been lying unoccupied. The economically weaker sections, however, face an acute shortage. According to the study, at the start of 2007, there will be 24.7 million people in urban India without houses and 97 percent of them will be from low income groups (LIGs) or economically weaker sections (EWSs), which implies that over 37 percent of the 66.3 million urban households, do not have shelter. Among the houseless, 18 million belong to the EWSs and the remaining 6.3 million belong to LIGs. The study projects a further worsening of the situation with a shortage of 26.5 million, at the end of the 11th plan in March 2012. The study has caused concern in the Ministry of Housing and Urban Poverty Alleviation which has proposed a project/ scheme for social and rental housing especially in the metros. The report further, said that growth in the total number of houses built during 1991-2001 was much less than those built in the previous two decades. (TOI, 25/11/2006).

Development almost always induces migration of labour, from depressed regions to developed/developing regions. Punjab's and Haryana's agricultural growth and prosperity post-green revolution would not have been possible without labourers from Bihar, Eastern U.P. and Rajasthan. Maharashtra's (especially, Mumbai's) industrial development was made possible by migration of labour from Bihar, U.P. and Orissa. Post-independence, with the rate of growth of the economy accelerating, migration of labour also gathered pace. Since there was no provision for housing migrant labour, vast slums came into existence in every developing city/town. Mr. M.S. Ahluwalia, Vice-Chairman, Planning Commission has stated that India would need $ 64 billions to build houses for the houseless by the end of the 11th plan.

With growth rate of the economy accelerating to 9 per cent or more during the 11th plan, immigration rate is likely to quicken and thus add to the slum population. Migration of relatively skilled and educated workers in IT, software, marketing and financial sectors would lead to boom in property value and push up rents. Unless therefore, steps are taken to launch a well-considered programme of provision of proper shelter for workers on a massive scale, with other attendant services, we would be creating further urban chaos, disharmony and crisis. Such a programme must include schemes based on "assisted self-help construction in which public authorities join forces with the future dwellers, whose work constitutes a form of non-monetary saving" (Sachs, 2004)

6.2 Affluence of the upper and middle class is being demonstrated through malls, shopping arcades and plazas, company towns, residential complexes, golf courses, expensive and latest model cars, sports cars and SUVs, fashion shows and designer clothes, gems and jewellry and the like. These classes can indulge in luxurious living, aping the western standard of living – all made possible, largely, by bank credit for housing and personal consumption, on installment basis. Newspapers are bringing out special supplements on real estate on week-ends. Marriages, birthdays and similar occasions are again used to display wealth and affluence. Political leaders, bureaucrats, public enterprise executives use the above occasions and special festivals, such as Diwali, Christmas, Eid etc. to receive solicited and unsolicited expensive gifts from clients in the private/public sector, with which they have business dealings.

6.31 Prof. Manmohan Singh, Prime Minister of India was in Sewa Gram in early July, 2006. He is known for his simple and unostentatious style of living. In his interaction with the media, he made the following significant observations to Economic Times(ET) i) Gandhiji told us "We must have the resilience and strength to stand up and uphold our beliefs and not be swept off our feet in the wake of integrating with the rest of the world at a time when the process of globalization is sweeping all over." ii) I am not unambiguously attached to reforms. I feel that India has to compete with the rest of the world on its own strength. *I am not enamoured of India copying the western consumption style"* (emphasis mine) Further he said. "We must be aware that, in the end, only a small proportion of the population will enjoy western standards of living and high consumption. We need to copy the west in production and raising productivity, and not in consumption." iii) "In India, we cannot raise our consumption patterns to levels that cause havoc with our environment." At another level, he was categoric that "FDI in retail, corporate investment in farming, huge capacity investment in SEZ's and captive mines are not the right solution to the problems of India's landless and marginalized people." Further he told ET; "India is a land of small farmers and we must do whatever we can do to increase the viability of their farming operations".

6.32 The challenge before the prime minister and the UPA government is: what policies should be adopted to stop the craze for western consumption patterns and ostentatious life style? With television and media glamourizing these life styles and consumption patterns, the demonstration effects on the youth and on impressionable rural and urban populace are not only powerful but also highly deleterious. Take for illustration, a news item in the 'know your consumer' section of Economic Times titled; Urban Middle Class; Baby Boomers – which tells of the huge market of urban kids under six years of age: 2.43 crores or 56 percent of the total of 4.33 crores were in households with annual income over Rs. 1.5 lakhs or 44 lakh kids under 6 years with annual family income of Rs. 3 lakhs and above, and then suggests: "Don't waste time and head straight to your biggest markets in Thane, Ahmedabad, Delhi and so on.

Another news item talks of rich (high net worth individual)- HNWI Indians' number rising by 20 percent in one year and it starts with " Stock images of an India full of half-naked beggars and hungry children may soon get a quick burial..... because more Indians are getting richer". I have already pointed out in section on savings and capital formation, about the high growth rate of two wheelers and personal cars and the projection of 16% annual growth rate of the automotive sector till 2016. Instead of developing a public transport system, and with expanding cities and easy availability of bank credit on instalment / hire purchase basis, the upper section of middle class has opted for personal cars and the lower segment of middle class going in for motorcycles / scooters. The sale of mobile phones has been rising at staggering rates. The subscriber base had touched 11.66 crores in August 2006, with numbers rising by over 58 lakhs in August. While mobile phones should ordinarily, be put as a luxury or non-essential item in the Kaleckian sense, it has had such powerful externalities, in flow of information, entertainment, crime-detection etc, and for India especially, along with BPO and software, a big export earner that this should be regarded as basic/essential sector.

6.4 Education, Health and Training

6.41 "Education is essential to development, due to its intrinsic values, insofar as it contributes to cultural awakening, conscientisation, understanding of human rights, enhancing of adaptiveness and growing sense of autonomy, self-reliance and self-confidence." (Sachs). The instrumental value of education in respect of employability can be clearly seen in the vast expansion of employment for the Indian educated youth in the ITC sector.

6.42 The National Policy on Education (NPE) 1986, as modified in 1992 emphasised three aspects in relation to elementary education, namely: (i) Universal access and enrolment. (ii) Universal retention of children up to 14 years of age, and (iii) a substantial improvement in the quality of education to enable children to achieve essential levels of learning.

The NPE had emphasised a positive and interventionist role for correcting social and regional imbalance, empowering women, the disadvantaged and the minorities. Priority was to be given to children with special needs, to women, SCs/STs and minorities.

6.43 NPE 1986 had set a goal of expenditure on education of 6 percent of GDP; Economic survey claims that the combined total expenditure on education by Central and State Governments was 3.4 per cent of GDP in 2004-05 (BE). RBI, however, states a figure of 2.7 percent (actual) for 2004-05, 2.9 percent for 2005-06 (RE) and 3.4 per cent for 2006-07 (BE). This implies that expenditure on education was cut to reduce the revenue deficit of central and state governments. This is despite the fact that "education cess" of 12 per cent has been levied on all central government taxes w.e.f. 2005-06. Further while the share of the central government has been increasing, that of the state governments in the states aggregate budgetary allocation for education is declining. Kerala has witnessed the sharpest decline of 13.3 percentage points, from 20.1per cent in 2000-01 to 6.8 per cent in 2005-06. Maharashtra has witnessed the second highest decline from 22.3 per cent in 2000-01 to 9.1 per cent in 2005-06.

6.44 It is heartening to note that the gross enrolment ratio (GER) of children in the 6-14 years age group enrolled in the elementary schools has increased progressively from 32.1 per cent in 1950-51 to 84.91 in 2003-04, with the rate of increase in GER of girls higher than that of boys. Drop-out rate at the primary level (classes I-V) declined from 39.1 per cent in 2001-02 to 31.4 per cent in 2003-04. The number of out-of-school children, is reported to have come down from 320 lakhs in 2001 to 95 lakhs as in Oct. 2005 (ES).

6.45 Sarva Shiksha Abhiyan (SSA) is the main vehicle for providing elementary education to all children launched in 2001-02. One of its goals was to see all children in school and educational institutions by 2005. The fact that lakhs of children are employed in road-side dhabas, restaurants, in domestic service, work as shoe shines, rag pickers etc shows that we are still far from achieving this goal.

6.46 National Literacy Mission (NLM) is the other instrument for banishing illiteracy from the country for making adults literate. Total literacy has been the strategy of NLM, implemented through Zila Saksharata Samitis (ZSS) i.e. District level literacy societies.

6.471 Education being the first condition for creating human capital, improvements in labour productivity cannot be ensured, without universal education, at least, up to the elementary stage. But with large sections of people living in poverty, this cannot be achieved without widespread and effective state intervention.

6.472 While education is a source of acquiring existing knowledge and skills, it is also the base for developing new knowledge and skills. Knowledge becomes the prime mover for creating opportunities for developing new technologies and new technologies, in turn, demand acquisition of new skills by the workforce. However, creation of new technologies require higher education and research facilities. It was for this reason that shortly after independence our first prime minister, Pt. Jawahar Lal Nehru, along with eminent scientist, Dr. Shanti Sarup Bhatnagar, created a chain of National Laboratories for conducting research in science and technologies. It is labour and more particularly the quality of labour that is the key determinant of the country's competitiveness, as is evident from a high correlation between skilled labour endowment and the GDP per worker across countries. Higher education enhances a country's capacity for participation in an increasingly knowledge-based world economy and has the potential to enhance economic growth.

6.473 India has a large working-age population and an extensive higher education system. While we are justifiably proud of our success in the IT services and IT-enabled services, it would be unwise to be euphoric about them. Several Indian studies have shown that the overall state of higher education is dismal; however, these studies have failed to map the contradictions in our higher education that exist. While undergraduate enrolment is large, enrolment in postgraduate and doctoral programme is small; curricula in most universities and colleges are out-dated. Higher education courses with occupational focus form less than 20 percent of the total. Last two decades have witnessed a rapid expansion of private providers of higher education, while the number of government institutions and private aided institutions has been almost stationary "It is primarily the non-subsidized private institutions that have responded to the demand for new kind of knowledge and skills required in the growing Indian economy that is now closely connected with the rest of the world". (Agarwal 2006) A majority of these private institutions offer professional courses. Government spends 0.37 percent of our GDP on higher education, as against 1.41 per cent in U.S., 1.07 percent in the U.K. and 0.50 percent in China, of their much higher GDPs. However, per student expenditure as a percentage of GDP per capita, is 83 per cent for India, as against 53 per cent in China, 26 percent in US, 31 per cent in the UK, 17 per cent in Japan and only 5 per cent in S. Korea. "For greater acceptability of Indian graduates in the global labour markets, standards of Indian higher education have to be bench-marked with the global standards" (Agarwal 2006).

Though we have many schemes for providing financial aid to the poor students, the amount given is extremely meagre and procedures to secure loans are cumbersome and dilatory. The question of opening up Indian higher education to foreign providers needs to be considered from the point of view of its impact on the quality of education and research.

6.48 Health

6.481 Access to health services should be part of the broader objective of improving the health condition of the people, with the latter depending on adequate food security, access to safe water, improvement of living and working conditions and preventive measures such as vaccination. Economic Survey mentions that considerable progress had been achieved in the area of health since independence, but the situation was far from satisfactory. The National Health Policy (NHP) 2002 had laid emphasis on providing increased access to decentralized public health system, enhancing public health investment, and convergence of public health programmes. The focus was to be on primary health-care investment and increased investment in programmes to control communicable diseases. It envisaged an increase in public spending on health to 2-3 percent of GDP, by increased contributions by Central and State governments. The National Rural Health Mission (NRHM) (i) was to be launched throughout the country with special focus on 18 states with weak public health indicators and/or weak infrastructure. (ii) It was to build synergy between health and determinants of good health like nutrition, sanitation, hygiene and safe drinking water (iii) To mainstream the Indian Systems of Medicine to facilitate comprehensive health care (iv) To involve the community in the planning process (v) To upgrade infrastructure and to build capacity of health care system to enable it to handle increased allocations.

The NHP had also laid down certain targets to be achieved by certain dates e.g. Infant Mortality Rate (IMR) to be reduced to 30 per 1000 live births by 2012, Maternal mortality rate (MMR) to be reduced to 100 per lakh live births by 2012, total fertility to be reduced to 2.1 by 2012 etc RBI mentions that the combined expenditure by central and state governments was 0.8 percent of GDP in 2004-05 it was to rise to 0.9 percent in 2005-06 (RE) and 1.0 percent of GDP in 2006-07 (BE). The combined expenditure was 3.0 per cent of total expenditure in 2004-05 and was projected to rise to 3.3 per cent in 2005-06 (RE) and 3.4 per cent in 2006-07 (BE) of total expenditure.

6.482 Even to-day, over 50 percent of deaths are due to communicable diseases, the commonest among them being diarrhoea, fevers and respiratory infections. 20 percent of deaths are among children below 4 years and of these, 75 percent deaths are among infants of 0-1 year and among children below 5 years, especially infants, mortality is higher among girls, than among boys, more in rural areas than in urban areas and more among deprived sections of society. The fact that social groups and gender are significant predictors of mortality is confirmed by the planning commission's statement that anaemia and under-nutrition are contributory factors in over 50 percent of deaths in under 5-year olds. A study of the causes of infant mortality shows that 35 percent of infant deaths are due to premature birth and low weight of babies at birth. Many babies are born with low weight at birth, due to under-nutrition of their mothers. Acute respiratory infection (ARI) mainly pneumonias – cause about 25 per cent deaths and diarrhoea another 6 percent. Low birth weight of infants is due to poverty.

6.483 A study of allocation of resources among various budget heads shows that over 60 per cent of the budget goes to department of family welfare, 32 per cent only to department of health (including public health) and 3 per cent to Indian system of medicine. This misallocation of resources needs to be modified in favour of public health. A study of number of health services personnel in the existing infrastructure showed a shocking shortfall of specialists in health care institutions. Data compiled by Centre for Social Medicine and Community Health, JNU showed a shortfall of 85 per cent in paedriticeans, physicians-80 per cent, gynecologists-73per cent and surgeons-73per cent "However, there is at least one doctor per primary health centre, at least on paper. At the sub-centres, there is a shortfall of 47per cent for male multi-purpose workers (MPW), mid-wives (ANMs). The shortfall of pharmacists and lab-technicians is 23 per cent and 50 per cent respectively" (Sagar & Qadeer, 2005). Many doctors prefer to work in the private sector and consider posting in rural areas a sort of punishment.

6.484 It is heartening to learn that "The Planning Commission having studied the Bangs' home-based-neo-natal care programme is convinced that this shows the way for replication in the rest of the country. The model will now be part of the National Rural Health Mission (NRHM) in three lakh villages in Uttar Pradesh, Orissa, Rajasthan and Maharashtra" (Swarup, Tribune 2006).

Dr. Abhay Bang and Dr. Rani Bang founded the Society for Education, Action and Research (SEARCH) which "has trained a number of barefoot doctors" in 60 villages to treat women and also organized a movement against alcoholism," Their work has significantly reduced infant mortality in the area around Gadchirola – a remote tribal area, bordering Andhra Pradesh, Madhya Pradesh and Maharashtra.

6.485 Welfare Programmes: "All the citizens must have access, on equal basis to welfare programmes for the disabled, mothers and children, and old age, directed at the compensation of natural and physical inequalities." (Sachs) Compensatory social policies, including doles for the unemployed, should be financed out of the budget. Since most of the workers, as shown earlier, work in the unorganized sector, and open unemployment is much less significant than under-employment, there should be provision for social security for them.

6.49 Unorganized Sector Workers' Social Security

6.491 The National Commission for Enterprise in the unorganized sector, set up in September 2004 has submitted its report to the Government of India. The Commission has also submitted a draft Bill for the purpose. The Bill covers the entire country and all workers in unorganized/informal sector with monthly income of Rs. 5000 and below, including small and marginal farmers, wage workers and home-based workers, as well as informal workers in the organized sectors without any social security. The number of workers likely to be covered is estimated at 300 million.

6.492 The social security package for workers will comprise a national minimum social security cover comprising of, (a) old age pension for workers 60 years and above; (b) health insurance for self, spouse and children below 18 years of age, (c) maternity benefits for women workers or spouse of men workers and (d) insurance to cover death and disability arising out of accidents. The central government will create a national social security fund (NSSF) for the purpose. The draft bill has engendered considerable debate which should be welcome; what is significant is that the health needs of unorganized sector workers are being addressed.

6.493 Crop Insurance: Farmers constitute the bulk of India's rural population. Their wealth and welfare depends upon income from farming. Farming however, "involves numerous risks – natural, social and human. The uncertainty of crop yields is one of the basic risks that every farmer has to face". Recently there has been a spurt of farmers' suicides in a number of states in India and an important reason for these suicides, studies suggest, is failure to repay loans, due to crop failures. Agricultural Insurance Corporation (AIC) has overall responsibility to implement the National Agricultural Insurance Scheme (NAIS) w.e.f. Rabi season of 1999-2000. Three policy goals implicit in the scheme are: (a) Social response providing support to the poor farmers who are affected the most during severe crop failures, (b) risk management –

improving rural financial services' ability to manage commercial risks-important for improving access to finance, (c) controlling fiscal exposure of the government, during disaster years. A total of 624.38 lakh farmers have been covered during the 11 seasons (6 Rabi & 5 Kharif) in the period from Rabi 1999-2000 to Rabi 2004-05, with Kharif coverage being over 76 percent and that of Rabi, under 24%. A study conducted at the instance of AIC, analyzing secondary data, interviews with the farmers and interaction with other stakeholders has thrown up some critical issues, the more important among them being: a) should crop insurance be a part of comprehensive insurance policy? (b) should the scheme remain compulsory in the notified area or be made voluntary? (c) what should be the strategy to extend the scheme to other areas and crops? (d) how can the problem of "moral hazard" be minimized? (e) how should the premium be fixed? (f) how should the threshold yield be determined? (g) how should the actual yield be determined and indemnities paid? (h) what should be the role of different stake-holders AIC, banks, central and state governments? and (i) how best can the AIC be geared to perform its role effectively? (Vyas, 2006)

The study has stressed the need for proper coordination with all stakeholders at the States level. It has also recommended AIC's presence at the district level, on the model of NABARD — one-man office of the AIC manager to act as its "ears and eyes". For extending the coverage of AIC, the study has recommended outsourcing, to undertake the agency function to Krishi Vigyan Kendras, an agri clinic, a vibrant NGO's or private sector enterprise. The arrangements with these agencies should be flexible & not follow a rigid model.

Section 7
Development Dilemmas, Conclusion – Summing up

7.11 Bhaduri (2005), writing shortly after the NREG Bill was introduced in parliament and before the NREG Act was passed, had observed: "It is a misfortune for both the theory and practice of economic policy in India that we have not yet worked out a coherent scheme about how to take advantage of *an expanding* *domestic market involving the poor and the marginalized* in this era of globalization. The expansion in purchasing power can come from public works financed initially, if necessary through deficits of central and state budgets. The panchayats must have the full financial authority to design and implement these projects. Transparency and the right to information at all levels would be the mechanism through which our political democracy is brought closer to our as yet grossly distorted economic democracy." (emphasis mine)

7.121 Bhatia and Dreze writing some months after the Act came into operation and after surveying two Blocks in Jharkhand, partly confirm Bhaduri's apprehensions and yet exude hope. This hope can be translated into reality with mass mobilization of rural and urban poor and the deprived, on issues of hunger and employment, with an effective use of the Right to Information (RTI) as an important weapon to fight corruption and irregularities.

7.122 It would be appropriate to spell out the elements of 'inclusive' development. Sachs has defined it very well: inclusive development calls, first of all, at ensuring the exercise of civil, civic and political rights. Democracy is a truly foundational value [Sen 1999], as it also guarantees the transparency and accountability necessary for the working of development processes.

7.13 A federal structure and multi-party coalition of various political parties, representing various interest groups, places certain restraints, but the common minimum programme (CMP), adopted by the UPA government, is proceeding with hiccups, though. The National Farmers Commission (NFC) has made certain recommendations regarding food security (sub-sections 5.63 and 5.64). The challenges are in the implementation of various public projects whether it is Food for Work, employment programmes or other anti-poverty programmes. Non-involvement of the affected people, and of the panchayats in the formulation, selection and monitoring of the works leads to failure of projects and disillusionment, anger and frustration among the poor and the deprived.

7.14 The foregoing sections have clearly brought out the dual nature of our economic development-the burgeoning upper and middle classes, constituting around 20 per cent of our population of over 110 crore and 80 percent of the remaining both urban and rural, a majority of whom are on the margin of existence, but who are daily being bombarded with high and luxurious life styles of the 20 per cent affluent. The media, political parties and the NGOs are also telling them that employment for 100 days is their right, and if, however, they are denied this right, what will they do? how would they react?

7.21 The middle class is educated/skilled, vocal and has political clout, it would not brook any curtailment of its consumption standards. However, specific type of cesses – say nutrition cess for food security, employment cess to implement the NREG project need to be tried. Similarly, special levies on conspicuous consumption goods/services – air travel, A/C travel by rail/buses/ taxis, marriage/ festival pandals etc. need to be imposed to restrain conspicuous consumption.

7.22 The imposition of new cesses/levies, need to be accompanied by vigorous steps to tackle leakages, corruption etc and for strengthening the financial powers of panchayats and panchayati raj institutions. Further Panches, Sarpanches, and other panchayati raj functionaries need to be trained for their new functions. Thus, if the gram sabha has taken a decision to undertake soil conservation work, they should be able to work out the number of man (woman) days required for the task (of course, they would get technical help for working out the details of the scheme/project).

7.23 The economically weaker sections (EWSs) consist largely of the depressed and the deprived sections of the people, who suffer from hunger and malnutrition, lack of education and training, suffer from disease and bouts of ill health, thereby affecting their productivity. They have suffered these deprivations and indignities for centuries. But they are beginning to have a voice and to organise and to mobilize. Various non-government organizations (NGOs), with the Right to Information as a weapon and public hearings (Jan Sunwais) as a sort of peoples' courts, they are going to assert themselves. despite delays, reverses and repression. But with media playing a positive role, the struggle is likely to gather steam. The bureaucracy, the shady politicians and businessmen are going to deflect, attempt to divide and defeat these attempts. How far our democratic polity can measure up to tackle these strains and conflicts? Obviously, there will be strong resistance by established and new vested interests. They would use various strategems such as powers of state legislators, who are unhappy at their power (of patronage) having been increasingly transferred to panchayati raj institutions and functionaries. If the vested interests are successful in creating a stalemate or in finding ways to delay implementation of various social measures, the under-class is likely to react violently and resort to direct action. We have witnessed recently the strong reaction which defiling of the statue of Dr. Ambedkar at Kanpur, has created in Maharashtra and elsewhere. One lesson which the last general elections might have brought home to the UPA government is that "high growth, a booming stock market or higher ratings by bodies like the IMF and the World Bank are not good enough for winning elections in a country of so many desperately poor and marginalized people" (Bhaduri, 2005). If the NREG scheme is implemented faithfully and vigorously, the food for work (FFW) merged with NREG, PDS strengthened and recommendations of the National Farmers' Commission, accepted and implemented then there is hope that the internal market of the poor and marginalized would expand, and growth with social equality, would proceed to a higher plane.

7.24 The NREG Scheme has thrown up a challenge for the UPA government and for the political parties, constituting the UP Alliance, more especially the Left parties. They need to organize the rural and urban poor, to demand their right to employment, adequate income and adequate and nutritious food. This is both a challenge and an opportunity for Indian democracy: "if economics has to be relevant and governments have to survive, both must be more people – rather than market-friendly in today's India" (Bhaduri, 2005).

7.25 According to reports in the media, the number of districts where insurrectionary groups called the Maoists have spread their base has increased from 165 in 2005 to 186 districts in 2006. The finance minister, Mr. Chidambaram would have to discard the 'growth' mount and get on to the development mount, which would be employment-led growth strategy. Here employment with dignity would be assured and a massive programme of education, cultivation of skills and training would have to be launched to raise productivity of workers. If this happens even in one or two States, its effects are likely to be infectious.

Notes

1. Former Member Secretary, Indian Council of Social Science Research (ICSSR) & former Director Institute of Development Studies (IDS), Jaipur. The paper is basically a compilation, with a surfeit of quotations from the sources on different aspects dealt with. The author has borrowed from five papers in the volume, "India's & China's Recent experience with Reform and Growth" edited by Wanda Tseng & David Cowen. The author wishes to acknowledge, his debt to Lord Meghnad Desai, Kanhaiya Singh & Suman Bery, Hu Angang, Hu Linlin & Chang Zhixiao, Lardy & Arvind Panagariya from whose papers he has quoted extensively. Economic & Political Weekly, as always has been a rich source of informed discussion on current issues of political economy and has been duly acknowledged in the discussion of various themes. The author has relied on Jeemol Unni's paper in the Volume on "India: Meeting the Employment Challenge," for discussion on employment in the unorganized sector. Economic Survey, 2005-06 and Reserve Bank of India Annual Report, 2005-06, have been important sources of official view point and data. Contributions of the Alternative Survey Group have been important source materials. The publication of the Group's 2005-06 Alternative Survey has been delayed, but the author had the benefit of access to Chalapati Rao and Ranganathan's contribution on the 'Stock Market'. It would be difficult to express adequately my sense of debt to Prof. Ignacy Sachs, whose contribution to Development Debate over the last 40 years has been phenomenal and from whose piece in EPW, I have borrowed heavily. The standard disclaimers apply.

2. There were droughts in 1957-58, 1965-66, 1972-73, 1974-75, 2000-01, 2002-03 and 2004-05.

3. IMF in its latest release or World Economic Outlook (Sept. 2006), has raised India's GDP growth rate from 8.0 to 8.3 percent for 2006 and from 7.0 to 7.3 per cent for 2007. FICCI has raised

the outlook for 2006-07, for growth rate of GDP to 8.6 percent, based on performance during April – Sept. 2006.

4. Maddison dollars or 1990 international dollars. Dollars, unless otherwise specified, stand for US$.

5. National income estimates covering a long period are by their nature, broadly indicative rather than precise.

6. Internationally renowned Polish economist, Prof. Michal Kalecki, during discussions on the five year plans in 1959-60 with Pt. Jwahar All Nehru, remarked, "Mr. Prime Minister, your land reforms have made further land reforms impossible", implying thereby that the former landlords, zamindars, jagirdars etc. who were allied to the British colonialists and were, therefore, hated, comprised only 2-3% of the rural population, had been replaced by numerous (about 20%) rich and middle farmers, who would strongly resist any further land reforms.

7. West Bangal Chief Minister, Buddhadev Bhattacharya is currently (as on 25/12/06) facing very strong resistance from Trinimul Congress (its leader, Ms. Mamata Bannerjee, who has been hunger strike for over 21 days), from the NDA and even, the leftist NGOs. This is despite the contention that the terms of the acquisition in West Bangal are more favourable than those in other states.

8. 'Health-care for all' were downgraded in the post-Deng period i.e. the second phase.

9. This sub-section is based on the paper by Dr. Jeemol Unni. All quotations and data in this section, unless otherwise specified, are from her paper.

Manufacturing industries have been grouped as under:

A-1 Growing value-added, growing employment and growing labour productivity.

A-2 Growing value-added, declining employment, growing labour productivity.

B-1 Growing value-added, growing employment, declining labour productivity.

B-2 Growing value-added, declining employment and declining labour productivity.

C Non-growth industries

C-1 Declining value-added, growing employment, declining labour productivity.

C-2 Declining value-added, declining employment, growing labour productivity.

C-3 Declining value-added, declining employment, declining labour productivity.

10. The Hindu caste system permeated other religions - Muslims, Christians and Sikhs also and inter-regional mobility could take place only according to caste rules.

11. NSSO collects detailed information on the employment status of the population through large-scale nation-wide sample surveys in which individuals are categorized as employed or available for work but not employed. The surveys conducted by NSSO take into consideration seasonal variations in employment and also identify the magnitude of under employment through the following types of measures of employment:

(i) **Usual Principal Status (UPS)** – Here people are counted as being in the labour force on principal usual activity basis, if they were engaged in economic activities (work) or reported seeking/being available for work for the major part of the preceding 365 days.

(ii) **Usual Principal & Subsidiary Status (UPSS)** – This provides a more inclusive measure, leading to a large proportion of the population as being in the labour force and lower unemployment rates relative to the UPS criterion.

(iii) **Current Weekly Status (CWS)** – People are counted as employed if they were engaged in economic activity for at least one hour on any day during the reference week. CWS unemployment rates tend to be higher, than the UPS & UPSS-based unemployment rates for the week.

(iv) **Current Daily Status (CDS)** – Based on the reported time disposition on each day of the reference week (in units of half day when needed by the presence of multiple activities within a day), person days in employment/unemployment are totalled to generate estimates of person days in employment/unemployment. This measure captures the 'within week' unemployment of those classified as employed on the CWS basis.

12. In international parlance, multilateral means basically that all countries are included, while 'Plurilateral' means a particular selection of countries.

13. Repo rate is the rate at which banks borrow funds from the RBI. The Ministry of finance and SEBI (according to Economic Times Nov., 13, 2006) are studying proposals for creating mechanism for hedge funds to invest in local equity market. Primacy will be given to funds which are willing to subject themselves to disclosure norms, have a record of a long-term investment perspective'? They would want to take a look at the global experience besides addressing the concerns of RBI "which want the quality of funds to be the cornerstone of any policy on foreign portfolio" Investment.

14. The number of SHGs had reached 18.30 lakhs on 31st December, 2005, according to Economic Survey, 2005-06.

15. This piece is almost wholly based on Sudhir Krishnaswamy's EPW piece.

16. I had the privilege of working on "Model of a planned mixed economy; India, a case study" for my doctoral dissertation under the guidance of Prof. M. Kalecki and Prof. Ignacy Sachs, at the Central School of Planning and Statistics, Warsaw (Poland) in mid-1960s. I have borrowed heavily from Prof. Sachs' paper.

REFERENCES

Agarwal, Pawan (2006), *Higher Education Policy – Many Contradictions,* Economic and Political Weekly (EPW), XLI (45), Nov. 11.

Aiyar, Yamini, Samji Salimah (2006) *Improving the Effectiveness of National Rural Employment Guarantee Act,* January, 28.

Angang, Hu, Linlin, *Hu and Chang Zhixiao (2005) China's Economic Growth and Poverty Reduction,* in Tseng, Wanda and Cowen David (eds.), India's and China' Recent Experience with Reform and Growth, Palgrave Macmillan.

Bhaduri, Amit (2005) First Priority : *Guarantee Employment and Right to Information*, EPW, XL (4), Jan., 28.

Bhatia, Bela and Dreze, Jean (2006) *Employment Guarantee in Jharkhand: Ground Realities*, EPW, XLI (29), July 22.

Blaas, Wolfgang (2006) *International Trade Negotiations and Strategic Forum Shifting* Paper presented at the International Conference on "Peace and Developemnt", CRRID, Chandigarh, Nov., 8.

Chaddha, G.K. (2005), *Pace and Pattern of Growth of Rural Non-Farm Sector in India*, Paper presented at the National Seminar on Accelerating Economic Growht and Regional Balance at the Institute for Studies in Industrial Development (ISID), New Delhi, September,16. 2005.

Deng, Kent G. (2000) *'A critical survey of recent-research on Chinese Economic History'* Economic history review, LIII (1) Feb.

Desai, Meghnad (2005), *India and China, An Essay in Comparative Political Economy* in Tseng, Wanda and Cowen, David (eds.) India's and China's Recent Experience with Reform and Growth Palgrave Macmillan.

Drache, Daniel and Froese, Marc D (2006) *An Empirical Analysis of Why the WTO is Broken and cannot be fixed – yet'* paper presented as the International Conference on Peace and Development CRRID, Chandigarh, Nov. 7.

Dutt, Amitabh Krishna (2006) *Flawed Logic of Capital Account Convertability* EPW, XLI (19) May, 13.

Government of India (2006) *Economic Survey, 2005-06* (ES).

Economic Times (2006) *Prime Minister's Sewa Gram Interview*, July, 3.

Economic Times (2006) *Prime Minister's Speech at the ET Awards for Corporate Excellence*, Oct. 9.

Economic Times (2006) *Prime Minister's Remarks at the Meeting of the Full Planning Commission for discussing the Draft 11th Five Year Plan*, Oct., 19

Gopal, K.S. (2006) *Is the Euphoria justified?* EPW, XLI (29) July, 22

Golait, Ramesh and Pradhan, N.C. (2006) *Changing Food Consumption Pattern in Rural India – Implications on Food and Nutrition Security,* Indian Journal of Agricultural Economics, 61(3), July – Sept.

Kalecki, M. (1993) *Introduction to the Theory of Growth in Socialist Economy* Collected works of Michal Kalecki, Vol. 4 ed. J. Osiatynski, Clarenden Press, Oxford.

Kannan, K.P. (2005), *Linking Guarantee to Human Development* EPW, XL (42) Oct. 15.

Kannan, K.P., Srivastava, Ravi & Sengupta, Arjun (2006) *Social Security for Unorganized Workers – A major National Initiative*, EPW, XLI (32) Aug. 12.

Krishnaswami, Sudhir, (2006) *Airport Privatization Case – Public Law and Public Sector Reform,* EPW, XLI (40), Oct., 7.

Lardy, Nicholas R. (2005) *Trade Liberalization and its role in Chinese Economic Growth* Tseng Wanda and Cowen, David (eds) India's and China's Recent Experience with Reform and Growth, Palgrave Macmillan.

Maddison, Angus (2001) *The World Economy A Millenial Perspective.* Development Studies Center, OECD, Paris.

Mehta, Jaya (2005) *'Poverty'* Alternative Economic Survey, India – Magnifying Mal-development, 2004-05.

Needham, Joseph et al (1954) *Science and Civilization in China* various volumes, Cambridge University Press.

Panagariya, Arvind (2005) *India in the 1980s and the 1990s: A Triumph or Reform?* in Tseng, Wanda and Cowen David (eds.), India's and China' Recent Experience with Reform and Growth, Palgrave Macmillan.

Parthasarthi, Ashok (2005) *Refashioning Rural Industrialization Programme*, EPW, XL (44-45) Oct., 29.

RBI – *Reserve Bank of India, Annual Report, 2006-06.*

Rao, P. Parthasarthy, Birthal, P.S., & Joshi, P.K. (2006) *Diversification towards High Value Agriculture – Role of Urbanization and Infrastructure*, EPW, XLI (26) July 1.

Reddy V. Ratna, Golab, S (2006) Agrarian Crisis: *Looking Beyond the Debt Trap* XLI (19), May 13.

Sachs, Ignacy (2004) *From Poverty Trap to inclusive development in LDCs*, EPW, XXXIX (18) May 1.

Sagar, Alpana & Qadeer, Imrana (2005) *'Health'* in Alternative Economic Survey, India – Magnifying Mal-development, 2004-05.

Sen, Partha (2006) *Case against Rushing into Full Capital Account Convertability* EPW, XLI (19) May 13.

Singh, Kanhaiya & Bery, Suman (2005) *India's Growth Experience* in Tseng, Wanda and Cowen David (eds.), India's and China' Recent Experience with Reform and Growth, Palgrave Macmillan.

Srinivasan, T.N. (2006) *China, India and the World Economy*, EPW, XLI (34), August, 26.

Swarup, Harihar (2006) *Doctor Couple in the Service of the Poor,* Tribune, Nov. 19.

Unni, Jeemol *Employment Trends and Eamings in the Informal Sector*, Paper presented at India: Meeting the Employment Challenge, Conference on labour and Employment issues in India, Institute for Human Development, New Delhi, July 27-29.

Vyas, V.S. and Jurgit Singh. Crop in surance in India: scope for improvement. EPW. Vol. 41 No: 43/44, Nov. 4, 2006. pp. 4585-94.

Williamson, Jhon (2006) *Why Capital Account Convertability in India is premature* pub. in It, XLI (19), May 13.

Wray, L. Randall (2006) *Currency Sovereignity and Policy Independence*, EPW, XLI (19) May 13.

Yadav, Sharad (2006) *SEZ Policy, a threat to Food Security,* Times of India, Sept. 18.

6

ECONOMIC LIBERALISATION AND GOVERNANCE: CHALLENGES AHEAD

B.S.Ghuman

Introduction

Both the theoretical and applied public administration has been undergoing fast changes. The mega events like globalization, liberalization, privatization, and decentralization, increasing media and citizen oversight and information technology have influenced significantly the theory and practice of public administration. With a view to absorb the profound implications originating from these events, public administration has relied heavily on other social science literature particularly that of new institutional economics, political science, and management. This literature has not only enriched the theoretical foundations of public administration but has also added a couple of administrative devices to its toolbox. In the changed environment, the focus of public administration has been extended beyond the mere provision of goods and services. Quality of service, transparency, accountability, time bound redressal of public grievances, consultation with users of service, value for money and ultimately enhancing citizens' satisfaction has become equally significant to administration. Further, the administration for performing its developmental, promotional, and service functions has started relying upon private sector, semi-private organizations and civil society organizations including NGOs. The outcome of the emerging combination of government and organizations other than government in the delivery of public services is described as governance. The objective of this paper is to examine the relationship between economic liberalization and governance in India. The paper is divided into five sections. In Section I conceptual framework has been described. An overview of economic liberalization has been provided in Section II. The relationship between economic liberalization and governance has been discussed in Section III. In Section IV the challenges for governance emerging from economic liberalization have been identified. The policy recommendations have been documented in Section V.

I
Conceptual Framework

Liberalization: Liberalization is a summary description of the progressive reduction in regulatory, promotional and entrepreneurial (i.e. government as producer) role of government in economic and social development. Liberalization has two dimensions–internal (domestic) and external. Internal liberalization consists of relaxing the control of government over domestic industry and other economic and social activities and also retreat of government as producer (i.e. privatization) within protectionist regime. External liberalization aims at exposing domestic firms to external competition by drifting away from protectionist policies. It comprises initiatives by nation states in the form of relaxation in regulations governing international trade, international investment, international finance and international technology including services. External liberalization, thus, provides a route for the domestic economy and economies of the rest of the globe for mutual exchange and integration. External liberalization is also promoted under Uruguay Round of trade negotiations culminating in the setting up of the World Trade Organization (W.T.O.) in 1995.

The theoretical foundations for the policy of liberalization including privatization are provided by several interrelated strands of literature mainly contributed by New Right Schools of Thought, property rights literature, the principal-agent relationship and organization and management literature. (Swann, 1988; Dunsire, *et al.*, 1988; Vickers and Yarrow, 1988; Bos, 1991; Ashford, 1993; Jordon, 1993; Mascarenhas, 1993; Gray and Jenkins, 1995; and Kirkpatrick and Lucio, 1996).

Governance: Governance is a buzzword these days. Ideas about 'governance' appear in a wide range of contexts (Larmour, 1997, p.383). There is no consensus on the definition of governance. According to Pai Panandiker two broad strands of approach to defining governance can be identified. One approach is shaped by developmental concerns whereas the other is concerned with the exercise of political power of the state (Pai Panandiker, 1997, p.2). In the discipline of Public Administration the issue of governance has emerged as one of the key areas of dialogue (Pai Panandiker, 1997, p.1). The emergence of this issue on the agenda of Public Administration is motivated by the increasing role of market in the delivery of public services and as a consequence of reforming administrative institutions particularly bureaucracy and increasingly enhanced role of indirect administrative saving devices particularly in the form of non-government institutions such as private and semi-private organizations in the delivery of public services. According to Dunsire, "Governments (of any colour) in the emerging climate are likely to search more for indirect administration saving ways of discharging their inalienable duty to guard against external threat and internal disruption, and of achieving their electorally legitimated policy programmes; the outcome may be described as governance rather than government", (Dunsire, 1995, p.34).

Keeping these developments in view, in the present study governance has been defined as administration and management of both direct and indirect institutions of administration, engaged in the public policy making exercise and in the delivery of public services.

II

Economic Liberalization Policies in India: An Overview

Liberalization policy in India was adopted during the early 1980s. Its pace improved during the mid 1980s. However, the liberalization policies of the 1980s were partial in coverage and ad hoc in approach. It is from 1991 onwards that a systematic and comprehensive liberalization policy was set in motion. Earlier the Nehruvian model of growth adopted during 1950s and patterned somewhat on Soviet model involved strict regulation in the most of the areas of the economy. However, economic liberalization policy is patterned on the philosophy of allocating scarce resources among sectors, strata and regions largely through market forces.

The Indian economy faced a serious crisis during the middle of 1991. The major component was a severe balance of payment crisis. During this period the economy had lowest foreign exchange reserves ($1.1 billions) bare enough to finance less than 3 week import bill, very high inflation (14 percent), high level of gross fiscal deficit (8.4 percent of gross domestic product), lowest rate of growth of the economy (less than 1 percent) and negative rate of growth of per capita income. Economic crisis, in part, deepened due to political instability in the country. India had two different Governments between December, 1989 and March, 1991. During 1991-crisis the country was ruled by a caretaker Government. The political instability adversely affected the confidence of international investors in the Indian economy. That period witnessed considerable withdrawal of foreign capital particularly by the NRIs and thus perpetuated balance of payment crisis. The day-to-day foreign requirements were managed by borrowing from abroad against gold.

The new Congress (I) Government constituted after June 1991 elections approached the IMF and World Bank for a loan to mitigate the crisis. In exchange, these financial institutions imposed comprehensive programmes of stabilization and structural adjustment. The aim of the stabilization programme was to restore stability in the economy by reducing the severity of the balance of payment crisis and inflation. Adoption of appropriate exchange rate, interest rate, fiscal and monetary policies were some of the components of stabilization measures.

The aim of structural reform programme was to attain a higher rate of growth on sustainable basis through efficiency and productivity originating from relaxation of government controls over production, investment and prices in the domestic economy and progressively opening up of the Indian economy to foreign trade, capital and technology. The structural reform measures constitute the core of the economic liberalization. Liberalization in India has two dimensions – internal and external.

The domestic liberalization policy encompasses all facets of the Indian economy. However, thrust areas are industry, public enterprises, taxation, financial and infrastructure sectors. The industrial sector has witnessed far-reaching reforms. The New Industrial Policy, 1991 (NIP, 1991) abolished compulsory licensing for all except a few industries. The reform has enabled the taking out of the licensing system for more than 90 percent of the industrial sector. In case of existing units all major expansions are exempted from licensing. The existing and new units are provided a new broad banding facility with a view to enabling them to produce any article without an additional investment.

In the area of public enterprises five major reforms have been introduced. First, monopoly of the state sector has been drastically reduced from seventeen to four. That is, thirteen industries have been opened to private sector that was hitherto the monopoly of the state sector. This is known as disguised privatization. Within existing public enterprises, sweeping changes favouring increasing role of market forces are in progress. These include performance improvement through a memorandum of understanding (MOU) system, referring of sick enterprises to the Board for Industrial and Financial Reconstruction (BIFR) for the formulation of revival /rehabilitation schemes or closure and enhanced autonomy to select public enterprises for enabling them to become global and domestic players.

Privatization has not been explicitly referred to in the NIP, 1991. Initially the word privatization, it seems has been avoided partly due to political considerations. In the first budget (1991-1992) immediately after the announcement of NIP, 1991, limited selling of government equity under the name of disinvestment policies was mentioned. The selling of government equity below 50 percent continued till late nineties. It is during October 1999 budget that a full-fledged privatization policy was announced. Under privatization policy, 13 public enterprises and 21 hotels owned by the government have already been privatized.

Based on the recommendations of Chelliah Committee and Raikhi committee tax reforms comprise moderate rate of taxation, broadening the tax base, simplification in compliance and extension of modified value added tax (MODVAT) to other areas. Financial sector reforms consist of slashing of Statutory Liquidity Ratio (SLR) and thus increasing the availability of funds with banks, allowing private banks to expand, encouraging new entrants, simplification and rationalization of the interest rate structure. The Government has also opened insurance sector to private sector. The capital market is undergoing similar reforms.

The infrastructure sectors particularly telecommunication, power and roads which were traditionally the monopolies of the state sector have also been opened to the private sector.

External liberalization (i.e. globalization) in India has covered areas such as trade, foreign exchange, capital and technology. The major initiatives include current account convertibility of rupee, allowing exchange rate of rupee to be determined by the market forces in foreign exchange markets, abolition of import through licensing except for consumer goods, drastic reduction in import duties overtime, automatic approval of Reserve Bank of India for foreign equity in select high priority industries, the provision of automatic approval for technology agreements in select high priority industries. In addition Foreign Institutional Investors (FII's) registered with RBI are permitted to operate in the capital market. Large number of incentives are provided to Non-Resident Indians (NRI's) and Overseas Corporate Bodies (OCB) to invest in India. Indians firms are also allowed to raise capital from International market through Global Depository Receipts (GDR's) and Foreign Currency Convertible Bonds (FCCB's).

Globalization of the Indian economy is also in progress through W.T.O. The Eight Round of negotiations under General Agreement on Tariffs and Trade (GATT) popularly known as Uruguay Round culminated in the form of agreement on agriculture, trade in textiles and clothing, market access, trade related investment measures (TRIM's), trade related intellectual property rights (TRIP's) and services. These agreements having varying time frames to come in operation. The phenomenal progress in information technology particularly Internet field has further accelerated the process of globalization of the Indian economy.

The liberalization process initiated by the Congress (I) Government has been followed by successive Governments led by Untied Front and Bharatiya Janata Party (BJP) with a minor move initiated by the BJP Government towards disguised protectionism by imposing non-modvatable levy on imported goods under the grab of 'Swadesi' to provide 'level playing field' to the domestic industry. Economic liberalization is near the completion of twelve years. Economic liberalization process seems irreversible in India.

III
Economic Liberalization And Governance

Changes in governance in India in response to globalization, liberalization and privatization policy have been uneven both in pace and distribution across fields, ministries, departments and the organizations. The economic ministries/organizations such as Finance, Industries, Commerce, Planning Commission etc. have witnessed fast and many changes. Other ministries have experienced very slow and only a few changes in response to liberalization. With a view to having a better understanding in changes in governance in response to changing economic policy environment, the discussion has been divided into two parts, namely, changes in economic administration and changes in general administration.

(i) Changes in Economic Administration: Economic administration as a specialized field of government activity has marked a significant turning point in response to the liberalization policy (Vittal, 1997, p.14). Many economic acts and regulations have either been amended or are in process of amendment. For example the Industrial Monopolies and Restrictive Trade Practices (MRTP) Act, 1970, has been drastically amended in September 1991 in tune with liberalization. The role of the MRTP Commission has also been made more specific in the form of ensuring that the enterprises do not act against public interest or indulge in unfair trade practices. The Foreign Exchange Regulation Act (FERA), 1973 has been replaced by Foreign Exchange Management Act (FEMA) 1999. Similarly the Import and Export Act, 1947 has been substituted by Foreign Trade (Development and Regulation) Act, 1992. The Patent Act 1930, Copy Right Act, 1957 is being amended in tune with the World Trade Organization (W.T.O.) agreement. The Indian Companies Act, 1956 has also been amended in the light of changed economic environment. Sick Industrial Companies (Special Provisions) Act 1985 has been amended in December, 1991 to cover sick public enterprises and subsequently to be referred to Board For Industrial and Financial Reconstruction for the formulation of revival/rehabilitation schemes or closure.

The ministries/institutions governing economic policy-making have also experienced considerable changes. The Planning Commission, once known as 'super-cabinet' has experienced erosion in its role in policy making. In the Union budget making exercise the contribution of the Planning Commission has declined over the time. According to Thimmaiah the World Bank (World Bank, 1996) has suggested that the role of the Planning Commission be reduced only to allocate loan funds on the basis of economic viability of specific projects and thus the Planning Commission would be constrained to play conventional role of helping to reduce regional disparities. Planning Commission may be better known as Investment Commission and in no way would be different from the development financial institutions like Investment and Development Bank of India (IDBI) [Thimmaiah, 1996, pp. 29-30). Ministry of Finance has emerged as super Ministry in the liberalization era. The setting up of Expenditure Commission has further strengthened its stronghold over other ministries. Creation of new institutions /authorities dealing with matters relating to economic administration is another outcome of liberalization. Ministry of Disinvestment, Disinvestment Commission, Foreign Investment Promotion Board have been set up in response to liberalization policy. In the liberalized era with a view to protect interests of consumer in areas such as telecom, insurance and power opened to the private sector, the government has constituted regulatory authorities, namely, Telecom Regulatory Authority of India (TRAI), Insurance Regulatory and Development Authority (IRDA) and the Central Electricity Regulatory Commission (CERC). The role of the capital market has increased during the liberalization era. For exercising control over the capital markets and ensuring its proper growth, the Security Exchange Board of India (SEBI) has been accorded a statutory status under SEBI Act 1992. The Government of India has also put institutional arrangements in place to deal with issues arising from W.T.O.

The governing pattern in public enterprises has also been experiencing changes due to reform initiatives such as granting of more autonomy and introducing effective accountability in public enterprises through initiatives like autonomy package (*navratna* and *miniratna* status to select public enterprises), bringing more public enterprises under Memorandum of Understanding (MOU) and professionalizing the board of directors by inducting part-time non-official members.

(ii) Changes in General Administration: General Administration restructuring has never been on the top on the agenda of the Indian government during liberalization period till November 1996 when reform issues concerning administrative institutions came on the scene in Chief Secretaries' Conference held for the said purpose. Chief Ministers' Conference followed it on *Action Plan for Effective and Responsive Administration* held under the chairmanship of the Prime Minister on 24th May, 1997. The Home Minister, Finance Minister, Law Minister, Minister of State for Personnel, Public Grievances and Pensions, Cabinet Secretary, Chief Secretaries of the States/Union Territories and senior officials in GOI also attended the Conference. The conference statement, "...strongly endorsed the need for ensuring responsive, accountable, transparent and people friendly administration at all levels and agreed that necessary corrective steps must be taken to arrest the present drift in the management of public services..., the Conference urged that measures should be taken to restore the faith of people, *particularly the weaker sections of the society, in fairness and capacity of administration...* Further the increasing establishment expenditure and large size of Government staff is adversely affecting the development process by reducing the investible funds. The ambit of Government interaction needs to be redefined, so that the superfluous functions can be dispersed with." (GOI, May, 1997, p. 1).

In response to the Chief Ministers' Conference and resolution adopted therein, various initiatives have been taken by the

Ministries/Departments of *GOI* and by the States and Union Territories. The Department of Administrative Reforms and Public Grievances (DARPG) has compiled information about these initiatives in two reports entitled, *Initiatives and Best Practices of Government of India for Effective and Responsive Administration* (November, 1997) and *Policies, initiatives and Best Practices in the States/Union Territories* (August, 1997).

The reform measures mentioned in the first report are classified into three subjects:

1. Accountable and Citizen-friendly government;
2. Transparency and Right to Information; and
3. Improving the performance and Integrity of Public Services.

The aim of new initiatives in the field of general administration is to provide effective and responsive administration. A close look, however, on the progress of these measures suggests that these initiatives have also not succeeded in fulfilling the laid down objectives (Ghuman, 2003).

IV
Outcome of Economic Liberalization And Emerging Challenges for Governance

As stated earlier the principal aim of economic liberalization is to attain a higher rate of growth on sustainable basis through efficiency and productivity originating from relaxation of government controls over production, investment and prices in the domestic economy and progressively opening up of the Indian economy to foreign trade, capital and technology. The supporters of liberalization further argue that growing rate of growth through 'trickle down effect' would take care of poverty, unemployment, income inequality and regional disparities.

Firstly, a quick perusal of ten years' experience of the Indian economy during post-liberalization phase reveals a gap between rhetoric and reality. Table 1 shows that the rate of growth experienced by the Indian economy during the 1990s are not markedly different from the 1980s (pre-liberalization period). During both pre and post liberalization periods the economy had

Table 1
Average Growth of Real GDP 1950-51 to 2000-2001

	1951-52 to 1960-61	*1961-62 to 1970-71*	*1971-72 to 1980-81*	*1981-82 to 1990-91*	*1991-92 to 2000-2001*
GDP (factor cost)	3.9	3.7	3.2	5.6	5.6
Per capita GDP	2.0	1.5	0.8	3.4	3.6

Source: K. N. Kabra (2002)

experienced almost same rate of growth and thus liberalization policy has not succeeded in accelerating the rate of the Indian economy.

The industrial sector and foreign trade, which are the central focus of amended and new economic laws, have remained more volatile. For example the annual growth rate of industrial sector during 1990s and early 2000s has fluctuated between 1 percent and 12.3 percent. Similarly the annual growth rate of export has oscillated between 2.7 percent and 35.3 percent

Secondly, changing economic laws governing both internal and external sectors simultaneously have not helped the Indian industries to improve efficiency and productivity. Rather these have helped the multinational corporations (MNCs) to enter India in a big way and take over most of the lucrative industrial activities, and also resulting in increased sickness among domestic industrial units.

Thirdly, the administrative ministries and bureaucracy have made consistent efforts to thwart the implementation of new initiatives in the field of the economic governance. For example the autonomy of new authorities/commissions such as Telecom Regulatory Authority of India (TRAI) and Disinvestment Commission was reduced drastically. The status of both these institutions was changed from obligatory to recommendatory. Further the core group of Secretaries formed for Disinvestment/ privatization programme had not taken serious note of very exhaustive recommendations of the Disinvestment Commission. The recent debate on privatization within cabinet suggests that the majority of the administrative ministries oppose initiatives of disinvestment ministry. Fourthly, India has not made adequate institutional arrangements to reap the benefits of globalization particularly originating from World Trade Organization.

The trickle down hypothesis has also not worked effectively during post liberalization phase. Again a quick look on equity aspects shows that the performance of the economy has not improved. In certain cases its performance has deteriorated.

The number of people below poverty line has increased both in the rural and urban areas. For example 231.9 million people were below poverty line in rural areas in 1987-88. Their number increased to 244 million in 1993-94. In urban areas the number of poor increased from 75.2 million to 76.3 million in 1993-94. In terms of percentage the picture has slightly improved. Prior to liberalization 39.1 percent people were below poverty line in rural areas, which has come down marginally to 37.3 percent in post reform period. In the urban sector the respective figures are 38.2 and 32.4 percent.

Employment scenario after liberalization has not improved as per the expectations of the policy makers. According to recent Economic Survey (2002-2003) there was slow down of the overall growth rate in organized sector employment (p. 214). The rate of growth of employment on Current Daily Status (CDS) basis has declined from 2.7 percent per annum in 1983-94 to 1.07 percent per annum in 1994-2000 (Economic Survey, 2002-2003, p. 214). The declining trend in the growth rate of employment is mainly attributed to a near stagnation of employment in agriculture (Economic Survey, 2002-2003, p. 214). Stagnation of employment in agriculture is partly due to decline in public investment in agriculture. The absolute number of unemployed as well as the incidence of unemployment (i.e. unemployed as percent of the labour force) has also witnessed an increase in the recent past (Economic Survey, 2002-2003). Import of capital intensive technology during economic liberalization is partly responsible for growing unemployment. This imported technology is resulting in jobless growth.

Regional disparities have a tendency to increase during post-liberalization period. Prior to economic liberalization the government through promotional and entrepreneurial roles was helping backward areas/states to get fresh investment. Orissa, Bihar, Madha Pardesh and other backward states benefited considerably in terms of direct central investment (i.e. setting up of public enterprises) and private investment under various promotional schemes. After economic liberalization market forces motivate fresh investment. State-wise break up of foreign direct investment (FDI) clearly shows that western states like Maharastra, Gujarat and southern states like Karnataka, Tamil Nadu, Andhra Pradesh are attracting maximum FDI. For example the share of Maharastra and Gujarat was 17.36 percent and 7 percent respectively in FDI between August 1991 and August 2002. The respective shares of Karnataka, Tamil Nadu and Andhra Pardesh were 8,8 and 5 percent. The land locked Northern and the North-Eastern states, have not gained much from FDI. According to a recent study in the post-liberalization phase due to the declining of the state and supremacy of market forces in allocation of resources across regions the gap between the highest and lowest per capita in the states has steadily winded. Only industrially advanced states like Mahrashtra, Gujarat, Karnatka, Tamil Nadu, and West Bengal have experienced a higher rate growth in the post-liberalization period. Another state is Kerala, which has registered a higher rate of growth. All other states have experienced lower rates of growth during post reform period. The coefficient of variation (C.V.) in the state income growth rate has increased almost twofold in during the post reform period. The C.V in the state income growth rate was, for example, was 28.39 percent in the 1980s, it increased to 56.23 percent in the 1990s (Srivastava, 2002, pp. 39-43).

Earlier in the planning era the state had plethora of policies and programmes to accelerate growth rate, mitigate poverty, unemployment and also economic, social and regional disparities. Now in the market forces regime most of these policies and programmes are either discontinued or are given lower funding and less care at the time of implementation. The combination of declining public investment in important sectors like agriculture, absence of social safety networks, the above mentioned outcomes of economic liberalization have far reaching economic, social and political implications and ultimately posing serious challenges to the governing institutions.

V

Policy Recommendations

Economic liberalization process seems irreversible in India. Adopting the following prescriptions by the institutions of governance can help to reduce the gap between the objectives and achievements of economic liberalization.

1. Acceleration of rate of growth on sustainable basis is the most important challenge before institutions of governance. For

this purpose more and more public investment should go to those sectors in which due to low return the private investment is not forthcoming in a big way, but the sectors are backbone of the economy. Agriculture and small-scale industrial sectors are most suitable examples of such sectors. Adoption of suitable mix policies aiming to arrest frequent fluctuations in industry and foreign trade is also required for sustaining a higher growth on long-term basis.

2. In a labour surplus and capital scarce economy over emphasis on privatization should be replaced by proper mix of public and private sectors. Privatization programmes should be implemented on selective basis. It should mainly confine to public enterprises producing private goods. Privatization should be used more as a disciplinary strategy for public enterprises rather than a channel to raise resources to meet fiscal deficit.

3. With a view to arrest jobless growth process, the government should give liberal tax incentives to corporate sector for investment in R & D for developing technology, which can promote both growth and employment.

4. The poverty alleviation programmes should be restructured so that procedure orientation is replaced by mission orientation.

5. With a view to reduce growing regional disparities, a regional policy aiming to motivate private sector to invest in backward and landlocked areas should be formulated and implemented.

6. The above-mentioned suggestions cannot yield result in the absence of improvement in quality of governance.

7. Quality of governance can improve considerably if existing government driven model in replaced by participating model of governance.

8. In the participatory model of governance all the stakeholders including the poor, disadvantaged groups and people from the backward areas participate as partners in policy-making, its execution and assessment.

9. Vested interests of those in power are likely to be stumbling blocks in the way of reform initiatives. In order to make reforms feasible and sustainable both political and bureaucratic institutions, should be reformed simultaneously. It is all the more necessary because liberalization policy is not formulated indigenously. For

this, strong political backing is a prerequisite. In this regard politically tall leaders from various political parties can give a lead. Building of networking among the NGOs, intelligentsia, seasoned and honest bureaucrats, professional associations, political parties and administrative institutions would provide an environment for governance to move towards good governance.

REFERENCES

Ashford, Nigel (1993), "The Ideas of the New Right", in Jordan and Ashford (ed, 1993).

Bos, Dieter (1991). *Privatization: A Theoretical Treatment.* Oxford: Clarendon Press.

Dunsire, A. *et al.* (1988) "Organizational Status and Performance: A Conceptual Framework for Testing Public Choice Theory," *Public Administration,* Vol.66, No.4.

Ghuman, B.S. (2003), "Impact of Globalization, Liberalization and Privatization Policies on Governance: The Indian Experience", coming in a book titled, *Public Governance and Decentralization*, edited by S.N. Mishra and Anil Dutt Mishra, (Sh. T.N. Chaturvedi Felicitation Volume), New Delhi, Mittal Publications.

Government of India (2003). *Economic Survey 2002-2003*. New Delhi.

———————— (24 May, 1997). *Action Plan for Effective and Responsible Administration,* Statement adopted at C.M. Conference, New Delhi.

Gray, Andrew and Bill Jenkins (1995), "From Public Administration to Public Management: Reassessing a Revolution?". *Public Administration,* Vol.73 (Spring).

Jordan, Grant (1993), "The New Right and Public Policy: A Preliminary Overview", in Jordan and Ashford (ed. 1993).

Kabra, K.N. (2002), "From Gradual to Galloping Liberalization: A Journey to Nowhere & Withering of Development State in India", *Alternative Economic Survey 2001-2002*, New Delhi, Rainbow Publishers.

Kirkpatrick, Ian and Miguel Martinez Lucio (1996), "Introduction: The Contract State and the Future of Public Management", *Public Administration.* Vol. 74 (Spring).

Larmour, Peter (1997), "Models of Governance and Public Administration", *International Review of Administrative Science.* Vol.63.

Mascarenhas, R.C. (1993), "Building an Enterprise Culture in the Public Sector: Reform of the Public Sector in Australia, Britain and New Zealand", *Public Administration Review.* Vol.53, No.4.

Pai Panandiker, V.A. (ed. 1997). *A Survey of Research in Public Administration* 1980- 1990. Delhi: Konark Publishers Pvt. Ltd.

Srivastava, R.S. (2002), "Regional Growth and Disparities", *Alternative Economic*

Survey 2001-2002, New Delhi, Rainbow Publishers.

Swann, D. (1988), *The Retreat of the State: Deregulation and Privatization in the U.K. and U.* S. New York: Harvester Wheatsheat.

Thimmaiah, G. (1996), "Redefining the Role of the Planning Commission", Dr. Malcom Adiseshiah Memorial Lecture (Institute for Social Sciences and Research. Vellore).

Vickers, John and George Yarrow (1988). *Privatization: An Economic Analysis.* London: The MIT Press.

Vittal, N. (1999) "Corruption as Aids of the Society," *The Economic Times,* May 24.

7

WORK CULTURE

(Veer Singh)

Charles Dickens, in the opening lines of his famous novel[1] on French Revolution said, "It was the best of times, it was the worst of times, it was the age of wisdom, it was the age of foolishness, it was the epoch of belief, it was the epoch of incredulity, it was the season of Light, it was the season of Darkness, it was the spring of hope, it was the winter of despair, we had everything before us, we had nothing before us."

Likewise, when we look at the contemporary society, and the social, political and economic settings, we find ourselves confronted with a host of new concepts some of which are: 'Future Shock', 'End of History'[2], 'Third Wave', 'Death of Distance', 'Clash of Civilizations'[3], 'Knowledge Society' and many more. All these concepts represent developing trends in the modern society, which would perhaps be known as the most productive period in terms of ideas, paradigms and thoughts.

India today stands at the cross roads of history in the new Millennium. A resurgent nation looks forward to its rightful place in the comity of nations. The economic upsurge and public welfare shall not come easy. In order to reach our goals. we have to change traditional mind-set on work, work culture, efficiency and discipline, individually and collectively and promote a work culture which shall bring in prosperity and enlightenment.

Work Culture: Is a neutral concept, which could be positive and negative. It consists of attitude towards work, efficiency and discipline. People who have positive work culture look at work as a value, a goal and an ideal and an instrumentality for individual and collective prosperity and well-being. Therefore, hard work and positive work cultures are appreciated by one and all. Negative work culture on the other hand, treats work as a burden, a punishment and an avoidable responsibility.

Historically, in material prosperity of a community, work culture has played a very crucial role. Max Weber[4] finds positive protestant work culture as a main cause of comparatively higher economic growth and development in Western Europe as against Eastern Europe with its negative catholic work culture.

Work culture could be defined as aggregate of qualities in organizations and in its employees that arise from what is generally regarded as appropriate to think act and work. It consists of a culture through which individuals, organizations and communities achieved their goals and expectations. It is work culture which defines the norms of acceptable conduct and makes individuals understand their roles in a larger picture. Thus, work culture could improve one's performance, efficiency and output significantly, whereas poor work culture would impede even the best efforts of change.

Indian Work Culture: Historically Indians have had a poor work culture and efficiency. Out – put of an Indian worker is considerably low in comparison to the Japanese, Germans and other communities. Therefore, inspite of being very rich in terms of bountiful natural resources, India has been a very poor country for centuries. On the other hand, Japan which is poor in terms of natural resources is one of the strongest economies in the world to -day because of the habit of hard work, discipline of its human resources. The ravages of World War II could cause only marginal and temporary interruption in their economic growth.

On an average, a Japanese worker, works for 2124 hours[5] per year, which is 200 to 400 hours more than the work hours of workers in France and U.K. Every Japanese on an average works 1 to 1-1/2 hours every day by way of extra work (Not overtime work). This extra work is generally neither recognized, nor paid for. On account of their hard work they are known as work alcoholics (Kroshi).

In India the man – days lost due to frequent strikes, *Bandhs, Gharao* and other practices are the highest on an average. National growth has moved at snails pace which Westerner with a sort of contempt call "Hindu Growth Rate." Added to that corruption is rampant and India happens to be 69th[6] most corrupt in the world according to Transparency international, Berlin. Black Economy is almost a parallel economy in India.

Some of the causes of poor work culture in India can be identified in brief:

(a) Primordial Value system and change resistant tradition: Through the ages, life in India has moved at a very slow pace and modernity has made its impact only in urban pockets and among the educated and relatively affluent elite. The Primordial value system and tradition has been resistant to change. Workers and artisans have had a comparatively low social status and esteem. Besides, tradition of religious and philosophical beliefs like Sufism decries worldly acquisition and preaches spiritualism, asceticism and simplicity. Work has no further value beyond providing for your frugal existence. Das Maluka, a famous poet had stated " God provides for all, although birds do not work and pythons have no paid jobs". The common ignorant Indian does not understand and realize the value of work. Majority of people still believe in predeterminism and fatalism that poverty is the misfortune and a divine curse for the misdeeds of earlier life and that no one can change one's destiny.

(b) Feudal Power Structure: In spite of an egalitarian and socialist polity under a progressive and liberal constitution with guarantee of equality, liberty and justice, the Indian social set up and polity remains feudal and personality based. The working class still does not enjoy high social status. The progressive labour legislation has been more on paper with cosmetic significance rather than a tool of securing socio – economic justice. The labour bondage, exploitation of workers in unorganized sectors, payment of unequal wages, child labour are even today the major problems. The feudal management techniques, lack of participatory management have accentuated a sense of alienation among workers. Workers lack sense of belongingness. The levels of motivation and morals are low. It is relevant to mention that alienation of workers in the erstwhile Soviet Russia with its extremely exploitative state capitalism led to alcoholism at work place, work shirking and consequently fall in labour productivity. Ultimately it led to the collapse of Russian economy and disintegration of Soviet State.

(c) Corruption: As stated above, India is one the most corrupt countries, Corruption leads to money accumulation in the hands of the persons having control over power levers. Lately, wage differentials, unemployment have increased and social security systems have weakened after privatization and liberalization. This would lead to further social frustration and may affect work culture, morale and efficiency. Corruption leads to further social frustration and may affect work culture, morale and efficiency. Corruption leads to vulgar consumerism and has a negative impact on human psychology of looking for easy money rather than " Earned money".

(d) Ineffective Socio – Legal control Mechanism: Work culture depends on two factor (i) either the inner realization by the individual that work is value, or (ii) coercive sytem which tries to maintain discipline and efficiency through coercive means. Our socio–legal control systems have proved ineffective. The legal procedures are too technical and time consuming. Moreover, the system does not encourage efficiency, discipline either through recognition or rewards. To quote Fukuyama societies in which accumulation of " Social Capital" is high, always grow faster and better. India lacks in corporate culture built on mutual trust (Social Capital) between the employers and the employees.

Toward better work culture: The Correctives:

The correctives for improvement of work culture could be classified in two broad categories:-

(a) Informal correctives: Include education, religion and social awareness, social reform movements and role of NGOs. These informal systems by their very nature are not very efficacious. They lack proper policy formulation; organizational structures and the requisite financial back up. At best, their impact on work-culture has been marginal.

(b) Formal Correctives: (i) Revamping of Management systems and build-up of social capital and (ii) effective legal control mechanics.

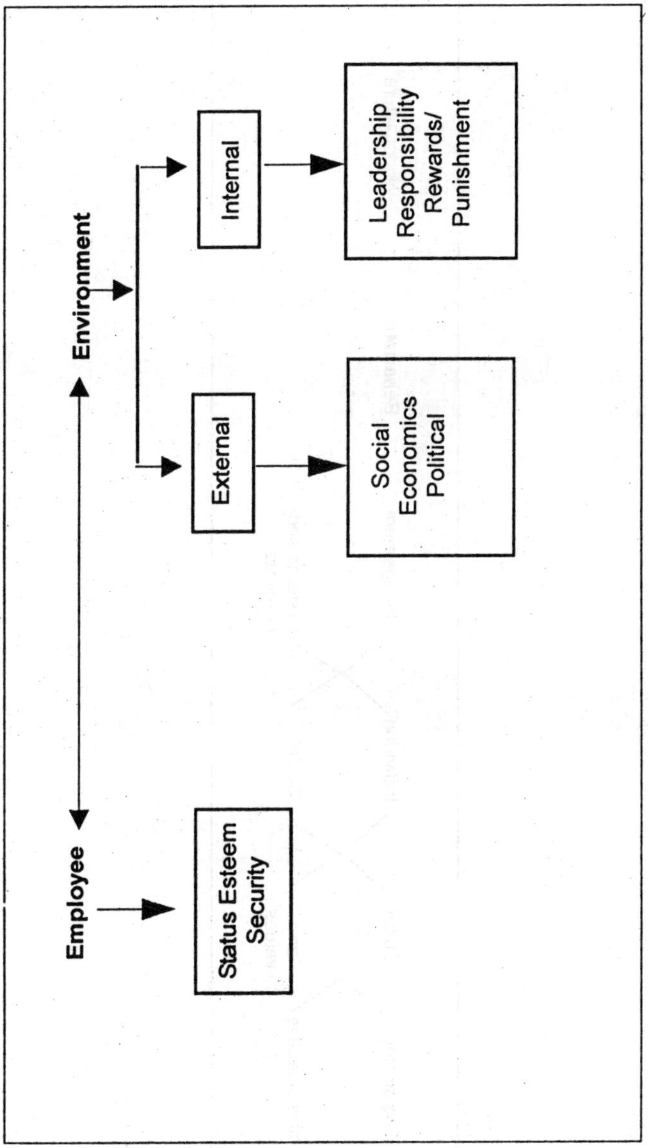
Employee
Environment
Internal
External
Leadership
Responsibility
Rewards/
Punishment
Social
Economics
Political
Status Esteem
Security

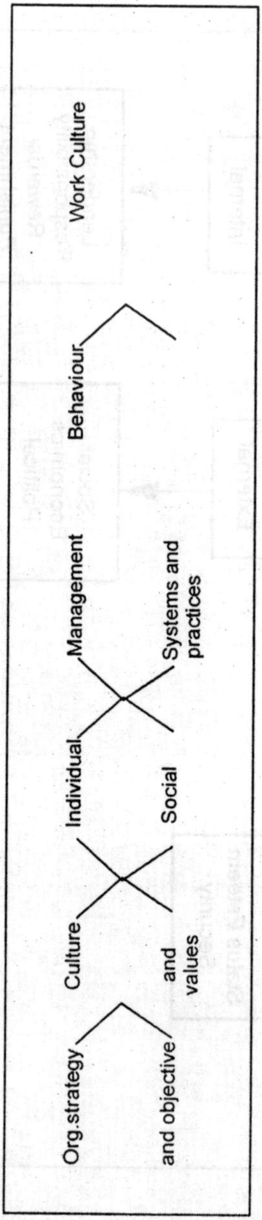
Org.strategy
and objective
Culture
and
values
Individual
Social
Management
Systems and
practices
Behaviour
Work Culture

The central question is why do people work and why should people work more?

(i) Human needs are the basis of human conduct and therefore, it is through work that an employee seeks status, self-esteem and economic security. In building up his perception on work culture multiple factors play their part: When there is dichotomy or gap between the goal the individual's and the goal of the organization, alienation of the worker increases which, in turn leads to erosion of work culture and standards of discipline. Conflicts arise when individual's goals eclipse organizational objectives. As far as possible, every individual worker has to be integrated into the work culture of the organization. Any indiscipline in the organization and poor work culture is symptomatic of organizational ill health and every organization should accept the basic value norm.

(a) That human beings are not a commodity but a creative human resource,

(b) That every organization is a welfare organization and therefore, welfare of their employees and their families is one of the priorities of the organization.

(c) That every employee is as an important part of the organization as are the owners and the managers. In other words, an organization is like an extended family.

(d) Organization should provide the optimum opportunities for self – growth in terms of higher skills, education etc.

(e) Leadership should be progressive and responsible and should lead by personal example rather than through autocratic management approach.

(ii) That role of the leadership is to align the organization's strategy and it could be expressed in term of inter linkages of multiple factors. The Japanese corporate culture is an example of integration of individual and corporate goals and as such the corporate entity become extended unified family with high levels of mutual trust, co-operation and common ethos. It is said of Japanese worker that he is born in the organization, grows there and ultimately dies there. The three pillars which have sustained high work culture there include:-

(a) A life time employment with minimum labour mobility
(b) Seniority based wages and
(c) Single company trade unions

Socialization at work place is very high and corporate entity is responsible for total well - being of its employees. People perform better when they are trusted and motivated. The organization should care about the careers, interest and well being of the people who constitute it. Improvement on the quality of work life of our people should be a prime concern. Initiatives like "Open House" sessions where every body gets an opportunity to raise concerns, discussion forums and get–to-gathers should be encouraged because these unleash hidden talents and give vent to creative abilities.

Work environment should promote a transparent work culture where open debate and constructive criticism are encouraged and information flow has no constraints. "Command and control" are old – fashioned practice. After all, brilliant ideas need not always originate from the top. Aim should be a high performance organization with a clear vision responsibility and openness. This is how a new work culture based on strong emotional, social and professional thrust can be built through these informal strategies.

(ii) Legal control mechanism: Law as the most important social institution has a vital role in building a positive work environment and a work culture. It is a vital tool of social control, social change and progress. As such it has a role where it can educate, lead and if need be coerce. Martin Luther King had rightly said Law "may not change heart but it can certainly restrain the heartless." The lazy, laggards, the work shirkers and the indisciplined have to be adapted back and integrated into a positive work culture. American Management Association observes: "Until human nature attains greater perfection, the fullest measure of freedom of action can be realized only within the frame work of expressed discipline. In social situation it takes the form of Law." As a formal tool, law has certain advantages over informal methods:

(a) It is formal enacted by a duly empowered legislature following the prescribed procedure
(b) Selection of goals and proper policy formulation precedes the formal law making

(c) Law makes adequate administrative and financial resources available for enforcement of law.
(d) Law provides for physical sanctions for breaches of Law.
(e) It provides for formal settlement of disputes through judicial adjudication and arbitration etc.

The entire service jurisprudence consisting of the constitutional provisions, Service Rules, judicial judgments and administrative instructions aims at provision for minimum security of service to the employee and the larger public interest of dismissal, termination of services of an employee found unfit to hold public office.

The legal control mechanism of disciplinary inquiry, action and punishment of delinquent employee are very technical and time consuming. Beside, it is very expensive to go through the long procedures, because courts look even at the smallest lapse in disciplinary procedure with suspicion and as acts of arbitrariness and vindictiveness and these punishments are generally set aside. As consequence, the employee who comes back with a sense of victory with favorable court judgment becomes more indisciplined and infects others also. Thus, formal disciplinary action has not proved very effective.

Failing the disciplinary action, the employers look for other alternative means to discipline the recalcitrant employee. Suspension, transfer, denial of promotion, bad annual reports are not technically punishments but the same are used as concealed penalties. These demoralize and humiliate the employee and cause financial loss to him. Such techniques worsen rather than improve the work culture and lead to further alienation of the worker with loss of trust in the fairness of the employer.

Our response to the issue of betterment of work culture requires a multi – pronged approach. The strategy of reward and punishment should be evenly balanced, leadership, motivation training, rewards and recognition are going to play major role in building positive work culture. Even punishments should be used as a tool to educate and to make the worker realize his mistakes.

McGregor's Hot Stove theory could provide a sound basis for perspective planning. Hot stove approach involves an advance warning, consistency, immediacy of action and objectivity. The purpose should be to bring out the creative faculties of each individual worker and harness them in national building and curb the negative tendencies of work shirking and indiscipline.

REFERENCES

1. ***A Tale of Two Cities.***
2. Francis Fukuyama.
3. Huntington, *Clash of Civilizations.*
4. Max Weber, *The Protestant Ethics and the Spirit of Capitalism,* 1905.
5. *The Times of India,*Sept. 17, 1995.
6. *Transparency International*, Berlin.

8

CORRUPTION: A SOCIAL SCIENTIFIC ANALYSIS

S.L. Sharma

Few will dispute the fact that corruption has assumed epidemic proportions in present times and that it warrants careful diagnosis and effective remedial action in right earnest. The challenge is both enormous and grave. Hence the choice of this theme. In the interest of systematic exposition, this presentation is organized into five parts. Part I seeks to clarify the concept of corruption and distinguish its various forms. Part II sketches its rising graph and increasing social acceptability in India. Part III probes deep into its social causes and consequences. Part IV examines the linkages between corruption and development. Part V outlines some policy positions and strategies to combat corruption.

I. Meaning and Forms

Derived etymologically from the Latin verb 'rumpere' meaning "to break" the term 'corruption' connotes different things to different people. However, three broad usages of it can be distinguished: moralistic, official and monopolistic. At the broadest level, there is the moralistic usage which views corruption as a morally improper conduct, or as deviance from a moral norm. In this usage, the term corruption encompasses all kinds of violations of moral standards, including social and sexual, apart from administrative and political. Next, there is the official usage of corruption which implies misuse of public office for private gain. Crucial to this usage is the context of public office. A public office carries with it a certain measure of authority, discretion and facilities that are required for serving public good. When the incumbent of a public office misuses any of these privileges for his private benefit that constitutes an instance of corruption. It may range from misuse of official facilities such as car and telephone to misuse of discretion for bribery, extortion, nepotism, and financial gain. The third usage is monopoly centred. According to Klitgaard, for example, corruption equals monopoly plus discretion minus accountability. Stated in a synoptic form, it is put as follows: C=M+D-A. Thus, corruption arises when someone has monopoly over a good or service, has the discretion to decide whether or not you receive it and is not accountable.

Of the three, it is the official usage which is the most common kind, and hence, of immediate relevance. Corruption, in its technical sense, is essentially a phenomenon related to the context of office. Accordingly, corruption can be best defined as betrayal of public trust by the incumbent of an office. It involves four main elements: public office, illegitimate use of office for unofficial ends, secrecy surrounding the misuse and damage to the third party or public in general. Broadly there are three kinds of resources available with an office: official facilities, funds and authority. Corruption signifies misuse of any one or more of these official resources.

Corruption manifests itself in various forms. Broadly, three forms of it can be easily discerned: misappropriative, collaborative and extortionist. Misappropriative corruption refers to misappropriation of official facilities such as an official car, telephone, etc, or official funds resulting in fraud or embezzlement. Unlike mispppropriative corruption, collaborative corruption involves two parties, i.e., the official and the private agent who collaborate in a mutually beneficial transaction. In this form of corruption, the official trades his authority for money or some other kinds of unlawful gains including material or sexual spoils. Bribery is the most telling example of it, as it involves exchange of an official favour by the bribee to the briber for some unlawful payment. The bribee receives the payment for bending a rule or for ignoring it to serve the interest of the briber. Thus it may be an act of commission or omission on the part of bribee in favour of the briber. Nepotism, influence peddling and political horse-trading are some of its other variants. In political horse trading, the roles get reversed, as the politician in power takes over the role of briber in order to retain his political office. It constitutes an instance of collaborative corruption nevertheless.

Like collaborative corruption, extortionist corruption also involves two parties, though the other party i.e., the private agent is an unwilling partner in it. He is actually coerced to pay by the official even for getting his lawful claim conceded, or his legitimate work done. The official uses delaying or harassing tactics in it. Extortion is the telling illustration of it. Extortionist corruption implies a setting of uneven power relations in which the private agent is at the receiving end. It represents a case of might is right, with the politicians and civil servants oppressing the citizens with impunity. The redeeming feature however, is that unlike collaborative corruption, extortionist corruption is not as much damaging to the interests of the organization concerned or of other individuals.

Besides, the above delineated three major forms, which are more illustrative than exhaustive, it is also important to distinguish between centralized corruption and decentralized corruption. Centralised Corruption is that in which one or a few, usually top officials, monopolize the booty. On the other hand, decentralized corruption is that in which the spoils are shared among a large number of officials from top to bottom.

In passing, it may also be useful to distinguish between traditional and modern forms of corruption. While we have had a culture of corruption in that the practice of gift-giving to the political or administrative bosses on festive occasions is old enough, in modern times certain new forms have gained in salience such as "speed money" and donations on demand. It is also possible to distinguish between types of corruption on the basis of the spheres. Two major forms are immediately discernible on this basis: bureaucratic corruption and political corruption.

II. Rise and Spread

Not a new phenomenon, corruption, is as old as human civilization. In his magnum opus *Arthashastra* which dates back to the fourth century B.C., Kautilya observes, "Just as it is impossible not to taste honey or poison that one finds at the tip of one's tongue, so it is impossible for a government servant not to eat up, at least, a bit of the king's revenue. Just as fish moving under water cannot possibly be found out either by drinking or not drinking water, so government servants cannot be found out (while) taking money (for themselves)". (R.P. Kangle, *The Kautilya Arthashastra*, Part 11, 1972, p.91).

Although corruption is not a new phenomenon, what is new about it is the phenomenal increase in its magnitude, spread and social acceptability. S. S. Gill in his book "The Pathology of Corruption" (Harper Collins) provides a detailed account of corruption from pre-Vedic times to the times of Narasimha Rao. In the ancient age of Ram Rajya, kings and ministers practiced corruption in devious ways. During Mughal rule, the rulers granted *khillats (*robes) in exchange for *nazranas.* The officers of the East India Company accepted bribes in return for the favour showered on the briber. That, however, changed when India came under the control of Viceroys, Governors and ICS who were highly paid and hence did not usually resort to corruption. But, the graph of corruption has gone upwards in a remarkable way in the post independence era, with scams galore, such as the cement scandal, the ITC scandal, the securities scam, the Bofors, the *chara ghotala* and many others, thanks to the quota permit Raj. Allegations of corruption against Narasimha Rao and several of his cabinet colleagues, including Pandit Sukh Ram, are too fresh in public memory to require any elaboration. When this is the sate of corruption in high public places one can well imagine its extent in ordinary public life.

Earlier confined to only a few departments of bureaucracy, such as the Public work Department, Police, etc., it has now pervaded all spheres of public administration, business and industry, professions and even the judiciary. Its incidence is on the rise. This is evident from the Annual Report of the Central Vigilance Commission for 1997 according to which it disposed of 363 cases during 1964-65 while it has disposed of 5700 cases in 1997. According to a report of the Transparency International, a Berlin-based anti-corruption organization, the increase in corruption in India in 1998 is 22 per cent over the 1980-85 level. Little wonder that in terms of the Corruption Perception Index of the Transparency

International, India figures among the "most corrupt" countries of the world. India managed to retain its 73rd rank for the second time in a row among 82 countries surveyed. This dubious distinction of India is further confirmed by a recently released U.N. Development Programme report prepared by the Mahbubul-Haq Development Centre which finds South Asia as the "most corrupt" region of the world and within South Asia, India and Pakistan as the "most corrupt countries". Not surprisingly, in a recent survey, every four of five respondents said the country had become corrupt, and only five per cent of them described either politicians or the police as completely honest.

What is alarming about corruption is not just its rising graph and its pervasive spread, but its social acceptability. Notably, attitudes of both officials and the people towards corruption have drastically changed. Take the attitudes of officials first. In the days gone by, officials used to spurn an offer of a bribe on the plea that God has blessed them with children and, therefore, they would not like to invite the wrath of God by committing the sin of corruption. Ironically, today the same plea of having children is used to rationalize acceptance of a bribe in order to provide for the children. What a change of attitude! Similarly, the older generation administrators tell us that there used to be only a counted few corrupt officials in their times who would get isolated, branded and blacklisted. Today, it is the other way round: an official of integrity is labeled as a black sheep and ridiculed. In such a corrupt environment it has become almost impossible for an official of integrity to perform his duties honestly. The price for being honest is at times too high to pay. No wonder, the Maharashtra bureaucrat Arun Bhatia earned his 26th transfer in his 30 year long career as a reward for his relentless crusade against corruption. The honest man is now considered a liability, or a thorn in the flesh.

Another point to note here is the self-protecting power of corruption. It is no secret that a corrupt official manages to go scot-free by means of corruption itself. That explains why in spite of all the scams and scandals so far only one minister from Kerala has recently been convicted of corruption. And, for the same reason, it has made big news in the media leading to commentaries and editorials.

Like the officials, peoples' attitude towards corruption has also softened. They no longer look down upon a corrupt official, like before. If any thing, peoples' attitude is marked by a measure of ambivalence: they like it as well as dislike it at the same time. They lament it in public but are too quick to take recourse to it as and when they are caught by a state agent for violating a rule, be it a traffic rule or a bye-law of building construction. As a matter of fact, no one of us today minds paying "speed money" for expediting our work. We find it more economical and less harassing than waiting for the law to take its own course. What is even worse, corruption has begun to acquire a respectability of a sort. It is being hailed as an instrument of efficiency. Accordingly, bribery has come to be viewed as "efficiency fee". By all accounts, corruption has become a way of life today. All the same, it signals a perturbing development. For, when an 'evil' becomes acceptable as a 'good' it must ring disturbing bells.

III. Social Causes and Consequences

Two board explanatory perspectives can be distinguished on the causes of corruption psychological and sociological. Psychological perspective and one of them locates corruption in the failure of character of the corrupt individual, his personal pathology, his faulty socialization, his personal compulsion or some weakness of his personality or character. Such an explanation carried conviction when the incidence of corruption was limited and its practice was confined to a few individuals. But when corruption has become so rampant and widespread as today, the psychological explanation holds no good. Hence the relevance of the sociological perspective which attributes it to the failure of the system. The systemic wrong is located in the prevailing paradigm of development which is viewed as faulty because of its lopsided stress on economism with little regard for culture, on material prosperity to the neglect of morality, and on individualism at the expense of holism. The prevailing craze for the culture of consumerism, decline of moral and social values and the disconcerting trend of loss of fear of law provide a conducive climate for the growth of corruption.

At this point it will be pertinent to ask under what conditions corruption tends to thrive? It flourishes under conditions of scarcity and shortage of goods and services heavy regulation, red-tape and procedural delay; lack of transparency and accountability; cushions of safety; low and inadequate salaries; and above all, culture of greed and consumerism. Some analysts have sought to link corruption to democracy. That is not a tenable proposition in the light of available evidence. First, because the totalitarian nations have not been corruption free. The fact is that there was as much corruption, if not more, in the erstwhile socialist Soviet Union as anywhere else. It is though a different matter though that it remained concealed because of the secretive character of the totalitarian nations. Secondly, because the countries which have figured among the corruption-free countries in the report of the Transparency International are well-known democracies of the world.

Whatever its causes, it has grave subverting effects on the system. It undermines the rules of the game, breeds injustice and discriminates against the poor, disrupts public services and endangers public health and safety; demoralizes the common man and errodes public trust in government, reflects poor governance and poses a threat to democracy; deters investment and impedes development; pulls down the national image in the international set up; exerts depraving effects on the practitioners and their families; and to cap it all, it sounds a death knell to civil society. Curiously enough, there are many, who see some merit in corruption and maintain that it performs some positive functions. It saves people from harassment; promotes efficiency in bureaucracy; expedites development; and, above all, leads to improvement in the levels of living of its practitioners as well as its beneficiaries.

IV Corruption and Development

The analysis in the preceding section suggests some linkage between corruption and development. The relationship between corruption and development can, in fact, be viewed in two ways: (i) how development affects corruption?; and (ii) how corruption impinges on development? On the bearing of development on corruption views are divided. The general impression is that development tends to breed corruption in its early phase but contains it in the later phase. For a systematic understanding of the effects of development on corruption, it is important to ask the following three questions; (i) Is there a relationship between level of development and degree of corruption? ; (ii) Is there a linkage between the kind of development and the degree of corruption?; (iii) Is there a connection between agencies of development and their reliance on corruption for development?

On the first question the ranking of various countries by the Transparency International on the Corruption Perception Index is suggestive of a correlation between a country's level of development and its rank on corruption. By and large, developed countries are over represented in the 'least corrupt' category and the developing countries in the 'most corrupt'. This is clearly suggestive of a negative relationship between the level of development and corruption. In other words, it implies that development tends to breed corruption in its initial phase and contains corruption in its advanced phase. In fact, the linkage between level of development and corruption is neither simple nor straight. It is quite a complex relationship. At first glance, it may appear that there is more of corruption in the developing nations than in the developed ones. On a closer examination, however, it becomes clear that there are large variations in the incidence of corruption among groups of countries at similar stages of development. For example, the Transparency international Corruption Perception Index ranks Chile, the Czech Republic, Malaysia, Poland and South Africa as "cleaner" than industrialized countries such as Greece and Italy.

There has now come to light another dimension of relationship between level of development and corruption. The recent survey of bribe-takers and bribe-givers by the Transparency International has come out with a startling revelation. While India and Pakistan, both in the transitional phase of development, have relatively clean records as far as paying bribes for boosting exports is concerned, Singapore, a relatively developed country, having a high rank among the non bribe takers, on the other hand, emerges with a dubious distinction of a high rank in the matter of giving bribes for boosting exports.

In respect of the second question pertaining to the relationship between the kind of development and the degree of corruption, for long it was believed that the capitalist nations have a higher incidence of corruption as compared to the socialist nations. However, the disclosures in the wake of the collapse of the Soviet Union have offered evidence to the country. In fact, corruption is reported to be one of the significant factors contributing to the break up of the Soviet Union. It is, therefore, difficult to take a definitive position in this regard chiefly because of the non availability of data on corruption in the socialist countries, thanks to the veil of secrecy in those countries.

Coming to the question of linkage between an agency of development and its reliance on corruption for development, it has now come to light that both the agencies of development, i.e., governmental organizations and non governmental organizations, have begun to take recourse to corruption in order to grab development projects. It is well known that the donor agencies have now started the system of bidding for development projects. This has led to close competition among the NGOs in the field of development, many of which have been unscrupulous in relying on corruption for getting their project proposals approved by the donor agency.

Turning to the effect of corruption on development, there has appeared a debate in recent literature. According to one view, corruption improves efficiency and helps growth. It does so by greasing the wheels of a rigid bureaucracy. The assumption of the "grease-the-wheels" argument is that bribery can be an efficient way of getting round elaborate regulations and burdensome procedures. In this respect, the following observation of Samuel P. Huntignton is worth noting: "In terms of economic growth the only thing worse than a society with a rigid, over centralized, dishonest bureaucracy is one with a rigid, over centralized honest bureaucracy" (1968, p.386). Thus, corruption may indeed foster development. A similar argument is advanced by Nathaniel Leff, who argues that corruption may introduce an element of competition into what is otherwise a comfortably monopolistic industry... (and) payment of the highest bribes (becomes) one of the principal criteria for allocation... Hence, a tendency towards efficiency is introduced into the system " (1970). Likewise, Francis Lui maintains that "bribing strategies... minimize the average value of the time costs of the queue... (and the official)... could choose to speed up the service when bribery is allowed" (1985).

As against this, another view is that corruption is detrimental to development. It creates inefficiency, and impedes the ability of developing countries to attract foreign investment. Citing the Sanathanam Committee on the Prevention of Corruption, Gunnar Myrdal in his book "Asian Drama" (1968) maintains that corrupt officials may, instead of speeding up, actually cause administrative delays in order to elicit more bribes. The prevalence of corruption raises strong obstacles and inhibitions to development. The corruption that is spurred by fragmentation of loyalties acts against efforts to consolidate the nation. It decreases respect for and allegiance to the government and its institutions. It often promotes irrationality in planning and limits the horizons of plans. While Myrdal made these observations in the context of linkage between corruption and development in the countries of South Asia, these are also applicable to such countries as Nigeria, Indonesia and Russia. The revisionists may, however, refute Myrdal's argument by citing the cases of countries like Thailand and South Korea which show higher growth despite corrupt environs. They could also add that Italy's economic might is growing and its GDP is at the level of relatively virtuous Britain.

In view of the above observations, it is not easy to take a definitive position in respect of the effects of corruption on development. On net balance, however, it appears that the arguments in favour of the efficient effects of corruption on development are not altogether irrefutable.

V. Combating Strategies

On the question of combating corruption several policy positions have appeared. For want of better terms, these may be described as: fatalist, moralist, statists, libertarian and voluntarist. The "fatalists" are pessimists: they believe that corruption has become so pervasive and deeply entrenched that no matter what we do, it cannot be eliminated. This is a cynical position, having no rational basis, and deserves to be discarded for the same reason.

The "moralists" have not lost all hope but they find corruption posing a formidable challenge which can be met only by restoring values for probity and integrity in public life. For achieving this end they stress the need for fundamental changes in the value system, animated value reform campaigns and value planning in education. All this is fine as an agenda, but how to implement it in real life situations? This is a question for which they have no convincing answer.

The "statists" bank heavily on legal and administrative solutions. They recommend strict anti corruption legislation, its ruthless enforcement, exemplary punishment to the offenders, strengthening of the vigilance commission, administrative reforms, transparency in administration, measures to determine accountability and an incentive pay structure for civil servants. These are, no doubt, useful strategies to combat corruption. What they need first is the political will. Where is the political will to implement these measures? It is well known that we excel in enacting legislation but flounder when it comes to implementation; we are quick to appoint inquiry committees and vigilance commissions but fight shy of carrying out their recommendations. So many cases of scams and scandals have been exposed, but curiously enough hardly any one of the culprits has been prosecuted and punished.

Viewing corruption as a by-product of a top-heavy administrative structure, the "libertarians" take an opposite stand. Accordingly, their solution is to 'roll back the State', promote deregulation and expedite economic liberalization and globalization. They hail the idea of the minimal state, as in their view corruption is induced by state activity by means of regulations and bureaucratic allocation of scarce public resources. Most of the regulations are there to serve the patronage-dispensing power of politicians and bureaucrats which only tend to breed corruption. In a sense, therefore, the easiest way to minimize corruption is to legalize the activity that is prohibited or controlled. The libertarians put their faith in market and contend that the more free and perfect the market, the losser the scope for corruption. In their opinion, the best solution to the problem of corruption is deregulation and liberalization.

There is of course some merit in the libertarian position in so far as it pleads for reducing over regulation but its advocacy for according primacy to the market is problematic. That is so because the market may not care for the social objectives. It can adversely affect the lot of the vulnerable sections of society. To be sure, there are regulations devised to grant permits and licences for economic activity, but there are also regulations that seek to serve social objectives, viz., the public distribution system. Deregulation in respect of the public distribution system is bound to adversely affect the lot of the poor and the deprived.

Finally, there is the voluntaristic position which places optimism on the role of the "third sector", i.e., non governmental organizations in eliminating corruption. The "voluntarists" maintain that neither the State nor the market is capable of eradicating corruption, as corruption suits both of them in different ways. What is therefore needed is the intervention of the civil society through its major agency of voluntary groups. The voluntary groups have the credentials to lead the crusade against corruption and to root it out, as they have no stake in it. People are wary of corruption. Voluntary groups represent the rise of people's power. As such, they are in a position to organize people against corruption. They are in a unique position also to involve people in diagnosing corrupt systems, as people know about the sources and locales of corruption. They may undertake systematic surveys, set up concerned citizen's watch groups, and conscientize and mobilize the masses.

Taken singly, each of the above discussed policy positions is incapable of tackling the problem of corruption. That is so because corruption is multidimensional and an intricately embedded phenomenon that cuts across the polity, economy and society. What is therefore needed is a multi-pronged attack on it. As such, there is a need for a combined strategy with judicious use of the above-referred policies and the measures implicit in them.

9

EDUCATIONAL MANAGEMENT IN THE EMERGING SOCIAL ORDER OF INDIA

(S.S. Mathur)

India of early twenty-first century is very much different from India of mid twentieth century. The progress made in this country in all parameters of progress and development is tremendous. In the last five decades its economy has drastically changed for the better. Its political system has moved in new directions. Its approach toward the welfare of its citizens even though not exemplary is marked with great enthusiasm for achieving higher goals. There have been rapid strides in the fields of education and health. Still these two areas of human welfare require much more to be done to make this country an advanced welfare state. It is a matter of great concern to the planners and administrators in general and social scientists in particular as what to do and how to do it so that this country in the shortest possible time achieves the target of advanced welfare state. Much of this concern is related to the management of these fields. The present paper is prepared with the objective of presenting a management model that may ensure rapid growth in these areas. Since both the fields cannot be adequately dealt in one paper, this paper is confined to the management of education only.

The model that is being presented is positive in its spirit. It means that instead of simply highlighting the deficiencies in the existing management practices it is concentrating on offering positive suggestions for improving the system of education. The format is not critical but constructive. It presents what has to be done to uplift the masses of this country to affluence and to a truly democratic and secular society because these are the two basic tenets on which the future of this country rests.

Emerging Social Order

In this country the social order of the past that was based on feudalism, casteism and the barbaric treatment of the down trodden and the people of lower castes has undergone through tremendous changes. Today the down trodden and the lower and backward castes and classes have found a voice to challenge the upper castes and the feudal lords. The process of breaking the caste barriers effectively began by Gandhiji is still going on but there have developed many aberrations in it. The caste is still playing a dominant role in the political and the educational fields. Unfortunately the politicians of all hues and shades are playing the caste card so as to establish their superiority in ruling the country. There has developed another evil in the form of minoritism. The card of minorities is being played not for the upliftment of the minorities but for their own benefit by the politicians of all hues and shades. In the garb of favouring minorities the opportunist politicians have grabbed the educational field. They are creating a divisive society. The caste and religion are playing a much negative role in developing an affluent and literate society.

It is a typical phenomenon of modern Indian social order that while lower and backward castes have been able to get political advantage they have failed to rise above the poverty line. Except a few leaders of the poor and backward classes and of minorities the vast multitude of them is poor and illiterate. In the field of education they are at the lowest level. Most unfortunate thing is that each political party tries to envelop education with in its political agenda, not to do something positive for education, but to befool the masses by posing as the guardians of the poor and downtrodden showing themselves as deeply concerned with their welfare. Many of the politicians in the name of serving the society have made education a commercial enterprise. They open expensive institutions and exploit the parents and guardians by charging high fees in the name of giving quality education. The mushrooming of ill equipped engineering, medical and management institutions are the examples. One of the states of Indian union had gone to the extent of opening universities in depleted buildings and small apartments. Not only this, the political parties find education as a vital tool for spreading their ideology. So one party when it comes to power propagates its agenda of safforonization and when this party is thrown out of the government the party in power vigorously pursue its agenda in the name of secularism and the welfare of minorities creating more rifts in the society. The idea of integrating the different castes and classes into an unity is of very little concern to them.

In such a social order the role the educational administrators, managers and self-proclaimed educational thinkers play, is quiet deplorable because they succumb to the will of their political masters in order to gain important positions. They bow down to the wishes of those who have the power to make their career. Independent thinking and right attitudes are the causality. In the present paper my concern is not to go on pointing out the deficiencies in the educational system in detail. My goal is to present what ought to be done to make this country a global power with a very sound economic foundation that can only be achieved by the implementation of well thought out plans for the management of education.

Recently in an article in the journal "India Today" in its Anniversary issue (dated December 26, 2005) Indian Prime Minister has emphasized the need for making more investment in education so that every citizen is made literate and adequately skilled and employable. But he is not contended with the quantitative change but also emphasizes qualitative change. He makes it very clear that for qualitative change first thing that is needed is change in our minds. He says, "We must learn to think afresh and anew, and not be afraid of new ideas, new ways of thinking and new ways of doing things." The new model of educational management that has to emerge out definitely requires a change in the mind set of the administrators and planners of education. The directions in which the mind set of the administrators and the planners have to be changed are being outlined in this paper. Five directions of change are indicated. Together these directional mind changers may constitute a futuristic model of educational management for an evolving cohesive social order.

First Direction of Mind Set Change (MSC-1):

It involves four Principles around which the change in mindset should be directed:

1. Universal education does not always result in making all those who attend school becoming functionally literate.
2. Education is not only concerned with the diffusion of information but should be knowledge based and skill oriented
3. Much of the education depends on the emphasis on common sense rather than on forcing the students to achieve high scores in the memory related tests and examinations.
4. Good management of teaching-learning depends on watching and listening.

We will now elaborate these points.

First principle: The research studies have shown that many schemes that are introduced in many developing countries to universalize education have failed to make literate all those who have been enrolled for learning. In India in 2001 Sarva Shiksha Abhiyan (education for all) was introduced. On the face of it was a very good move. It aimed to have all the children aged six to fourteen in primary schools by 2007 and in upper primary schools by 2010. It was a much stiffer target than the "UN Millennium Development Goal" of universal primary education by 2015. The objective of completing six to eight years schooling as planned by Serva Shiksha Abhiyan is to gain skills that translate into higher wages and less poverty. But according to Ernesto Schiefelbein, former education minister of Chile, research shows that while literacy improves income significantly, additional years of schooling contribute little extra. This is because as Aiyer (Times of India, Dec 25, 05) points out that in many countries with near universal education, students cannot read simple texts or do simple sums. They may have completed school, but they are functionally illiterate.

Surveys in seven Latin American countries reveal functional illiteracy of 40% in Chile and over 50% in other countries. Maria Cristina Mejia, Education Minister of Bolivia, says her country has greatly increased school enrolment and ended the gender gap in education, yet incomes are not rising. One obvious reason for the failure of the schemes of universal education for a number of years for achieving the aim of improving the learning outcomes or incomes is that educational quality is weak. Many rich countries like USA are spending billions on improving quality but the results are not very encouraging. According to Aiyar the reason is rich-poor divide. It is very evident in the case of India. As we have pointed out earlier in this paper the Indian social order is very much stratified. There are rich, very rich, poor and very poor people. It has been found that while the children of those who are in the brackets of well to do attain functional literacy after the completion of schooling at the primary level the children of poor do not gain much from being in the school for a number of years. Aiyer points out that in India we ascribe this to poor teacher training and high absenteeism. But even in Latin America, where teaching quality and school completion is far superior, the poor-rich divide is staggering. According to Schiefelbein over 90% of the children in the richer half of the society are functionally literate but only 10 % in the lower half, even though virtually all complete schooling. Thus in the management of education this aspect is to be kept in mind. The mind set of the administrators has to be changed towards providing universal education. They should not think that only by raising the allocation of more funds for education and by bringing all the children of educable age to school they will be able to raise the functional literacy level or the increase in the incomes of the poor.

For making the children functionally literate there is need for concentrating on their reading skills. It has been observed that if children cannot read after two to three years of education, they probably never will. A shortcoming that has to be seriously tackled by the educational administrators and the managers of education is that the vocabulary of the children coming from poor and backward areas is very short as compared to the vocabulary of those coming from affluent families. Schiefelbein found that better off children typically enter school with a vocabulary of 2000 to 4000 words, and have often started reading already at home. But poor children typically have a vocabulary of only 600 words, and have never read at home. Those who frame the policies for education must realize that the skills needed to teach a child with a 600-word vocabulary are totally different from those needed to teach a child with 3000 word vocabulary. Hence it is essential that while planning for the education of backward and poor children there should be put emphasis on developing reading skills by specially trained teachers. One of the well known NGO Pratham in its surveys has found that half the children aged six to fourteen cannot read simple sentences. In rural India, about 80 % of students in class VI can read at the level of Class II to III.

A 29-month long survey was conducted in Maharashtra, Karnataka and Andhra Pradesh, which found the existing literacy levels to be dismal. The survey in Maharashtra was carried out by the State Education Secretary, Sumit Mullick and former Director of Education V.L. Deoskar. "We found the standard of education in the state as abysmal," said Mullick. "In order to measure the 'illiteracy level', a specially designed test in mathematics and language was administered to 7.5 lakh students across Amravati, Akola, Yavatmal, Buldhana and Washim. The test included simple mathematical problems and also tested the abilities to write words. Those who scored 75% and above were considered literate, 65-75% were considered semi- literate and those with less than 65% were illiterate." The survey found 82% of students in any classroom in a zilla parishad or municipal school was illiterate or semi-literate. When SSC students were tested, those who had scored 80-90% in their exams scored only 20% in the baseline tests. The conclusion arrived at is that it is possible for a child to go through the entire educational system and he will not be literate. "The results were all the more appalling because the government had lowered the standard of the test below the 'World Bank's Bench Marks' for literacy. While the bank defines literacy as the ability to read and write short sentences with full understanding, the state merely tested the ability to write words orally dictated from the syllabus." (The details of survey given herewith are reported from the feature item in Times of India, Mumbai Edition of December 27, 2005).

As we have described above the situation regarding literacy is so dismal yet the mind set of the administrator does not go beyond introducing more tests and punishing the teachers for cooking up the results. The proper approach would have been to concentrate on the causes of this dismal picture and to develop such methods of teaching that might serve the poor and backward classes. As we know that only the poor and those students whose parents cannot pay higher fees go to the municipal or zilla parishad schools the results are not at all surprising as these children are exposed to similar type of teaching-learning process that is meant for those who come from affluent sections of the society. Those who manage education must realize that in India and many other developing countries there are a large number of students who are the first learners in the family and the handling of those, needs specific and well directed approaches towards learning and teaching. Equity does not mean exposing all categories and classes of students to the same type of teaching- learning situations.

Second Principle: This principle states that education is not only concerned with the diffusion of information but should be knowledge based. The way in which our educational system is organized is directed towards filling the minds of the students with mere information. The students must be taught to obtain knowledge and to develop the skills to put their knowledge to use. According to De Bono (1990) "Education is not only concerned with collecting information but also with the best ways of using information that is collected." Hence those who are concerned with the management of education should have a mind set change in the direction of giving a meaning of education as a means of obtaining knowledge and utilizing that knowledge in the best possible manner. This aspect we may clarify by giving an example. In history texts there has recently developed a controversy whether Aryans were the original inhabitants of India or have migrated from other lands specifically from Central Europe. The historians of a particular ideology consider them to be the original inhabitants of this country. The historians with a different ideology have the opposite view. The problem is what is to be taught to the students. Unfortunately this ideological divide is reflected in the text books of the students. One school of thought when it comes to power propagates its ideology and when the other school of thought gains power it makes all out effort to change whole of the text of the books. This creates much confusion in the minds of teachers and taught. The right approach here has to be to present both the view points as objectively as possible and encourage the students to analyze the arguments and the facts that are presented by both the ideologies and thereby increase heir knowledge base and learn how these different ideologies are going to impinge on the social order. Merely providing information of one or the other ideology through the particular ideological oriented textbook writers would be counter productive. It is bound to create fissures and dissentions in the social order.

Third Principle: This principle states that much of the education depends on the emphasis on common sense rather than forcing the students to achieve higher scores in the memory related examinations. Most of those who are concerned with the management of education stress the results of memory-based tests as the indicators of learning. This is not a proper criterion of leaning. One may score very high in examinations that are memory based but may be a complete failure in the affairs of life. High scores may help him in getting a job but the success on the job very much depends on his skill of common sense. What is common sense is difficult to define and very difficult to teach. Therefore those who manage education do not talk about it. They have a mindset that follows the common misconception that the goal of education is passing the examinations with high scores. We have described in explaining the first principle that in Maharashtra when administrators found the schooling has not resulted in literacy they chalked out a plan to hold regular tests and not that the efficient methods of teaching the poor and neglected sections of the society should be developed.

All of us have common sense. An illiterate person may also have it. An illiterate mason for example knows how to lay the bricks. What literacy does to him is to calculate his wages and to raise to some extent his standard of living. Education, in fact should help him to develop his aesthetic sense of laying the bricks. This aesthetic sense, we may call as his common sense. Hence our approach in education should be to develop a better understanding of one's life and job. This understanding is what we may describe his common sense. Howsoever hard you may preach for restricted family by having one or two children unless the person applies his commonsense that a small family means better living standard our efforts will fail. The neglect of nourishing the common sense has resulted in many evils in our society like child marriages, abortion of the girl child and dowry deaths. Many a times the educators wonder why these evils are rampant even among the educated. The reason is evident that they have passed the examinations but they lack in their common sense.

The three terms common sense, intuition and gut feeling even though are not synonymous yet are interchangeable. Intuition refers to our inner- voice, the gut feeling refers to our inner feeling while commonsense means our inner understanding. Since in education the understanding is prime factor we have used this term for changing the mind set of the administrators and the managers of education.

Fourth Principle*:* Good management of teaching –learning depends on watching and listening. In our educational system there has been given greater importance in learning on reading from the text books or by going through the notes dictated by the teachers. The class-room teaching is mostly done by the teacher being active and the students being passive listeners. While listening is important the teaching is a two way process in which listening to the voice of the teacher is as important as the listening of the voice of students by the teacher. Teacher can get much insight into what is going on inside the minds of the students while he is teaching and while they are in the school through active listening to the students' questions, views and remarks about himself and others. He will be able to assess the impact of his teaching and schooling to quite an appreciable extent.

Equally important to listening is observing. The students learn much by observing how the teacher is conveying his ideas through his body language. The teacher can also be able to interpret the feelings and understanding of the students by observing them closely. Today when technology is advancing at a rapid pace the keen observation by the learners is all the more necessary. The students can learn much by computer education. But computer education can only be successful if the students have learned to observe carefully the contents of the computer lesson.

In educational management and for that matter in any type of management listening and observing play a very vital role. In the words of Mark H. Cormack (1984), "The ability to listen, really to hear what someone is saying has far greater business implications, then simply gaining insight into people." In fact by listening what one is saying the manager will be able to understand what is going on around him. He will also be able to know the real feelings of his subordinates, fellow workers and superior officers about himself and the programmes he is introducing or executing. In our culture the talking part is done by the superior and listening part by the subordinate. This mind set has to change. What Cormack is emphasizing is that gaining insight into people is no doubt important but if you wish to get work done you must carefully listen to what they are saying. For example, you as a Principal of a school know that the Mathematics teacher is a good teacher but when you assign him some work he may not like it and may protest. Hence having insight into the capability of the teacher to teach mathematics will not help you in assigning him some task that may be very important for the good of the school or students if he raises his voice against it.

Further, McCormack considers that "observation is an aggressive act. People are constantly revealing themselves in ways that will go unnoticed unless you are aggressively involved in observing them." When you watch any one closely you are performing an act that may be considered as an aggressive act. But such an act will enable you to understand the people in a better manner. The people by and large reveal themselves, their impulses, their motivations and resentments in many ways. Careful observation will be able to reveal their potentials and inclinations. Hence we may clarify that it is extremely important for the managers of education to be good and aggressive observers.

Second Direction of Mind Set Change (MSC-II):

It concerns with selecting personnel for efficient educational management. There is no doubt in it that our system of selecting teachers and other personnel for teaching and managing educational enterprise is defective. We select teachers and administrators for education on the basis of a brief interview. The senior positions like that of the director and secretary of education are filled by promotion from lower ranks or by the incumbents of the Indian Administrative services. There are followed various other methods like the results on specially administered tests. But the basic fact remains that if one has some required academic qualifications and has successfully faced the interview is capable of managing education. The mind set that any one who fulfils the above criteria could be a good administrator or the manager of education needs a change For managing educational enterprise at any level we require many other considerations.

According to Jack Welch and Suzy Welch (2005) for choosing the right persons the principle of 4-E (and 1-P) framework can be followed. For the selection of right type of people for educational management we can do no better but to follow this framework. But for following this framework the change in the mindset has to be first achieved. We will now describe this framework.

(a) The first E is positive energy. It is most important that the managers and administrators possess the energy to move in the positive direction. They should not utilize their energy just to criticize others or to find fault in the work of their subordinates or fellow workers.

(b) The second E is the ability to energize others. The managers should motivate others to vigorously pursue the goals that are set for effective education.

(c) The third E is edge, the energy to make tough yes or no decisions. The managers should be such persons who are not afraid to take tough decisions in problematic situations. They must have the courage to express their views and take decisions even under acute pressure from their superiors or the politicians.

(d) The fourth E is execute—the ability to get the job done. The managers must possess the ability to get the work done by others in order to get the goals set are achieved.

(e) If a candidate has four E'S, then you look for that final P-Passion. By passion it is meant a heartfelt, deep and authentic excitement about work. The managers must have keen interest in their work. They must have genuine excitement towards the job that they have undertaken.

Third Direction of Mind Set Change (MSC- III):

This direction of mind set change is about the process of management. In the process of management, the most important required change in the mindset, we are describing below.

A manager must be very clear in saying what he wants. He should not beat about the bush or say something that he does not mean. He must say what he means. Many administrators and managers do not express their true feelings for the fear that their views will not be liked by the others. They know that there is some wrong doing yet they keep silence showing their indirect approval. They remain passive. *"In Company of Fools: A true story"* Kurt Eichenwald relates how Enron's leaders engaged in massive book-cooking with little interference from the dozens of managers, lawyers, and advisors who had a pretty good idea of what was going on. Judith Samuelson and Mary Gentile in an article in Harvard Business Review (Nov. 2005) entitled "Get aggressive about passivity" ask this question: Why should simply speaking out about outrageous conduct be so difficult and so rare? In answer to that question they report that psychologists have studied the "by standard effect and other theories of why people who are aware of wrong doing fail to intervene. Passivity, it seems, is epidemic everywhere. Managers and executives, generally, have right 'values'- that is they know what they should do when circumstances call on them to take a stand or make hard choice. If managers acted on those values and if they applied the same skills they drew on when making a tough sell or marshalling resources for a new business venture then the misconduct might never escalate to the point where heroic whistle blowing is required."

Unfortunately our administrators and managers of education do not act on their values. This may be because they might consider that such action will not be appreciated by the people in general and their superiors in particular. This type of mind set must change. They must realize that it is not sufficient to think right thing but also to do it. Samuelson and Gentile emphasize that "managers have a responsibility to help employees over their mental hurdles. Leaders who act ethically themselves are necessary but not sufficient. They must also make clear that correctly resolving ethical and moral questions is part of everyone's job and that time spent doing so does, in fact, serve the business."

Fourth Direction of Mind Set Change (MSC-IV):

The fourth direction in which the mindset change of the managers and administrators is required is concerned with the achieving of social equity. We have already explained above that the Indian social order is very much stratified. For achieving social and economic equity the framers of constitution visualized a system of reservations for the backward and down-trodden classes in services and in educational institutions financed by the government. To some extent the reservation policy has been successful in raising the status of so-called schedule and backward castes. But reservations have benefited only a limited number of the socially neglected classes. The benefit to the masses of these classes is almost negligible as is evident by the number of people who are still much below the poverty line. Our administrators have the mind set that by extending reservations to higher percentages and to more classes they will ensure social and economic equity. This mind set needs radical change.

According to Bhiku Parekh (Dec. 26 2005), Indian Society is deeply divided, even fractured, along caste and communal lines. The post-independence strategy of dealing with these divisions by co-opting the elite in the power structure, the policy of reservation for the SCs, STs and increasingly for OBCs, and granting considerable cultural autonomy to Muslims has certainly yielded some worth while results, but it has also left much of ugly social reality untouched." The social reality is that the caste system has become more rigid. In Parekh's view, "Among the urban and rural poor, who feel cheated by the political parties and the state, castes have increasingly become the only vehicle of improving their access to power and promoting their economic interests." Parekh laments that even after over fifty years of independence, the quality of Dalit life shows little improvement. Parekh further observes that "Although understandable, the Dalit response is equally worrying.

They have turned the Dalit into a new identity and some even view it as a privilege because of the petty rewards it brings. Dalithood is thus in danger of becoming a rigid and relatively permanent category of our socio-political life." Whatever Parekh says seems to be very true. The Dalits instead of trying to improve their quality of life are harping on the crutches of reservation and special treatment to them for being Dalits. In fact what happens is that the so called Dalit leaders in the garb of serving the Dalit cause grab all the advantages for themselves and their offspring leaving a large mass of Dalits untouched with any progress in educational or economic fields. Therefore, it is not at all surprising that the vast majority of Dalits as well as STs and backwards are still basking in the glory of their backwardness. The cause of the socially disadvantaged will never be served if the managers of education go on harping on reservations with their present mind set and do not take positive steps with a changed outlook to provide that type of educational opportunities to them that may lead to the amelioration of their living conditions.

It is a psychological truth that no one wants to forego his or her privileges willingly. This is why the policy of reservation is very difficult to change. The vote bank politics will never allow it to lapse. An interesting case study may be cited why bestowing of favours in the educational field and for that matter in any other field is counter productive. The author was at one time serving as head of a university campus in a backward hilly region. The government of the sate sanctioned money for helping the poor and backward for partially fulfilling their financial needs for higher education. The author was surprised when more than 80 % of the students applied for the financial help. The author asked the Dean of Student Welfare and the office-bearers of the students Union Society, to prepare the list of those to whom aid may be given. To the utter surprise of the present author the list could not be prepared till the time the academic session was nearing to end. All sorts of claims, counter claims were made for getting aid by almost all the students on the campus. Ultimately it was decided to give some financial aid of about Rs.100 to all those who have applied. It was a very small amount that each individual was to get. Meanwhile there was an offer by All India Radio for conducting a survey of its programmes in some rural areas for which the volunteers were to be paid substantial amount. The work was only for a few days. In spite of putting the offer on the notice board and asking the union society to sponsor some of those who are in financial need, not a single student opted for work. Just to know why no student among those who were fighting hard for the financial aid of a few rupees is not offering for work the author questioned the student representatives. The reason cited by them was that "when they can get an amount without working why should they work?" It is perhaps the same story everywhere. Those who are habituated to get doles and money without effort will shun work. It is where the reservation policy has its greatest weakness. It has created a class that seeks favours without giving any thing in return rather it feels that it is the duty of the state and society to give them all they want.

The author agrees with Parekh that Dalithood may seem attractive to Dalits for obvious reasons but it is essentially a negative concept and reinforces a sense of passivity and victim hood. Hence the direction of mind change should be towards rewards for work and not for being born in a particular caste or class. By all means the socially disadvantaged are to be helped. But this help should not be regarded as a birth right of a particular caste or class. Those who can do should be encouraged to do and those who cannot because of environmental or economic reasons should be helped to do. In spite of our commitment to democracy we are finding deep fissures in our social order. The educationists should deal with it and try to bring in the social order cohesiveness and equity.

Fifth Direction of Mind Set Change (MSC-V):

We have already seen that our society is greatly fractured. In it there are extremely poor people and also there are fabulously rich persons. The society is stratified in castes, religions, regions, languages and races. Yet it is not static. It is dynamic and moving ahead. It is about the direction in which it has to move in the coming decades is where the mind set change of our educators is needed. We cannot cope with the forces of modern and progressive world with the old notions of our educational system. Much dynamism is needed in planning education for the future if India has to win the battle against repressive and divisive forces and march towards a just, free and affluent progressive society.

The managers of educational enterprise should pay heed to what our Prime-Minister Man Mohan Singh is saying. He says, "We must shed fear of the unknown and have the self-confidence to take risks, to experiment, to think, and act differently. A more humane and caring India, which is also a more creative and daring India, is what we need." Unfortunately the mindset of our educational administrators is confined to follow the routine. They cannot think beyond changing some text books or some topics in the old text books and remain tied down to a rigid system of examinations. A change in total approach towards education is unthinkable for them for they are afraid of unknown and lack self-confidence for bringing drastic changes in the system of education. But till we do not think afresh about our education system we will fail to achieve much progress and prosperity. No doubt today we are finding India moving ahead in many fields. Still we will fail to make this country a developed one till we make all out efforts to equip our youth for facing the challenges that may be thrown before them in the course of time. The youth will be able to meet the challenges through their increasing fund of knowledge. It is knowledge that is at discount in our educational system. It may be argued that it is due to our knowledge base that we are today pioneering information technology movement and computer engineering as well as space research. There is no disagreement with this observation. However, in a population of one billion these may only be considered exceptions. A large mass of population is ignorant and shows insignificant level of achievement.

The latest statistics released by the National Sample Survey presents a gloomy picture about our higher education. It comes to the conclusion that the unemployment rate is indirectly proportionate to the level of education, that is, there are fewer unemployed among the uneducated and that too among youth in the 15-29 age group. According to the Survey, in rural India, every 187 men out of 1000 who have completed at least their graduation remain unemployed against 9 out of 1000 who are not literate. The same is true for rural women. Every 387 educated women out of 1000 remain unemployed as compared to only 2 out of 1000 who are not literate. Urban India also follows the same trend. Every 207 out of 1000 graduate men remain unemployed while only 10 illiterate men in urban areas are unemployed. In case of women, 370 in a sample of 1000 graduate women remain unemployed, whereas all illiterate women are employed. The survey points out that in rural and urban areas, the unemployment among the educated was higher than that among those whose education level was lower than secondary. The unemployment rate is high among all categories of educated youth—whether you look at it in terms of gender or rural and urban (Extracts of Survey published in The Times of India dated Jan 1, 06). As may be evident from the results of the survey described above the more you are educated the less are your chances of getting employed. It seems that our educational system has failed to develop youths who are employable and hence drastic changes in it are needed.

From our discussion two things clearly emerge out. One is that our education system should be such as that the product of it is employable and second is that employment and progress very much depend on the development of knowledge base. Thomas Friedman in his book, *"The World is Flat, A brief History of the Globalized World in the 21st Century," writes,* "There may be a limit to the number of good factory jobs in the world, but there is no limit to the number of idea generated jobs in the world." Those who manage education should focus their mind on the idea generated education specifically in the area of higher education.

In an article Sujata Dutta Sachdeva in *The Sunday Times of India, Mumbai,* (Jan.1, 2006) writes, "It's the success story of the decade and it's getting better all the time. As India's ITES juggernaut gets more and more knowledge –driven, it's opening up a world of opportunities for the Gen Next- not just for the Techs and MBAs, but also for BAs and PhDs." She further quotes Sunil Mehta, VP, Nasscom who explains, "The ITES Sector is creating jobs of all kinds. From PhDs in operational research to degree-holders in literature, everybody has a chance." An Evaluserve study says that by 2010 India will have the lion's share, 70% of the $ 17 billion global knowledge process out-sourcing (KPO) pie which translates into three lakh new jobs in fields as diverse as back-office work, clinical research in pharmacy and biotech, legal services, publishing, and automotive aero-space R&D. With in a decade we will find India needing qualified persons in all the fields for knowledge outsourcing. Nasscom estimates the Indian ITES Sector will generate 50,000 jobs in clinical research by 2009 and the demand for accounting graduates will be around 100,000. Gartner predicts 85% of US companies will outsource at least one component of their HR function by 2006, many of them to India. But the main problem is that will there be enough talent to fill up jobs as more and more jobs may be available? We have already emphasized that with the present system of education we are not able to make all those children who go to school literate in the sense that they can read or write most simple sentences. They remain virtually illiterate even after a number of years spent in schools. We have also noted that those who have graduate degree are less employable than those who have not attended colleges. Hence it is a challenge to our educational thinkers, planners, administrators and managers of education to revamp education in such a manner that our youths are able to get employment in various fields.

It may be emphasized that our education should be knowledge based. Friedman (2005) says, "The more we put out the boundaries of knowledge and technology, the more complex tasks that machines can do, the more those with specialized education or ability to learn how to learn, will be in demand, and for better pay. And the more those without that ability will be less generously compensated." What we need is developing of ability among our students to learn how to learn instead putting undue stress on memory based learning for public examinations. The mindset of those who are to manage education should change so that they plan for knowledge, for learning how to learn and for specialized education.

Friedman (2005) paints a rosy picture of Indian democracy and expresses appreciation of the Indian people. He writes, "I am keenly aware of the implications of Indian democracy, starting with the oppressive caste system. Nevertheless, to have sustained a functioning democracy with all its flaws for more than fifty years in a country of over 1 billion people, who speak scores of different languages, is something of a miracle and a great source of stability for the world." It is a tribute that should enthuse and encourage us to build a better India and a world in which peace will be the ideal.

REFERENCES

Aiyar, Swaminathan S Anklesaria (Dec. 25, 2005). "Pitfalls of Universal Education," *Times of India, Mumbai edition.*

Aiyer, Swaminathan S. Anklesaria (Jan1, 2006). "The Challenge of Functional Literacy", *Times of India, Mumbai edition.*

De Bono,Edward (1990). *Lateral Thinking*, Penguin Books, London.

Friedman, Thomas (2005). *The World is Flat, A Brief History of Globalized World in the 21st Century,* Allen Lane, Reprint of Penguin Books.

Harvard Business Review (Nov. 2005).

India Today, Anniversary Issue, Momentous Years 1975-2005 (Dec.26, 2005).

Karnik, Kiran (9Jan., 2006). "Dreaming of a New India", *Times of India, Mumbai Edition.*

Mc Cormack, Mark H. (1984). *What They don't Teach You at Harvard Business School, Notes from a Street-Smart Executive*, Baton Books, New York.

Mukerji, Anashita/TNN (Dec. 27, 2005). "*State* Plans Primary Education Revamp, *Times of India, Mumbai edition.*

Singh, Mahendra Kumar (Jan.1, 2006). "Higher Education a Disqualification? Fewer Jobs Among Less Educated: Survey, *Times of India, Mumbai edition.*

Sachdeva, Sujata Dutta (Jan 1, 2006). "Non-Techies take the KPO Call", *Times of India, Mumbai edition.*

Welch, Jack with Welch, Suzy (2005). *Winning,* Harper Collins Pub. London

10

QUALITY OF MEDICAL PERSONNEL A CORE ISSUE IN HEALTH CARE SERVICES IN INDIA

S.P. Kaushik

'Health for all by year 2000' The Alma Atta declaration has remained an unfulfilled dream. Though progress has been made in that direction, the goal has not been achieved. Commenting upon the National Health policy: approach of the Government and the Indian Medical Association, Dutta, had outlined and supported the need for a policy of active involvement of the people for the success of the programme. One would agree largely by the seven objectives suggested by him but a major drawback of that package had been that it did not dwell with the quality control of the medical manpower. In my long years as a Medical educationist (more than four decades), I have strongly felt that quality control of medical personnel remains a core issue in development of health care services in any country and particularly so in India.

In a society which is openly corrupt, it would be out of place to write about quality controls. The basic pre-requisites of quality control are honesty and sincerity of purpose by all concerned. Nonetheless, the need for quality control cannot be over looked any more, if progress has to be made. The society at large, its leaders and medical administrators have to rise above their own selfish interests so as to help the ailing medical fraternity to get out of the present rot, in order to serve the Nation better.

Medical profession, by tradition has been considered as a vocation. However, being part of society which harbours individuals and organizations with near total moral and ethical degradation, it may be expecting too much from doctors? If thing have to improve there has to be an upgradation in holding moral values in all compartments of the society in general, and in particular the health care sector.

Health care in our country consists of three-tier slab system ie. Primary, Secondary and Tertiary care. It includes primary health care centres, village hospitals, district hospitals, medical colleges, post graduate and apex institutions. The other medical personnel besides doctors are paramedics, nurses and technical staff. The present chapter exclusively deals with quality status of MBBS and specialized doctors, who are main (central) persons delivering health care at all levels in all situations. Let us therefore examine the major issues effecting quality status of these persons and, how it is getting compromised at every step and what could be done to improve things in years to come?

Admissions to MBBS and Postgraduate Courses

In order to enter a medical college a student after 10+2, having attained the age of seventeen years is required to appear and pass a pre-medical test, held at national as well as state level.

The ingenious Indian mind is always at work and certain percentage of back door entries are invariably made by foul means. This results into a group of students, with sub standard merit, gaining entrance to medical courses by successfully clearing examinations.

The remedy lies in making these competitive examinations as clean and transparent as possible, in order to allow entrance of only meritorious students, both at MBBS and postgraduate level. For the want of space and the risk of deviation form my central theme, I would leave this aspect here and not go into the details of foul practices and means used for this purpose, except to emphasize the point that the dilution of merit pool begins by such entrants.

A greater set back to the merit pool at the entry point is mandatory 'reservation' of seats for various categories of candidates belonging to certain castes and religions. The society needs to consider dispassionately this aspect in details. Since the percentage marks for clearing the examination are lower for reserved categories students, the pool of selected candidates consists of two streams, one with high merit and the other with low merit, clubbed together. This mixture of heterogeneous categories results in significant merit dilution and lowering of standards. It is almost impossible for teachers and taughts to improve the low merit over the years and bring the low merit group at par with high merit students. The end result is that in order to create equilibrium and uniformity in the two groups, the overall merit as a whole suffers. Since the objective is to improve further the over all merit, this amounts to a major start point failure and reflects badly on the final quality of the finished product. The society therefore has no option but to finally decide now about continuing with the practice of reservation of seats in professional courses in its present form, where the product has a vital role to play in alleviation of human suffering and the responsibility of directly saving lives.

However, if reservation has to stay, there could still be two ways in which the system ought to be modified and the gap between the two merit groups is reduced to a minimum. One, that the merit of the reserved category candidates is brought at par to the rest of them before every one competes in open selection with each other on one to one basis. The state should provide all kind of support to the reserved category prospective candidates and their families, in the form of financial, social and material wealth i.e. money; furnished houses and fulfill their other day-to-day requirements. An alternate option could be that only one time reservation at step one is practiced for any such candidate once in his/her whole professional career. This way the number of dropouts after basic degree qualification is likely to be more, but it would ensure no further dilution of merit at higher levels of specialization. This hard choice has to be made if professionalism is to survive in this country.

Faculty Selections and Promotions

The faculty is supposed to be the torchbearer and/or showpiece of an institution, and plays a pivotal role in shaping of the best quality of final product. Unfortunately, one is aware of the fact that most of the faculty selections are not fair in our country. Merit is either not a criteria at all or at best is a secondary consideration. Money power, connections and patronage seem always to get the better priority over deserving candidates. Inbreeding, automatic promotion schemes, not permitting lateral entries at higher levels of faculty positions, domination of a select group of candidates from a particular medical college of a geographical area and many such other manipulations are done in such a manner that the merit becomes the primary casualty. These practices have a tremendous demoralizing effect on the meritorious candidates, who are otherwise trying to work hard with all sincerity and honesty, to improve their contribution for the betterment of society. The class of faculty which actually comes up are in contrast 'second raters' with inadequate proficiency and capabilities for training and teaching medical graduates, the so called future of India. The left out faculty members not only loose out all desire for coordinated team approach, they also give up firm commitment to work. There is no ambition left any more for originality and advancement. Total violation of concept of academic hierarchy i.e. lecturer, assistant professor and professor with or without headship of the department has also resulted into free autonomy of work and has made most of the departments a battle field for one-upmanship, rather then happy and healthy places of work. It would be an eye opener if one checks out on how many teachers part take in teaching activity regularly, keep there time schedules and assignments. It is the selection of low merit faculty, on the basis of 'other considerations' which remains the main cause of this discontent amongst the larger faculty mass. The negativity of mind thus inflicts and further potentiates 'no work' culture and at the same time kills new input of any fresh ideas by otherwise talented faculty.

The end result is a compromised pool of students, as well as a compromised pool of teachers. If both the faculty as well as student don't have the best available merit and healthy work culture, it should not be difficult to imagine the quality of outgoing product. Fair and impartial selections and promotions of only meritorious faculty, based on best performance, is the only way to improve the overall situation and ensure best quality of care delivered by these professionals.

The Training Programme

A significant number of medical institutions in the country don't have a structured training programme for undergraduates and/or postgraduate students, even today in spite of best of efforts by medical council of India. If a programme does exist on paper, its implementation and/or upgradation has often legged behind. Surprisingly some of the institutions don't even have a well-defined course curriculum defined in details. The curricula often mention the administrative schedule alone and does not include any syllabus.

Violation of procedures in starting a new superspeciality degree course has also been observed now and then. Short cuts have been made in meeting many of the pre-course essentials. The essential requirements of creation of an independent superspeciality department for a minimum of three years, constitution of bodies like Board of Studies and others, recommendations of Peers in the speciality field and interaction with national associations/societies etc., are some of the examples of these omissions, particularly by non-MCI postgraduate institutions. The MCI finds itself in a helpless position, unable to do any thing because of the constitutional autonomy of such institutions.

The ratio of teacher and the taught is yet another deficiency which is commonly prevalent. The number of teachers is often not adequate as per MCI norms. For the medical council inspections the faculty is either borrowed or hired on short-term contracts, and disappear soon after MCI approval and/or recognition of the college/course.

Clinical Proficiency, Patient Care and Research

The standards of patient care expected by the society from the medical fraternity are indeed and ought to be very high. Any neglect is intolerable, often highlighted in vernacular press and even taken to consumer courts. However, at times like these one forgets the common proverbial saying that 'You reap what you sow'.

The diluted merit of teachers and taught, the unhealthy work ethos and environment, naturally influences and effects adversely the quality of patient care programmes, as well as the research potential of the faculty.

The main thrust areas in medical research are laboratory based, experimental (including animal studies) and problem oriented clinical research (pertaining to patient related data collection and analysis). In a country like ours majority of medical institutions have lagged behind in laboratory based and experimental research. The main emphasis is usually on clinical research. Unfortunately even in this area one has failed to make any great international mark. The number of scientific papers published may well be in thousands per year, but very few of them attain a significant Citation index and/or have a high Impact factor. This is largely the result of poor record keeping, lack of honest audit, data collection and plagiarism. All these factors influence the quality improvement of one's publications and reflects poorly on the quality values of the man doing such research.

The ethical conduct and control of the medical manpower is also a consideration of vital importance. The extension of boundaries of malpractices arena have engulfed all moral, financial and legal limits. The common unethical practices have included patient snatching, undercutting (as there are no uniform fee structures), kick backs and reward systems, toutism, advertising, making false indications for intervention, cooking up data, making tall claims, running down other colleagues etc. etc. By and large no ethical monitoring and/or control of this manpower seems to exit. A large number of medical colleges and/or PG institutions do not even have a properly constituted ethical committees or at best these committees have poor monitoring authority and controls.

The Infrastructure Support

A Compromised manpower with inefficient faculty having poor research and ethical standards is hardly expected to have an excellent grade of performance. The matter gets further compounded by the fact that even the best of our public institutions (medical) are unable to provide a good infrastructure support. The equipment is usually old, outdated and not necessarily in good functional state. The new equipment is not easy to procure because of government procedures, red tape and financial constraints. The non-functional machinery is neither repaired, nor updated or replaced for want of expertise, good workshop facilities and budgetary difficulties. The resultant deficiency further erodes the capability of medical manpower to learn, practice and innovate new methodology in order to deliver adequate and better patient care.

The Reject Pool

The author has always felt greatly concerned about the quality value of those medical graduates who qualify MBBS from sub-standard private and/or public or public medical colleges in India or from abroad. Large number of these doctors don't progress any further in improving their qualifications. This group along with those who are unable to make to the Post-graduate courses by an open competition, in spite of having made repeated attempts, constitute the so-called 'reject pool'.

The size of this 'pool' is indeed quite large. This MBBS manpower often or usually gets distributed to middle and/or small set ups in the rural and urban areas and work unsupervised as general duty and or resident medical officers, before finally settling down on their own in practice after three to five years.

No one has ever bothered to monitor the quality of experience gathered by this group in their formative years. This experience plays an important role in making of good or bad doctor for the life. The experience gained is the by own effort of the young doctor, the training is totally unstructured and there is absolute lack of guidance or help available to them for picking up the correct methods and knowledge in order to deliver good medicare in later years. The health care capabilities and performance of this manpower has always remained compromised and well below average.

Regulatory Controls

In order to verify the capabilities of a medical person to deliver quality care after graduation and/or post-graduation, many countries in the world have strict regulatory controls. Regular participation in continuing medical education programmes, compulsory audit of one's results, record keeping, ethical monitoring and periodic recertification by competent authorities are some of these measures. The Indian Government is yet to implement such regulatory controls, and should ensure the best possible training and quality of experience gathering to our young graduates and postgraduates.

Conclusions

The write-up is not meant to be a negative report but a factual narration of the ground realities. Our health care system revolves around the quality of medical manpower available to us. We must therefore, strive to improve the quality status of this individual if we want better quality of care and thus rise above the prevalent 'mediocrity'.

The poor merit of selected candidates, deficient training and infrastructure, unethical practices, non-existent commitment of authority and faculty, demoralized cadre primarily because of non-recognition of good performers and manipulations by the senior medical administrators are few of the major factors, which have largely contributed and potentiated this 'mediocrity'.

Unless the society can ensure that only the best talented students get the opportunity to enter basic medical and/or specialized courses, and are trained by the best available faculty, under the best possible support systems and environment, it would not be justifiable to expect better health care delivery and performance.

The author does not mean any gender bias by using the word 'manpower'. Please read this as either male or a female doctor.

REFERNCES

Dutta PK. National health policy: approach of the Government and the IMA. *Journal of Indian Med Assoc.* 1979 Mar 16; 72(6): 129-31.

S.P. Kaushik. Surgical Training in India. *The National Medical Journal of India, 2002* 15(5) 282-283.

S.P. Kaushik. Surgical Audit: A Must for Speciality Development in India. *Tropical Gastroenterology* 2000; 21:41-42.

S.P. Kaushik. Ethics in surgical practice: An Indian viewpoint. *The National Medical Journal Of India*, 2002 15(1) 34-35.

Independent External Quality Control of Medical Services. Rendered by Private Health Care Providers. http;// dec2.bumc.bu.edu/Russian Legal Health Reform/Project Documents.n940.IG1b.com pd.

J.Schilling, R. Cranovsky and R. Straub. Quality Programmes, Accreditation and Certification in Switzerland. *International Journal of Quality in Health Care* 2001 13(2) 157-161.

11

DISTANCE EDUCATION AND THE CHALLENGE OF THE UPGRADATION OF KNOWLEDGE AND SKILLS OF THE WORKING CLASS

Satyavan Bhatnagar

Distance Education is comparatively a new system of education, tracing its emergence to the early years of the last century. Looking back at its development, it had made its debut in the western world as also in India (though at a much later stage) as a supplementary channel to the conventional system of education. Its main focus was to provide the facility of higher education to those of its aspirants who could not get into the conventional institutions either because of the awfully limited number of the latter or the financial incapacity of the former. Speaking strictly in the context of India, Distance Education has done a highly commendable service to the nation in the sense that it has shared remarkably the burden of the conventional institutions, especially at that time when neither the government nor those philanthropic organizations that had already been in the field was in a position to bear the brunt of the tremendously escalated demand for higher education. Today, when the process of industrialization has gone into strides and there has correspondingly arisen the demand for a larger number of new types of personnel, both technical and administrative, as also for the up-gradation of the knowledge and skills of the existing work force, a need is being felt for some sort of an institutional mechanism that may fulfil this demand. Though the existing system of education could also play the new role in as effective a manner as it has been doing all the while and it is certainly not going to abdicate that role, yet one aspect of the new requirement is that the existing work force cannot afford to leave their workshops and get back to schools and colleges. They need to be trained right at their doorstep without being displaced from their present jobs. Any such arrangement would not only suit the workers but also the industry, for neither of them would be derailed from their normal tempo of work. In such a situation, Distance Education alone could foot that bill. Realizing its responsibility toward the nation, Distance Education has once again responded to its call. While elsewhere in the world it has fully shifted its focus to the newer field, in India this change-over is still in the transitional stage. For, the demand for conventional education, though abated a little, is still there (the reason being that the expansion of the conventional type of institutions has not been able to keep pace with the growth in the demand for the same). Moreover, the demand from the industry has not become so pressing as yet. However, the indications are that the day is not far when the demand for the workers to be deployed form one trade to another will be as much pressing as it is elsewhere in the world. However, Distance Education in its new '*avtar*' will have to gear it up suitably in order to meet the new responsibility. For, the challenges ahead are quite formidable. In this paper an attempt has been made, first to highlight how this mode of education has meandered its way from stage to stage and then to focus on the new challenges.

I
Post-Independence Phenomenon of Escalation in the demand for Higher Education

Having already had 'a tryst with destiny' India could not afford to waste any more time to recover the loss sustained over the centuries. No sooner did it free itself from the British yoke than it set its foot on the fast track of development. While on one side, the Constituent Assembly hastened to give to the nation a first rate constitutional arrangement that may help facilitate the fulfillment of the hopes and aspirations of a newly-freed people, on the other side a massive development drive for an all-round reconstruction of society with 'democracy' and 'development' as two driving concepts was put into operation. The day was not far when that campaign began to yield its fruits. Hardly an aspect of our public life was left that might have escaped its impact. Every one began to feel the warmth of the glow of the newly established democracy. The spirit of equality that it unleashed and further reinforced by the periodic conduct of electoral exercises and the attendant political campaigns, further bolstered by numerous types of multi-pronged development measures undertaken by the government and the NGO's - cumulatively galvanized the psyche of the rank and file of the citizenry. The youth in particular began to nurse new hopes and ambitions.

One interesting and significant dimension of that new surge was the unprecedented demand for higher education. Earlier matriculation was considered to be the optimum level of education for every school-going child. Only very few of those who had the wherewithal to meet the cost of college education alone went in for it. The rest would stop after having done their matriculation and engage themselves in bread-earning pursuits. The dawn of the new age that opened vast new avenues both in the fields of education and employment, heavily discounted the value of matriculation. In the estimation of the common man, it came to be looked upon at best as an entrance qualification for admission to the institutions of higher learning. Graduate degree became the new goal for even those who earlier terminated at the matriculation level. One important secret of the escalation in the demand for higher education was that those jobs in public employment that hitherto were denied to the Indians were thrown open for them as well. Since these jobs mostly belonged to the superior cadres of the various administrative services, they obviously required comparatively better-qualified persons, armed with a minimum of graduate degree.

To meet the escalated demand for college education, both the government and those religious and philanthropic organizations that had already been engaged in the noble cause of providing higher education reinforced their efforts. As a result, the number of colleges marked an unprecedented increase just in a couple of years. Those small cities and large towns that hitherto were denied this privilege also began to have at least one degree-level institution.

However, the demand for higher education was unabated and even the reinforced effort to cope with it miserably flopped, the reason being the radical change in the mindset of the post-Independence generation as well as the ever-recurring phenomenon of population explosion had combined together to swell tremendously the stream of the seekers of higher education on a continuum basis. To provide a glimpse of the latter phenomenon, our population had increased from 369.88 million (1951) to 445.86 million and 555.04 millions, respectively in 1961 and 1971. *(Census of India Reports).* Having already taxed their resources to their optimum level, the government and the philanthropic institutions did not find it possible to go in for more colleges. However, they did make an effort and instituted evening shifts in most of their existing colleges. In due course, that experiment too proved inadequate in more than one way. At long last, Correspondence Education, as Distance Education was then described, came to be looked upon as the only viable supplementary channel to overcome this problem on a long-term basis.

The Delhi University was the first to go in for that experiment. Conceived and designed in the context of the mid-twentieth century philosophy of Correspondence Education, the Delhi School of Correspondence and Continuing Education made a resounding success. Based on the economies of scale, it enjoyed the dual advantage of not having a very elaborate infrastructure, on the one hand and of having no constraint on the number of students that it enrolled, on the other. As for the infrastructure, a simple institute of Correspondence Education that imparted instruction through the triple media of printed lesson scripts, periodic contact programmes and response sheets would not require elaborate infra-structure, typical of a college/ university department. For, all the three components of its instructional package could be handled conveniently by outside teachers, engaged on contract basis. Or at best a small faculty could be recruited for the needful. Following that pattern, the enrollment of the Delhi School, in its initial stages exceeded 15,000. If that much strength of students was to be absorbed in conventional colleges, it would have required no less than three to four of them Thus, Correspondence Education system helped fetch to the institution concerned handsome returns, besides, of course absolving the university of the recurring problem of the absorption of the overflow of students from colleges and the university departments. Above all, it kindled a ray of hope for those persons who had been condemned for one reason or the other to reconcile themselves with school education only.

In due course, Correspondence Education became an envy of the rest of the universities. Motivated partly by the missionary zeal of providing education to the economically as well as the socially handicapped college education-hungry people and mainly by the handsome monetary returns that it assured, a number of universities supplemented their study programmes with this stream. By the end of the seventies, 22 of them had instituted directorates/departments of correspondence courses. These Institutes, by and large were evenly spread over the length and breadth of the country. Hardly any region was left uncovered by them. The eighties pushed this process of expansion still further.

As Correspondence Education struck roots in the country and people learnt about the novel system that brought instruction to doorstep of the learner, demand for higher education began to be echoed from many a hitherto unfamiliar quarters as well. Among the newer seekers for higher education were, in the first place, those middle-aged (and in certain cases even elderly) people who were already employed in various offices (government as well as non-government) and who had been struck at comparatively lowlier positions of their cadres on account of their not being adequately qualified for higher positions. They too saw a ray of hope in correspondence education and began to clamour for it.

The second category that felt equally perturbed over the lack of facilities for higher education comprised those people who did not have any worthwhile activity during their spare time. Prominent among them were the housewives and the retired persons. With the passage of time, women too had gone in for higher education. After their marriage, they did not have much to do at home. But for a negligible section of them who went out for jobs, the rest found time hanging on their minds, for the domestic chores had no longer remained as time-consuming as had been the case with their mothers/grand-mothers-in-law. Similarly, with the enhancement of longevity, people would retire from active service comparatively at an age when they still had strength in their sinews and ambition in their mind. Both of these categories of the 'unemployed' who frantically looked for some sort of meaningful vocation to keep themselves occupied had found in Correspondence Education an ideal medium to satiate their hunger for higher education. That system suited them all the more for the reason that while they would not be required to go to the colleges and rub shoulders with the teen-aged collegians, instruction would be available to them at the threshold of their houses.

To revert to the emerging scenario of Distance Education in the country, the eighties marked not only its entry into many more conventional universities but also (more significantly) the ushering in of the system of Open Universities. The latter helped Distance Education develop an independent base for itself, for no longer shall it have to lean over the shoulders of the conventional universities. Andhra Pradesh was the first state of the country to set up an Open University. It dedicated it to the memory of late Dr. B.R. Ambedkar by naming it B.R. Ambedkar Open University, Hyderabad (1982). Almost immediately on its heels, came the Indira Gandhi National Open University (IGNOU) (1985). *(Bhatnagar. Distance Education: a system under stress).* The establishment of the latter marked a highly significant mile stone in the development of this system. Not only did the IGNOU enjoy the patronage of the Union Government and was inaugurated with a lot of fanfare but it was granted an overarching status, far higher than that of all other Institutes and Open Universities. It was vested with the authority to oversee and coordinate the development and functioning of this system in the country as a whole. In other words, all Institutions of Distance Education whether run by the conventional universities or by the State Open Universities would fall, directly or indirectly under its purview. To discharge the latter responsibility, it constituted the Distance Education Development Council.

By April 2001, Distance Education was being imparted by as many as 64 Institutions/Directorates of Correspondence Education (run by the conventional universities) and 10 Open Universities.

They absorbed in themselves 25, 75 619 students (the former 12, 21, 490 and the latter 13, 54, 129). In other words, they shared with the conventional institutions more than one fourth (26. 68 per cent) of the total responsibility of providing education to the incoming generations. (In the year, 2000 there were 96, 53, 619 students on roll in both the conventional and the distance streams as) *(Report of the UGC. 2000).*

To come to the nature of courses that the Institutes of Distance Education/Open Universities provide, way back when this system was introduced in early sixties its exclusive thrust was on arts subjects of the degree level education. For, the main objective keeping in view of which this system was thought of was to absorb the overflow from colleges and university departments and since a graduate degree in arts was the charm of the day (partly for the reason that, as it was then perceived it enhanced one's status in society and partly for the reason that it helped people to get a somewhat dignified job in some government office), almost all the Institutes of Correspondence Courses went in for arts subjects. Great demand for the same notwithstanding, it also suited to the convenience of the universities concerned, for instruction in arts put comparatively less financial burden on them.

It may not be out of place to mention here that even though Distance Education had struck roots in Europe, North America and Australia, our traditional educationists had a lot of reservation for it. They looked down upon the system with great suspicion and berated it as sub-standard. Whenever the issue of its introduction came up before their respective universities, they not only opposed it but also created obstructions at every stage of its institution. But since the demand for bachelor's degree was so great and correspondingly the traditional channel of formal education was quite unable to cope with it, little option was left for them but to silently acquiesce for the supplementation of the formal system with the non-formal channel. But by no means did it imply that they had recónciled with the new experiment. They continued to ridicule the system with unabated breath.

Opposition of the rank conventionalists notwithstanding, the moment the new system had set its foot on the Indian soil it had caught the imagination of the students and more particularly of the working people. For, they could not find a better method to improve their qualifications than the one that served their purpose eminently well without displacing them from their work. Meanwhile, much water had flowed under the bridge. The fast growing tempo of industrialization, coupled with the scientific and technological advancement of the country discounted the value of the arts courses and instead put greater emphasis on science, commerce and such other job-related educational qualifications. In due course, the latter became a craze of the new generation. How could the Institutes of Distance Education remain a silent spectator to that major development? The demand for the new courses became so acute that they too had to step in and discharge their part of the responsibility. The added factor that spurned them to jump into the new field was the immense lucrative potential that they sensed into it. As a result, a few years had hardly elapsed when almost every Institute began to dispense with one new course or the other.

Of all the new job-oriented courses, it was the bachelor's courses in education and commerce (B. Ed: and B. Com:) that excelled all others in their popularity. Keeping in view the wild demand for them as also the unusually handsome returns that they fetched, there ensued a rat race among the Institutes to start these courses. Sooner than later, every second or third Institute began to make a provision for them. However, most of them failed miserably to maintain the requisite standard of instruction because of the lack of adequate infrastructure they provided for. As was but inevitable, they fetched a bad name not only for themselves but also for the system as a whole. Its rank opponents got a handle to flog it with. At long last, the National Council for Distance Education stepped in and streamlined their dispensation.

That ugly development was just a minor storm in the tea cup. The system went on beating new grounds. It did not lag behind the conventional system in responding to the fast multiplying demands of a society in a hurry to modernize itself. Besides concentrating on graduate and post-graduate level courses of both the conventional and non-conventional nature, it instituted a variety of short-term job-oriented diploma courses for which demand was generated from time to time. Side by side, the system had also marked a vertical growth in the sense that quite a few of the Institutes had upgraded some of their study programmes to the master's level and even beyond that. However, the proliferation of the courses was not a smooth affair for the conventional university-run Institutes, the reason being that since they had been tied to the apron strings of their masters and the bulk of the decision makers there hailed from the traditional stream, they faced a lot of opposition at the hands of the latter. Thus it required a lot of persuasion (and in the process a lot of humiliation as well) on the part of the heads and faculty of the Institutes to bring the decision makers round.

The establishment of the Indira Gandhi National Open University, however, revolutionized the whole perspective of Distance Education in the country. Unlike the conventional university-run Institutes that depended upon their parent body for the line clear before instituting any new course, the IGNOU being a fully autonomous institution went ahead without any let or hindrance to institute all such courses as were in demand. Sooner than later, there was hardly any branch of human activity where one or the other of its courses might not have sought to provide to the learners academic instruction/ training. In due course, the range of its study programmes became quite fantastic.

When the IGNOU and other Open Universities began to expand their study programmers in newer directions, the decision makers of the conventional university-run Institutes also got a jolt and they had to cast off their old worn out inhibitions about Distance Education. They too had to yield ground to the demand for newer courses, thereby preparing their Institutes to face the challenges ahead. The net outcome of all these developments was that Distance Education geared itself so well that it was now in a position to shoulder the entire responsibility of providing adequate academic assistance to the working class to sharpen its tools and techniques befitting the requirements of a fast developing nation.

Yet another development in the filed of Distance Education that needs to be highlighted is the revolution in the technology of its instruction. Way back in the early twentieth century when Distance Education made its debut in the realm of education, it had only one agency to communicate with its students and that was the postman. The Institutes would prepare their study material in print form and dispatch that through the conventional mail to their students who on their part would take the help of the same agency to transmit their feedback to the Institutes. This system of Correspondence study did not forge a very lively contact between the teacher and the taught. There have been instances where a student even after having been on the rolls of an Institute for years had not got the opportunity to meet the person(s) who had been instrumental in improving his (their) qualifications so much. The exclusive dependence of this mode of instruction on the correspondence medium of communication had made this system bear the name of Correspondence Education. Such however is no longer the case. The new electronic technology has revolutionized the entire approach and methodology of this system. The vast array of new gadgets that this technology has placed at the disposal of Distance Education has completely obliterated the distances between the teacher and the taught. Hardly any difference is left between the students of this mode and those of the conventional system. If audio technology could make the voice of the teacher heard by the students in their bedrooms and video technology could enable them to catch the glimpses of his face and gestures, video-conferencing recreates the atmosphere of a class room and make the teacher and the taught interact face to face with one another, posing and answering questions with as great felicity as the conventional students do. Thus, electronic technology has overtaken the system completely, relegating the old postal agency very much behind, though it serves it as a supplementary channel of contact. This revolutionary development has made distance educators rename their system from Correspondence to Distance Education.

II
The New 'Avtar'

The Indian economy that had thus far been rigidly controlled and regulated by the state had begun to feel, from the mid-eighties onward the impact of the new twin-creed of liberalization and globalization. As a result, the stringency of state control over it relaxed a little and the private sector that had till then been totally out of bound for it was granted limited entry. Besides giving an unprecedented fillip to industrial expansion, this radical change in the development pattern cast its side effect on the psyche of our workers. When they found the tempo of industrialization gaining momentum and various new types of employment avenues opening before them, a realization dawned upon them that unless they improved their qualifications and refined their tools and techniques, they would not be able to catch the new opportunities by their forelock. Thus, there set in a trend, though very feeble that the workers would increasingly look for avenues to improve their qualifications and working skills so that they could seek premature retirement from their existing job and shift over to another that may be more lucrative and dignified. Who would help them realize that ambition? Their biggest handicap, as alluded above was that they would not leave their workshops for obvious reasons and revert to schools and colleges to replenish their knowledge or to learn something of the newer trades. They wanted the instruction at their doorstep without being displaced. That requirement could be met by no other system than Distance Education. Once again, Distance Education was thus called upon to meet another challenge of the developing society. Rising to the occasion, it shifted its thrust, as highlighted above from conventional arts and science subjects to such job-oriented courses as had become the craze of the day and also put greater emphasis on the use of the newer electronic technologies. In a way, this development proved to be a serious turning point in the growth and expansion of Correspondence Education. For, thus far it had been engaged mostly in sharing the burden of the universities by providing a supplementary channel to share their workload. But now onward, it had to provide services to the working class in refining their skills so that it could bear the responsibility of taking the nation on a fast track of socio-economic growth.

Yet another development that is unfolding itself today, though by and by in the realm of public employment, is the gradual replacement of the system of life long tenure by the system of employment on contractual basis. To dilate upon this development, as the sphere of private enterprise expands, more and more jobs will be thrown open for various types of technical and non-technical personnel. But the private enterprise based as it is on the sole concept of earning profit would prefer to recruit them on contractual basis, for, it can ill-afford the luxury of providing them permanent life-long tenure, the reason being that under this type of tenure the workers tend care more for their own personal comfort and perquisites than for the welfare of their employers, as we see them behaving day in and day out in government offices. It may not be out of place to mention here in passing as to why the private entrepreneurs are presently putting so much of pressure on the government to radically modify the existing labour laws, the underlying reason being that these laws, as they are structured today, leave but little manoeuvrability with them to discipline their labor force. It may further be underlined that India is perhaps one of those very few countries in the world that still carries on with the legacy of the system of the life long tenure in its public employment. When the system of contractual employment gets entrenched into the country's soil, the workers will have to face competition even for the renewal of their contract. That will further reinforce the trend of deployment from one job/trade to another. To facilitate them is do so, the workers will have to equip themselves quite adequately with the knowledge of those developments that had meanwhile taken place in their respective discipline/trade, thereby ensuring that someone who may be better qualified may not outmanoeuvre them? Here they would need the assistance of distance education. Such a situation has begun to make its impact. For, we no longer find the things in the government offices as smooth or easy-going as these had been until recently. For, the *babus* are now required to clear a few departmental examinations or attend a couple of seminars before they are considered for promotion to the next higher tier. They have now started realizing that they require some sort of outside assistance to pass the said examinations.

Finding the demand of the existing work force for providing to them the knowledge of the new tools and techniques of work fast escalating, some of the enterprising individuals have taken the initiative to do the needful by setting up their own private institutes of Distance Education. Independent of their own, they, unlike the universities and colleges are not hampered by hard and fast rules and regulations and are, therefore in a better position to adapt their courses of study as per the requirements of the day. They are doing a yeoman service to the fulfillment of the cause. In the same manner, some of the industrial houses too have made arrangements on the same lines for the training and retraining of their technical and the other personnel. In this way, the interests of the workers' as also those of the industry are being served reasonably well.

Distance Education appears to have entrenched itself so deeply in the Indian soil that it has provided a new feather to the indigenous system of education, namely outsourcing of education to the needy students beyond the borders of the country. It is a well-known fact that not all students are either bright or dull. There are always some who, by and large do not fare well in their studies. They need some outside support to consummate their studies. This is a fact that transcends the boundaries of states. Some countries meet their requirements on their own whereas the others are not in a position to do so. Information Technology further combined with the Distance Education mode has facilitated the task of the latter in particular. Their needs are met from outside their borders. Some of the enterprising individuals step in and do outsourcing of instruction in whichever field of studies they find a scope for the same. In India, a number institutes have come up in various parts of the country that cater to the needs of such outside students. By and by, outsourcing of education has also become a source of foreign exchange to the country, like any other industry in the field.

III
Challenges Ahead

The new assignment for Distance Education brings along with it many new challenges. Unless these are tackled suitably, the system will not be able to deliver effectively. The most important of them comes from the realm of modern communication technologies. Unless our Institutes own and suitably harness these technologies, their instruction would remain as weak as these had been thus far. Unfortunately, our conventional-university-run institutes as also the State Open Universities (the Indira Gandhi National Open University is perhaps the only exception) still continue to put their main, rather the exclusive reliance on the age-old communication methodology of printed lesson scripts, periodic class-room capsuled teaching (personal contact programmes) and the like. How ironical does it look that even in the twenty-first century when electronic technology has placed at the disposal of the distance educators numerous such gadgets as have mitigated the hurdles of distance (the only difference that separates distance learners from classroom students), most of them do not make use of these tools and techniques?

If we look into the reasons why they have not gone in for the new technologies, we find that neither the faculty nor the Institutes is interested in harnessing them. While the former consider them as an unwanted additional burden on their otherwise easy-going routine of work, the latter find themselves handicapped on account of the paucity of resources. In their own respective way, both the faculty and the Institutes are right. Their limitations need to be suitably appreciated.

As for the faculty, their primary role is to develop lesson scripts that may not only provide for the latest knowledge on the subject but should also be written in a lucid way so as to enable the distance learner to comprehend their subtleties without any type of external assistance. All this involves the expertise of a subject specialist who, besides having an in-depth knowledge of the subject concerned also devotes hours in the library to constantly keep him abreast with the day-to-day developments in his field. To expect such busy bees to further reduce their lessons into screen worthy scripts is to put the demand at too high a premium. Falling altogether in a different domain, the work of the conversion of the written lesson scripts into screen-worthy presentations requires not the subject specialists but those who have the knack and knowledge of rehashing the simple prose (the general form of the written scripts) into a live comedy that may be full of drama, suspense, humour, horror, satire, the like, and is couched in interesting and hilarious dialogues and, if possible that may further be laced with passion and light poetic verses. All through this exercise, the endeavour is to ensure that the interest of the viewer is sustained from the beginning to the end, lest he may not at any stage find the presentation boring and switch off the television/computer and go away. After the script has been refashioned that way, it is passed on to another set of personnel, consisting of cameramen, voice recorders, mixing experts and the like. Each one of them would work on it in one's own typical way. Thus, we find that the task of converting the conventional black and white scripts into the screen worthy lessons being so subtle, multi-pronged and one that that involves such a vast array of technical expertise cannot be a cup of tea of the conventional teachers. By no means can they cope with it and it would therefore be highly unjustified to entrust it to their care.

The subtlety of the task and the huge variety of the personnel that it involves apart, the preparation of the screen worthy lesson requires a fantastic range of electronic gadgetry and costly laboratory equipment. By itself, this is too tall an order for any institute. No one can afford to go in for it. If our Institutes have not so far ventured into this field, it is precisely this limitation on their part that prohibits them from doing so.

Limitations of the Institutes notwithstanding, one thing however is clear that unless they modernize their modes of communication by harnessing these technologies, they can neither compete with those Institutes/Universities that have already done so nor can they provide academically effective instruction to their learners. Keeping all these factors in view, the only viable course is that the higher level funding agencies such as the University Grants Commission, the Indira Gandhi National Open University or even the State/Union Governments should come forward to assist them with grants-in-aid for this purpose. But since the number of Institutes/Open Universities is so large in the country that it is quite impossible to dole out massive grants for this purpose to each and every one of them individually. In the fitness of the situation, it would be advisable if the requisite facilities are created at the regional level which the Institutes falling in their territorial domain may conveniently avail of. That is the only viable method to enable them to modernize their tools and techniques.

The second challenge to Distance Education comes from the phenomenon of an ever-escalating demand for it. The basic issue that shall have to be suitably addressed in the very near future is whether the system as managed today as an extension arm of the conventional system would serve the purpose or whether it needs to be detached from it and put on an independent pedestal of its own. For, the days ahead would pose various different types of problems to it that the system in its present form may not be able to suitably answer them. We may give a glimpse of the future scenario, as under:

(a) In the days to come, the type of the students who would come forward to avail of the services of these Institutes will be markedly different from the ones that join them today. The present lot comprises those who crave for the university degree largely for the reason that under the existing system of public employment, university degree forms the basic qualification, ironically for almost every type of public employment, ranging from a petty clerk to the highest cadres of the administrative services. That is why every young man or woman aspires to be a graduate. Sooner than later, this scenario is going to change very radically. Already, the process of change has set in. With the passage of time, this process will gather greater momentum. Fast expanding economy of the nation, coupled with the spread of the scientific temper of the people has gone a long way to provide technical bias to the bulk of the system of public employment, if not to the whole of it.

The twin phenomenon of liberalization and privatization has given a fillip to this process of change. Thus far, our *leviathan*, the state, controlled and regulated every aspect of our public life. That regime of awesome control and regulation required more *of babus* than perhaps the entrepreneurial or managerial personnel. The fast current of liberalization has begun to erode that regime. Obviously, as this erosion makes headway, the role of the *babus* will correspondingly shrink and that will make a great difference. Privatization will further reinforce this process of change. When more and more of public services, especially those that have a direct or even indirect bearing on commercial/industrial activities are taken out of the purview of the state and transferred to the realm of private enterprise, the role of the state would obviously shrink, leaving but little scope for its officials to interfere, much less control or regulate them The cumulative impact of all these developments would be that the older craze for the university degree, especially in pure arts will receive a serious setback. The impact of this change is already visible in the classrooms of our traditional colleges and universities. The number of students opting for the bachelor's and the master's degrees in such subjects as Hindi, Punjabi, History, Political Science, Fine Arts, Sociology and the like has gone down considerably whereas the Colleges of Medicine, Engineering, Architecture, Pharmacy, Computer Science, Information

Technology,.etc. are overflowing with students. Similar is the case with science departments of the universities and colleges. This change in the scenario of our public employment system is bound to spell disaster, among others on the Institutes of Distance Education that cater, by and large to the educational needs of the aspirants of the bachelor's and master's degree. Either they switch over from the conventional courses to the modern ones or face extinction.

(b) The process of change will not stop at that stage. Today, students accept what the system has to offer to them. Their choice is limited to a few select combinations of subjects, such as medical, non-medical, pure arts etc. The future requirements of the distance learners in particular will not fit into these cast-iron combinations. Like any other market, education too will be governed by the choice of the buyers and not by the dictates of the producers. What a learner has to study will be determined not by the system but by him and him alone. For, it will be he who would tailor his demand according to his own needs. He may, for instance like to combine physics with photography, or history with chemistry and the like. The system will have to concede to the learners the due degree of autonomy in deciding their choice.

In case a certain Institute does not make a provision for some course of study that a particular learner wants (there will be many such Institutes that do not make a provision for every course under the sun), the learner should not be denied admission nor should he be compelled to modify his choice. Eventualities like these will be very many, not necessarily arising out of the choice of subjects of the learners but on many other different accounts. All of them warrant that the various Institutes the country over should develop a suitable system of networking among themselves, borrowing/lending courses of studies from one another, instead of instituting them by themselves. The latter option will help them conserve their resources rather then frittering them away in the rat race of instituting each and every course.

The distance learners will have to be conceded yet another type of autonomy, namely that of allowing them to suspend their studies whenever they are forced by the circumstances to do so and to resume it whenever things improve at their end. To dilate upon this aspect, the future learners of distance education, unlike most of them who are there in this stream today, would be busy bees, badly occupied with their tight routine of work. Yet if they want to fulfill their aspiration for a better station in life, they will naturally have to make a compromise both at the workplace and at home. If at any time, some unforeseen contingency arises, they will be forced to suspend their studies. If after sometime, the situation marks some improvement, they may think of resuming the disrupted studies. To deny them the benefit of what they have already studied and the credits earned thereof and ask them to start the course *de novo* would be doing too great an injustice to them. The present university system under which a student if fails to complete a course within a certain specified number of years and that too year by year or semester by semester, will have obviously no room for such type of distance learners.

The foregoing glimpses of the future scenario of Distance Education lead us to the conclusion that the system as it operates today ill suits to the requirements of the distance learners of tomorrow. Thus, it needs to be modified in a somewhat radical way.

The biggest shortcoming of the present system lies in the lack of autonomy of decision-making on the part of the conventional university-run Institutes in particular. Quite often, they had to forego some highly ambitious study programme, simply for the reason that it did not fit into the mindset of the decision-making authorities of their parent universities. The author of this paper had to face humiliation on this account at a number of occasions. To quote just two instances from his sad experience: Once during his tenure as Director, Correspondence Courses, Panjab University, Chandigarh (1983-91), the local Post-Graduate Institute of Medical Education and Research (PGIMER) suggested to him to explore the possibility if his University could institute a correspondence course on nursing. As for the technical support, the PGIMER held out full assurance for the same. At his request, the Vice Chancellor constituted a committee comprising some senior faculty members of the University as well as of the PGIMER Institute of Nursing. The necessary blueprints were prepared. But when the proposal went to the Academic Council (the highest academic decision-making body of the University), the vested interests manipulated in such a way that the item concerned was put at the bottom-most level of the agenda so that little time be left for the Council to consider it. As was but obvious, the limited time of the meeting was exhausted in the consideration of the other items and the said item was not touched at all. Thereafter it could not see the light of the day and died the death of a still-born baby. After a couple of years, another proposal was mooted. That related to a course on Environmental Awareness. Again, a high-powered committee was constituted and the blueprints were readied. It too flopped at the level of the Academic Council. That time the item did come up for consideration but sadly those members who had endorsed the proposal made it a point not to present themselves on the occasion concerned, thereby lending support to those who were opposed to it. Ironically, not many years had passed when the Indira Gandhi National Open University picked up both these courses that our conventional teachers had not found fit to be administered through the medium of Distance Education and instituted them with a great fanfare. They are in strides today.

However, with the passage of time, the conventional educationists appear to have read 'the writing on the wall' and have become more realistic. No longer do they resist the introduction of the new courses, as a result almost all the Institutes have gone in for the non-conventional type of study programmes. This happy development notwithstanding, there is still the need to provide to them more of autonomy of decision-making. For, it is not the question of the institution of new courses alone. There are numerous other areas where independent decision-making is vitally important. Day in and day out, those who administer the various study programmes feel the need to modify the content of those courses, their duration and even the mode and manner of their administration. If for every little thing, they were to approach the higher authorities for the needful, it would imply the wastage of the precious little time of the latter. These things apart, there may be study programmes that may be common to both the conventional and the distance students. The requirements of the latter with regard to the modalities of their administration may require some variation from what applies to the former. In this way, there is an indefinite number of issues that may demand a different type of treatment for distance learners. Thus, the case for greater autonomy of decision-making to these Institutes is quite strong and it needs to be urgently addressed in the larger interest of this system.

In the fitness of the situation, the ideal solution would be that these Institutes should be withdrawn from the purview of their parent universities and then those of them that are viable, both academically and financially may be elevated to the status of Open Universities whereas those that do not qualify for that status may be merged with some nearby Open University. Though such a step would be too radical yet the parent universities can be persuaded to part with their administration in the larger interests of the system at large.

Once Open Universities are formed on these lines, many a problem that has become a source of deep concern for the managers of Distance Education would be suitably taken care. As for instance, one of the problems that has been defying solution at the hands of these Institutes pertains to the non-provision of the multi-media instructional mode. As discussed in detail above, the lack of such a provision has cost the system a good deal. The above-suggested model will effectively take care of this problem for all times to come. For Open Universities, that will then come up will have enough of resources, both academic and financial to provide for the same. If need be, Distance Education Council can also provide some funds to them for the purpose. Similarly, the grievance of the distance learners that they do not enjoy the freedom of taking up their studies, suspending them and then resuming them as per their convenience will also be suitably redressed. For, then these Institutes will live on their own, without fear or favour of anyone else. Their only concern will then be the well-being of their own learners and to that end they can take any decision they deem fit.

REFERENCES

Bhatnagar, S. Distance Educaton, a system under stress. *New Delhi. Concept Publishing Company. 2000.*

India, Census Reports. Government of India.

Annual Report, University Grants Commission, New Delhi. 2000

Annual Report, Indira Gandhi National Open University. New Delhi. 2000.

12

MANAGING ORGANIZATIONAL CHANGE: DIMENSIONS AND STRATEGIES

S.L. Sharma

Human Society is confronted today with a challenge of change as never before. Not that it has not experienced waves of change earlier. The last that if witnessed a momentous wave of change was in the wake of industrial and political revolution in Western Europe. However, the prevailing wave is remarkably different from the earlier one. What distinguishes it is the rapidity and velocity of change. This is evident from the manner in which extraordinary advances in information and communication technology as also the transformative forces of globalization have put every thing on an incredibly fast track.

At a time when swift change has become almost a credo, every institution, organization and group is faced with the challenge of keeping pace with it. All spheres of society are faced with the challenge of change and its management. In the sphere of economy, for example, globalisation signifies a call for change. So does the rise of civil society in the sphere of polity. In the sphere of administration, the idea of new public management warrants change. In the domain of family and community, social justice, including gender justice and justice to the deprived represents an advocacy for change. Every organization, formal or informal, every institution including family, school, office, industry, state and church and every group, especially the oppressed, is thus confronted with the challenge of change and its management.

There have appeared two perspectives in social science literature with respect to coping with the challenge of change: liberal and radical. The liberal perspective addresses the question of managing organizational change, i.e. change in a formal organization for enhancing its efficiency and growth. The radical perspective, on the other hand, is concerned with the question of organizing the deprived and the oppressed for emancipatory mobilization. The former focuses on the agency of management in initiating organizational change while the latter highlights the agency of NGOs, particularly social action groups, in organizing the alienated for seeking egalitarian transformation. The former projects sensitization and incentivization as strategies of organizational growth while the latter underlines the importance of conscientization and dialogical communication. Little wonder that the former is patronized by management studies while the latter by movement studies (Papa et.al 2004). As is indicated by its title, this paper is about managing organizational change. As for the theme of empowerment of the deprived, I have already dealt with it in some of my earlier publications (Sharma 1992, 2007).

For a systematic treatment of the theme under reference, it is important to ask the following three questions: (i) why to change? (ii) what to change? and (iii) how to change? The first is concerned with the need for organizational change, second with its dimensions and the third with its strategies. Accordingly, the paper is organized into these three sections.

Need for Change:

This section seeks to provide an answer to the first question, i.e., 'why to change?' Alfred Shutz, a celebrated Sociologist, makes a valuable distinction between two types of motives which he calls "because of" motives and 'in order to' motives. In terms of this distinction, the 'because of' motives behind organizational change are the following: rapid developments in a) manufacturing technology; b) information technology; c) management philosophy;

and d) people's expectations for something new and different. In view of these 'because of' motives, there is a need for organizational change because the 21st century is a century of change and innovation. As for 'in order to' motives, the need for organizational change is felt in order to survive, thrive, and excel. To elaborate on the 'in order to' motives, the importance of the first, i.e., 'to survive' has to be appreciated in view of the prevailing ethos of globalization. Globalization is a process of economic reordering of the world by means of integrating the markets of the developing nations with those of the developed. It marks an end of the era of protectionism thus exposing domestic economies of the third world countries to the global markets. As a result, it has created a climate of global competitiveness and generated pressures of unimaginable magnitude for swift changes. In such a climate of global competitiveness only those organizations are likely to survive which are quick and keen to change their ways.

Moving on to the second 'in order to' motive, i.e., 'to thrive', its importance can be gauged from the fact that change proneness is a common coordinate of all the thriving organizations. A number of studies including those by Peters and Waterman (1982), Bhattacharyya (1989), Baghai, Coley and White (1999) have revealed that the organizations which refuse to change are also those that stop to grow and they eventually go in the red. Nothing illustrates it better than the following observation by Garder: "Most human organizations that fall short of their goals do so not because of stupidity or faulty doctrines, but because of internal decay and rigidification. They grow stiff in the joints. They get in a rut. They go to seed". The third 'in order to' motive is the urge to excel. Excellence signifies a striving for continuous improvement, for outperforming others and, above all, for transcending one's own earlier standards. It implies an attitude of proactive change, a capability of anticipating change and a courage to introduce change while the going is good.

From the above, it is clear that the need for organizational change arises from a lack of fit between an organization and its surrounding ethos. If the surrounding ethos is buzzing with change and the internal environment of an organization is sluggish, the organization is bound to lose the race. This is the story of many of our organizations. Little wonder that the nation is faced today with the paradox of grudgingly changing organizations in a rapidly changing global scenario. Hence the need for infusing change proneness in our organizations.

Dimensions of Organizational Change:

This section addresses the question 'what to change?' the question begs three sub-questions: (i) where does an organization stand and where do we want to take it?; (ii) which domains of an organization have to be targetted for change; (iii) what kinds of changes are needed? An answer to the first question, i.e., 'from where to where' requires a realistic appraisal of the existing status of an organization. It also warrants a clear vision of the direction in which it is to be moved within a specified time-frame. This exercise will provide a critical input for injecting dynamism into the organization. There is a Japanese saying which claims: "that which gets measured, gets done". Hence the need to take this exercise seriously.

The second thing to do is to identify those organizational realms which may be critical for a change project. Broadly the following four spheres need to be distinguished for the purpose: technological, institutional, personnel (related) and cultural. It is necessary to ascertain as to in which of these domains is there an urgent need for change. Is it needed in the realm of technology? If so, in which area of technology: production or information and communication? Is it needed in the realm of institutional structure? If so, in which fields, restructuring of existing units, rationalization of rules and procedures or decision-making process? Is there a need for change in the filed of personnel management? If so, in which sub-fields: recruitment policy, training curriculum and methodology, or motivational inputs? Finally, is there a need for change in the work culture? If so, in which specific aspects of it: distribution of autonomy and accountability, system of supervision and control or modes of performance appraisal.

As for the kinds of changes, in addition to the above frame of reference, there are three contemporary advances that constitute a common agenda for all the organizations. These relate one each to the realm of technology, management philosophy and social ethic. In the realm of technology, we have the remarkable advances in information and communication technology. In the realm of managerial philosophy, the new advances bank on what McGregor calls the 'Human Side of Enterprise' (2006). In the realm of social ethic, there is the emergence of some new social sensibilities, including egalitarian and civil.

Given the startling advances in information and communication technology, their significance for organizational development can hardly be overemphasized. The need for their incorporation is too obvious to require any elaboration. However, it is essential to point out here that while it is easier for an organization to adopt latest technology, the same does not hold good in respect of acceptance of progressive managerial philosophy. This is so because material culture of an organization generally tends to advance at a fast pace, while its non-material culture tends to lag behind. This leads to what Ogburn calls 'cultural lag' which exerts an adverse effect on organizational development. In order to have smooth development, it is necessary for an organization to catch up with progressive management philosophy as fast as it adopts latest production and information-cum-communication technology. In view of the above, it is in order here to take stock of the latest trends in managerial philosophy. These include growing realization of the crucial importance of human capital, human resource development, 'Theory Y' as against 'Theory X'. All of them have to do with the human dimension of organizational development and have become parts of the prevailing management lore. While the thrust of human development has been on building human capabilities and sharpening competences, the accent of 'Theory Y' is on cultivating the finer instincts in human nature. Looking at the various management strategies, McGregor observes that they derive from two sources which he calls 'Theory X' and 'Theory Y'. The two theories are premised upon differing conceptions of human nature 'Theory X' is based on the assumption that humans are shirkers by nature and as such they work only under conditions of control and supervision. 'Theory Y', on the other hand, maintains that humans are generally inclined to work on their own, and they work better if they develop a stake in what they are doing, and if they are trusted upon. The two theories accordingly patronize two different sets of strategies. The practitioners of 'Theory X' favour strategies of strict control, standardization, performance appraisal and sanctions. The practitioners of 'Theory Y' patronize strategies of appealing to finer sensibilities, involving employees in decision-making, valuing their self-appraisal and suggestions, harmonizing their individual interests with organizational goals and investing in their overall well-being. Understandably, McGregor commends 'Theory Y' over 'Theory X'. Quite in tune with it is the concept of 'human engineering' which lays stress on managing motivations and emotions of employees. It seeks to secure full engagement of employees with organization's projects by means of what has come to be known as 'internal marketing'. Internal marketing is about raising the motivation level, the energy level, the efficiency level and the effectiveness level of employees. This is done by means of incentivization and investment in employee satisfaction. More about it later

Besides new advances in manufacturing technology and managerial philosophy, there have emerged some new social sensibilities also. These include egalitarian, ecological and civil. Egalitarian sensibility has emerged as a dominant sensibility of our age. Egalitarianism does not necessarily imply equality of rank or power. Instead, it signifies a certain basic equality in interchanges among persons occupying unequal positions (Beteille 2001: 291). What it denotes is a state of openness and respect for other viewpoints. Given the overwhelming concern of our age for equality, it is time for work organizations to imbibe the value of equality. This underlines the need for transforming our organizations from vertical to flat. Available research evidence shows that flat organizations perform at higher level of efficiency and effectiveness than vertical organizations. The former have also been found to be more productive than the latter. Most important of all, they are also known for promoting more equitable access of people to their output and services by making them available at affordable cost.

Rising concern for environment and ecology is another prevailing sensibility of our times. This calls for incorporation of environmental concerns in organizational culture. Green setting of an organization is conducive to both the physical ambience and the psychological facilitation for enhancing work efficiency. It will therefore, be only rewarding to make environmental budgeting a regular feature of the development planning of an organization. In the same way, it should form a part of the organizational ethic to undertake environmental impact assessment of its projects, ongoing as well as envisaged, so as to ensure that they do not pollute the environment and damage our ecology.

Upsurge of civil sensibility is yet another distinguishing mark of our age. Civility refers to a set of values pertaining to public conduct. The notion of civility is open to several different interpretations. Without going into its conceptual semantics, it will be in order to figure it out in terms of some common coordinates. It includes: (a) norms of good public conduct such as 'polished' or cultured behaviour, reasonableness and concern for others; (b) values of liberty, equality and fraternity; and (c) sensibilities such as secularization, pluralism and respect for human rights. At a time when civil values reign supreme, a formal organization will do well to imbibe them within itself. The most important measure of civility today is the human rights sensibility. Among other things human rights include the right to human dignity, liberty and equality, apart from the primary right to life. Of these the right to human dignity is of critical importance for an organization, both in respect of treatment of its personnel as also of clients or users of its product or services. It will help an organization to be in sync with the emerging social sensibilities of our times to incorporate them into its internal milieu.

Principles and Strategies of Change Management

'How to change?' is the toughest question to answer, as tough as it can get. A look at the prevailing situation in various organizations reveals four critical problems of change management: (i) ambivalent attitude towards change; (ii) top-down approach; (iii) resistance from below; and (iv) lack of knowledge about change management.

It is well known that in most of the organizations top management has an ambivalent attitude towards change. It feels the heat of change on account of the all-pervasive climate of change. But it is afraid of initiating change on account of the risk involved in such an endeavour. Michaevelli puts it succinctly in the following words: 'There is nothing more difficult to carry out, nor more dangerous to handle than to initiate a new order of things. For the reformer has enemies in all those who profit by the old order and lukewarm defenders in all those who profit by the new order.' No wonder that they act more as 'Hem', a change resistant character, than as 'Haw', a change prone character, and certainly not as 'sniff' and 'scurry', the quick change characters of Johnson's "Who Moved My Cheese" (1998). Stated in plain words, they prefer to stick to their 'secure zone' over moving into 'risk zone'.

Even in the cases where top management has a pro-change orientation things go awry at the manner of initiating it. The usual strategy followed by management is the top-down strategy which seeks to drive down the change through the organization. This is invariably resented by other functionaries. We have had occasions to see this strategy going flop in a number of cases, mostly because of its authoritarian character. More often than not, this leads to the problem of resistance to change. The reasons for resistance to change are not difficult to identify. Rick Maurer in his book "Why Don't You Want What I Want?" has identified three reasons: (i) 'I don't get it'; (ii) 'I don't like it'; and (iii) 'I don't like you'. The first is indicative of a lack of understanding of the change initiative. It implies a measure of ambiguity about the nature of change and its rationale. The second is indicative of disapproval of the proposed change on account of its perceived adverse implications. The third is indicative of one's grudge or prejudice against management in the light of one's earlier experiences. Stated in plain words, the functionaries may resist change because: (a) they do not quite understand it; (b) they suspect some design or ulterior motive behind it; and (c) they perceive in it a threat to their immediate interests. Whatever the reasons, resistance to change poses a serious problem.

The task of change management gets further complicated because of lack of knowledge about change management. Change management is not an ordinary act, it is a skilled task. It has principles of its own. The first principle of change management is that it should begin with the self. For a change agent, it is necessary to first change himself before thinking of changing others or an organization. The enormity of the task will become clearer as soon as one tries it on oneself. One will soon discover how difficult it is to change even one's simple habit, let alone one's mindset. As such, what it needs is patience as well as perseverance. A second principle of change management is trust building. A change agent has to have the skill of inspiring confidence in others and of convincing them of his sincerity of purpose as well as his genuine concern for their well-being. A third principle is to know the difference between what can be changed and what cannot be changed. A change agent has to know for himself as to what is within his sphere of control and what is not. Similarly, he should also be aware of what is within the sphere of control of the people who he wants to change. There is a need for him to synchronize his sphere of control with the sphere of control of his target group. A fourth principle is to acquire the knowledge of techniques of attitudinal change and behaviour modification. For this purpose, an elementary knowledge of human psychology is of vital importance. Besides that, knowledge of the techniques used by animal trainers may as well be of great value. Some of these techniques include: rewarding desirable behaviour and ignoring undesirable behaviour, 'approximations' which means rewarding the small steps toward learning a complex behaviour, 'incompatible behaviour' which means creating a situation that renders undesirable behaviour incompatible, and 'least reinforcing syndrome'. Most important of all is the knowledge of professional strategies of managing people such as bottom-up approach, human engineering, internal marketing, etc. For devising and developing such strategies of change management, importance of units like Research and Development (R&D) division, Management Information Systems (MIS) and Cell for Change Management (CMM) cannot be emphasized enough.

From the above, it is clear that most of the problems of change management arise from the manner in which a project of change is launched. Therefore, it is as important, if not more, to know how not to change as to know how to change. Some of the refrains that need to be kept in view are : avoid (i) top-down approach; (ii) adhocism and arbitrariness; (iii) communication through notices and circulars; (iv) desensitized handling of misgivings and misperceptions; (v) threatening implications for job security; (vi) phenomenal or fundamental or radical change at one go; and (vii) disregard for dissent.

In the light of the above, it will be apt to think of certain strategies of change management. These can as well be derived from the experience of the organizations which have made their mark as success stories of change management. Given below are some such strategies which are time-tested.

I. Pro-active Top: For an organization to be change-prone, it is necessary that its top management imbibes a pro-active change orientation. This calls for a change in its own self-image. From a reactive agency it has to turn into a pro-active one. As a pro-active agency, it has to cultivate three Cs, signifying capability, courage and commitment. It has to have a capability to envisage change, to anticipate it and to initiate it at the right moment. It has also to have courage to take risk, to launch change while the going is good and to continuously reactivate it. Above all, it has to have a conviction and an honest commitment to change itself before seeking to change others. It must be credible and transparent in the perception of the employees. It must follow Drucker's policy prescriptions of 'organized abandonment', 'systematic innovation' and 'organized improvement' (which Japanese call Kaizen).

II. Bottom-Up Approach: This is a strategy commended by one and all, including the Harvard Management School. David Stauffer considers it crucial for setting the stage for change. He observes: 'Want to drive change down through an organization? Then do not lose sight of the bottom-up perspective'. The bottom-up perspective is just not about avoiding imposition of change from the above. Instead, it is about cultivating change potential from below. This is not to say that the top management should not do its homework, or that it should not have a vision of change. Nor does it imply that it should wait for a call for change from below, or that it should uncritically accept whatever comes from below. The idea in fact is to involve the functionaries at all levels in thinking about the direction and content of change. This is best done by seeking their suggestions on a continuous basis with regard to the kinds of changes that they feel are needed for the growth of their organization.

III. Harnessing Change Potential of Middle Management: A widely held view in management circles is that middle-level-management like middle class in society, is usually conservative and status-quoist. Mike DeNoma CEO of a global concern, for example, maintains that initial reaction of a middle manager to organizational change is often to suspend judgment. Our field observations, however, show that middle level management is the best bet for a change initiative. It has its ideas about what to change, where (in which organizational domain), and how. Like new middle class in society, middle-level management has a professional proclivity to become a pace-setter of change. This is understandable, because a middle manager perceives grater prospects of upward mobility in a dynamic organization than in a static one. For the same reason, it will help the cause of organizational change to harness the change potential of middle-level management.

IV. Evolving a Shared Vision: Another golden rule of organizational change is to evolve a shared vision of all concerned, including not only the functionaries but also stake holders and customers. Usually it is mistaken for participatory decision-making. In actual fact it means a lot more than that. Participation is a formal proposition and it usually stays put at the level of tokenism. Evolving a shared-visions calls for active involvement of all concerned in thinking, feeling and articulating their views about the changes needed in the organization. It will require a measure of concern for the organization among those who are associated with the organization in one way or another. Such a concern can be generated by the top management by giving evidence of its own concern for the well-being of all the members of the organization.

V. Promoting Multilateral Communication: The prevailing practice of communicating about change is marked by a unilateral approach, i.e., form top-downward. Generally it is done by means of issuing office orders or official circulars. It is time to rethink it. A better alternative is multilateral communication at the very stage of envisaging change. A climate of free flow of communication from all sides, including vertical consultation, will make a big difference. In order to commend it, I can do no better than cite the example of the pattern of communication followed by Kiran Bedi in her endeavour to change the image of Tihar Jail from a centre of detention to a centre of reformation of prisoners (Dangwal, 1995). She provided suggestion boxes at various points in Tihar and encouraged inmates to offer their suggestions for improving the working of the institution. She would get the suggestion slips collected every evening, study then all at home, adopt the useful ones and publicly reward the authors of the accepted suggestions. To inject a personal touch in her dealings with the inmates and the staff, she followed the philosophy of management by 'walk, talk and walk again'. This provided her opportunities galore to exchange views with the inmates, take them into confidence and thereby involve them into the act of organizational change. The upshot of it all is that the top management has to create a climate of free, fair and fearless communication from below. This would require confidence building among the employees such that they feel that their organization cares for them. Apart from winning them over, this will also pre-empt the possibility of resistance to change.

VI. Re-engineering for Change: In popular parlance, the term engineering carries a technological connotation. In managerial circles, however, it has acquired a broader connotation. The term re-engineering in managerial circles refers to reorientation of business processes as also of social processes. In these days of rapidly advancing technological engineering, there has emerged a compelling need for institutional re-engineering, procedural re-engineering, business process re-engineering and, above all, for social and psychological re-engineering. A change-prone organization has to have a continuous engagement with all the above sorts of re-engineering with particular stress on social and psychological re-engineering.

VII. Moving Towards Flat Organizations: Studies have discovered that flat organizations are more conducive to change than vertical organizations. This clearly suggests the need for collapsing the existing managerial hierarchy of ranks and positions into two broad categories, i.e., executive officers (EO) and chief executive officer (CEO). This will make a significant difference to the change proneness and dynamism of an organization.

VIII. Investing in Internal Marketing: Internal marketing provides a stepping stone to growth of external marketing. As hinted earlier, it is about boosting morale of the employees and enhancing cohesiveness among them. In order to achieve it, there is a need to invest in promoting their comfort, their job satisfaction and their overall happiness. There is a need to do every thing possible to keep them in good humour and to retain them for as long as they are productive. In this regard, it is important for an organization to find ways and means to balance the corporate commitment of its employees with their family commitment. Strategies should be devised to prevent aggravation of family tension caused by corporate commitment.

IX. Phasing the Change Project: A grand project of change is not a workable proposition, certainly not at one go. For, it may appear bizarre to the employees and may generate a sense of insecurity among them. A better thing to do is to break it into manageable phases. Little wonder that Pierre Mourer, an expert on organizational affairs, observes: 'A huge project presented to employees as smaller bits-sized projects helps you win commitment by showing momentum and progress'. The phasing should be guided by a sense of prioritization and a clarity about interim goals set out for each phase.

X. **Commencing Institutional and Attitudinal Changes Simultaneously.** For any systemic change to take effect it has to be backed up with attitudinal change and vice-versa. It is necessary to dovetail the two. The irony is that more projects of organizational change suffer from a lopsided approach than not. They bank heavily on change initiative either at the institutional level or at the attitudinal level. For example, so many laws have been enacted to change the structure of gender relations in work organization but these have met with little success on account of inadequate investment in attitudinal change. On the other hand, considerable investment has been made in training aimed at generating attitudinal change in the prison administrators to transform the image of prison into a reformatory. But in the absence of necessary change in the Prison Act and Jail Manual, it has produced little effect. A rational approach requires that the two are pursued simultaneously.

Generally, organizations are quick to appreciate the value of investing in latest technology or even in rationalizing rules and procedures. But they are loath to appreciate the value of investing in training. They may sometimes not mind investing in training for enhancing occupational skills. But when it comes to investing in training for attitudinal change, they fail to appreciate it. This is so inspite of plethora of research evidence that indicates that attitudes and feelings play a more vital role than technology and skill in the successful completion of change projects.

XI. Setting up a Cell for Change: Finally, it is time that each organization sets up a cell for change. This may serve as a think tank in collaboration with R & D (Research and Development) wing for harnessing knowledge management for change. This should also serve as a nodal agency for anticipating and envisaging change by cultivating the change potential of work groups and functionaries at various levels. This should also be entrusted the responsibility of devising strategies to smoothen the process of organizational change and to prevent and overcome resistance to change. It has also to be a part of the 'change implementation team'. Identification of training needs and organizing or arranging training programmes is another important task that it has to handle. Above all, it has to monitor the ongoing change project/s of the organization.

Before closing, it will be only apt to lay bare the theoretical premise from which the above outlined strategies are derived. For want of a better term I would call it an 'inclusive and integrative approach'. It is inclusive in that it lays stress on involving all concerned, including the top, the middle and the bottom level functionaries, in designing and implementing a change project. It is inclusive also in that it puts premium on a shared vision and multilateral communication. It is integrative in that it sets its focus on commencing systemic and attitudinal changes simultaneously. It is integrative also in that it underlines the need for reconciling the corporate commitment with family commitment of the functionaries. Last of all, it is integrative in that it integrates internal marketing with external marketing.

In closing, it may be remarked that there is no set formula of organizational change. Every change project is a new challenge and a new experiment. The above outlined strategies can, nevertheless, serve as preliminary guidelines for planning and implementing organizational change.

REFERENCES

1. Baghai Nehrdad, Stephon Coley and David White. 1999. *The Alchemy of Growth: Kickstarting and Sustaining Growth in Your Company.* London. Orient Business Book.
2. 2. Beteille, Andre. 2001. Civil Society and the Good Society. *Sociological Bulletin.* 50 (2): 286-307.
3. Bhattacharyya, S.K. 1989. *Achieving Managerial Excellence: Insights from Indian.Organization.* New Delhi. Mc. Millan India.
4. Dangwal, Oramesh. 1995. *'I Dare' Kiran Bedi: A Biograpghy.* New Delhi. UBS Publications and Distributors.
5. DeNoma Mike. 2003. In David Stauffer. "Setting the Stage for *Change' The Hindustan Times Careers,* Chandigarh. 17 July, 2003.
6. Drucker Peter F. *Management Challenge for the 21st Century.*
7. Johnson. Spencer. 1998. *Who Moved My Cheese: An Amazing Way to Deal with Change in Your Work and in Your Life.* London. Vermilion
8. Maurer, Rick. 2002. *Why Don't You Want What I Want?* Arlington. Bard Press.
9. MgGregor, Doglas. 2006. *The Human Side of Enterprise.* Tata McGraw Hill. Delhi.
10. Papa, Michael J, Arvind Singhal and Wandy H. Papa. 2005.*Organizing For Change: A Dialectic Journey of Theory and Praxis.* New Delhi. Sage.
11. Peters, Thomas A. and Robert H. Waterman Jr. 1982. *In Search of Excellence: Lessons from America's Best-run Companies.* New York. Harper and Row
12. Sharma, S. L.. 1992. 'Social Action Groups as Harbingers of Silent Revolution. *Economic and Political Weekly.* Vol. XXVII. No. 47
13. Sharmam S. L. 2007.Community Participation: An Effective Agency of Rural Development. *Kurukshetra.*January.
14. Stauffer, David. 2003. Setting the Stage for Change. *The Hindustan Times Careers.* Chandigarh. 17 July, 2003.

13

LEADERSHIP FOR THE FUTURE

S.S. Mathur and Sanjay Mathur

What makes a great leader? Historians, political thinkers and psychologists have debated this question for quite a long time. A number of theories were formulated to answer this question. One of the theories, which was very often debated and researched, was great person theory. This theory maintains that certain key personality traits make a good person a good leader. A combination of the traits of intelligence, charisma, and courage were speculated as the hallmark of a successful leader. But the researchers were able to establish only a modest relationship between personal characteristics and leadership. Another viewpoint which was put forward was that for leadership the personality traits alone should not be taken into consideration. We should take the social situation into account as well. While we have to acknowledge that personality characteristics do influence the leadership behaviour to some extent the situation in which the person is leading should also be acknowledged. This view of the leadership states that "it is not enough to be a great person; you have to be right person at the right time in the right situation". There have been proposed many other theories. Most have been found deficient in one aspect or another. Hence none of them gives us a perfect model of leadership.

Recently the thinking about the organizational set up is undergoing revolutionary change. Organizations are not thought to be rigid, static and unchangeable. They are considered dynamic, forward moving, divisive in smaller units, having limited number of permanent jobs and flexible in their planning and execution of their work. Let us now look into this new concept of organization so that we can understand the needs of these organizations for effective leadership. We may then be able to formulate our ideas for the type of leadership, which will be needed for the future.

Emerging Concept of Organizations

Most of the managers in the past and also in the majority of cases in the present as well think of the organization as a machine, some thing that can be designed, measured and controlled which conveys the idea of being managed. This concept was working well in the past, when the organizations typically produced efficient machines of one sort or another. In the future organizations will be very different much more like networks than machine (Handy, 1996. p.3).

There is emerging a new language of organizations. In connection with organizations we talk of "adhocracy", of "federalism", of "alliances", "teams", "empowerment", and "room for initiative". The key words, which we are now trying to use in relations to the processes in the organizations, are options, not plans, the possible rather than perfect, involvement instead of obedience. This is the language of politics, not of engineering, of leadership, not of management. The organizations are dropping the title of manager and replacing it with terms as team leader, project coordinator, lead partner, facilitator, or chair. It is expected that in future it will be recognized that organizations are communities of individuals, not arrays of human resources (Handy, 1996, p.4).

It is expected that the managerial field would become the predominant political theory in the future. When will this happen depends upon when the whole new range of concepts replace the old conceptual thinking about organizational functioning? In the opinion of Handy the three new concepts are: Subsidiary, Earned Authority, and Virtuality. We describe them briefly with the help of the examples from the Indian context, as under:

Subsidiary: The principle of subsidiary holds that a higher-order body should not assume responsibilities that could and should be exercised by a lower-order body. For example, the State should not try to usurp the role of the family, because to do that is to demean the place of family in the society.

The organizations, at present, particularly the public or State sponsored are designed in such a manner that mistakes never happen. The result of it is huge expenditure in terms of control and they have become uncreative. No mistakes also meant no experimentation. This situation is now undergoing gradual change. It is now increasingly emphasized that individuals or groups have to be trusted to deliver until it is clear that they cannot do so. The task of the leader is to make sure that individuals or groups are competent to exercise the responsibility that is given to them, understand the goals of the organization, and are committed to them.

The organization of the Indian government is such that there are layers after layers of control. Any one who deals with the governmental organizations is very well acquainted with how these layers function. In any office of the government from the lower division clerk the important file of governance travels to the highest authority passing through the hands of the numerous functionaries at the various levels of hierarchy of officialdom. Interestingly the return journey follows the similar route. The result of it is that precious time is lost in arriving at a decision and conveying it to the concerned persons or the establishment. In case it is a financial matter or some controversial event the decision-making becomes the game of table tennis in which the ball is thrown backward and forward among the various functionaries who have to deal with it. Tremendous time is lost in worthless notings on the file and the scheme or plan or the activity for which the decision has to be taken loses all its vitality. The plan or the scheme becomes a financial disaster because by the time it is sanctioned for implementation its cost escalates to huge amount, which sets in motion, once again the same process for the sanctioning of additional grants. In future this system cannot survive. The world is moving very fast and those who move at snails pace are bound to perish. The future organizations have to create the climate for the delegation of authority and the sharing of responsibility. The doubting of the integrity of every one, which is enshrined in the concept of control, will have to be replaced by trust.

Earned Authority: According to Charles Handy (1996, p.5) the second concept that is evolving out is that of earned authority. In machine organizations, power stems from one's position. In political organizations leaders have to prove their competence. All authority has to be earned before it is exercised. The leaders must be given the time and space to prove themselves. Leaders grow they are not made. A career is now not so much a ladder of roles, but a growing reputation for making things happen.

Virtuality: It is the third concept. The new organizations are dispersed. Workers are employed in many different offices and locations. They do not necessarily owe their loyalty to one organization. The new organization is typically a 20/80 place, with only 20 percent of the people involved being employed full time by the organization. The others are suppliers or contractors, part-timers, or self-employed professionals. The organization is a "Box of Contracts" rather than home for life for its entire people. A virtual organization is one that you do not necessarily see, certainly not altogether at one place, but that nevertheless delivers the goods.

The traditional public or private organizations in India are so constituted that most of the jobs offered in them are on permanent or quasi-permanent basis. The personnel are appointed to do particular jobs in keeping view their qualifications. No efforts are made to diversify their job assignments with the result that they become stagnant in holding particular positions. Their on job training remains confined to limited fields and in case the organizational needs demand some other type of work from them they prove to be totally unfit.

Handy (1996, p.6) says, "Virtuality means managing people you can not see and can not control in any detail. This kind of management by remote control can work when trust goes in both directions. Trust like authority has to be earned, tested, and, if necessary withdrawn."

The Necessary Attributes of a Leader

In the type of the organization as envisaged above in which there is a tough task to run a community of individuals where authority has to be earned, the necessary attributes of the leader in Handy's (1996, p.8) views are as follows:

1. A belief in oneself which will give the individual self-confidence for undertaking tasks which hitherto have not been attempted but this has to be accompanied by a decent doubt that one can be also wrong on occasion, others ideas may also be listened to.

2. A passion for the job which will provide energy and focus that drive the organization but this has also combined with its opposite an awareness of other worlds. The leader must read, meet people and recognize that there are other worlds than his own personal self. In them he is prepared to enter in.

3. A love of people and its opposite a capacity for aloneness. It is not that leader always gets the approval of others for his initiative. Many a times he may have to move alone. He may also drive satisfaction from the success of others giving them the recognition that they themselves are often denied.

Living with these paradoxes requires strength of character. It also requires a belief in what one is doing. Money alone will not be enough to provide motive to live with these contradictions. "Great leaders are bred from great causes, but leaders, at their best also breed great causes."

Three things that shape the kind of Leadership we require: According to William Bridges (1996, p.13) there are three things that characterize the way we are getting more and more of our work done today, and that together they shape the kind of leadership we require. These three things are:

1. The organizations, industries and societies in which we work change quickly and often.

2. Most of us spend much more time manipulating information about things than manipulating the things themselves.

3. The production and support activities that used to be integrated within a single Organization are now more and more frequently "unbundled" and parceled out among different organizations

These three things are further clarified as below:

1. **The Speed of Change:** The world's total knowledge is increasing at a very rapid pace and so is the speed of change. But

the relevant changes are those that force us to reconfigure the organization in order to profit from them or even to survive them. These changes are usually related to technological developments. For accepting relevant changes the organizations must have responsiveness and flexibility. No doubt organizations try to be responsive to change and remain flexible. Yet they do not always succeed because of in built inflexibility and unresponsiveness in their structure and system. According to Peter Ducker "Every organization has to build the management of change in its very structure."

Jobs make it hard for an organization to respond to change effectively. The market changes but people keep doing their job instead of shifting their attention to whatever most needs to be done. They are paid to do their own job for which they have been initially appointed.

In a rapidly changing environment a company can go bankrupt while its entire employee are doing their job perfectly. Hence the desirable changes in the work environment will not be brought in by those who make a balance sheet of "this is my job", "this is not my job" but by those who do that which has to be done to keep the organization moving ahead.

According to Lawler iii (2001, p. 22), "It is increasingly likely that individuals will have multiple careers in the sense that they will switch their areas of technical expertise several times during their work lives. This is a virtual necessity given the rapid changes in technology and the importance of individuals' staying in tune with current organizational capabilities and core competencies."

2. **Knowledge- based work** Another factor that makes jobs dysfunctional is that more and more work is knowledge based rather than industrial. It is not merely labour which may lead to the achievement of the organizational goals. Knowledge work is difficult to divide work into separate jobs, each with different job description. Knowledge work is often done by cross-functional teams. On such teams cross training is common. This erodes the outlines of the jobs.

Leadership passes back and forth from person to person as the phases of the project succeed one another and different skills become essential. The resources needed to complete the project also change so that people come and go with each new need.

Lawler iii (2001, p.18) emphasizes that there are number of problems with the job-based approach, all of which btem from the fact that it fails to give sufficient importance to human capital." He emphasizes that a far superior approach, given the needs of an organization, is to focus on the knowledge and skill needs of an organization and to make these the basic molecules of the organization. Instead of job descriptions, organizations need person descriptions that outline what individuals need to do in order to perform the tasks that need to be performed.

3. **Unbundling the Organization:** It is now considered uneconomical to employ all the workers the versatile organization would need to do all the work that needs to be done. Instead the people should be hired for no more time than necessary, drawing some from temporary agencies and others from informal pools of consultants and individual professionals. The organization unbundles its activities. It depends on its full time workers for only part of its needs. It out sources or uses sub contractors for the rest.

Leaders for De jobbed Organizations

Who will be the leaders in de jobbed organizations? What does it take to lead an organization where people forget their job and do, instead, the work that needs doing? The answer is that it takes a new kind of leadership. It requires new leadership because the de jobbed organization poses new leadership challenges.

"De jobbed organizations are patterned like an energy field, and leaders function as energy nodes around which energy clusters" (Bridges, 1996, p.17). They emerge in the natural course of business. Leadership is the thing that people do whenever and wherever it is needed. The de jobbed organization require more leaders and leaders with more sophisticated skills. For developing sophisticated skills there will be needed comprehensive training programme.

For Indian governmental organizations it is imperative that they reduce their fat by de jobbing a majority of its employees. It should have the minimum of the core group in each department or in each organization or sub-organization. The rest of the work should be done on contract basis by offering the contracts to the organizations which have developed the expertise in the type of work needed by the governmental organizations, or employ specialists and other workers on part-time basis to do the job.

According to Drucker (2003, Reprinted, p.101). "The foundation of effective leadership is thinking through the organization' s mission, defining it and establishing it clearly and visibly. The leader sets the goals, sets the priorities, and sets and maintains the standards." Many a times leaders have to make compromises but effective leaders always weigh the pros and cons before they make compromises. They make a choice between right and desirable and wrong and undesirable. Thus Drucker considers that " leader's first task is to be the trumpet that sounds a clear sound."

Drucker further feels that the effective leaders consider leadership as responsibility rather than as rank and privileges. If things go wrong he is prepared to take the blame upon himself rather than throwing it on his juniors or subordinates. An effective leader encourages brilliant and hard working subordinates.

The third requirement for effective leadership according to Drucker is to earn trust. He says that " trust is the conviction that the leader means what he says. It is a belief in something very old- fashioned called integrity."

According to Kemp (1999, p.15) an effective manager is one who has the skill to become a role model for his employees. It means that the managers have to practice what they preach. They must set a clear example of an effective and committed worker. Kauzes and Posner (2001, p.87) put emphasis on self-awareness as an important quality of a successful leader. The Indian philosophical ideal "Know thyself' is considered as a *MahaMantra* (great formula) for the success of leadership by these authors as well as by Kemp, (1999, p.15). Kemp says, "Stephen Covey describes this as working from inside out. It implies that managers continue to explore ways of managing themselves effectively before trying to manage others." Kauzes and Posner consider that Warren Bennis called the "management of self' (knowing your skills and deploying them effectively) a leadership commandment. Bennis says that the "management of self is critical, because without it, leaders and managers do more harm than good. A good leader takes delight in changing. Tom Peter suggests, "Leadership is learning to love change." Drucker (2003, reprinted, p.281) says that "We live in a very turbulent time, not because there is so much change, but because it moves in so many different directions. In this situation the effective executive has to be able to recognize and run with opportunity, to learn, and constantly to refresh the knowledge base." An effective leader is also a visionary. Kemp considers that "for change to be effective, there needs to be framework for the delight in change. Having a clear vision of where you are going provides this framework."

Emotional Intelligence for Effective Leadership: Besides a clear vision the effective leaders are required to have emotional intelligence. According to Goleman, Boyatzes, and Mckee (2003, p.3) " Great leadership works through the emotions." If the leaders fail in driving emotions in the right direction, nothing they do will work as well as it could or should. These authors consider that a leader, who connects to the people's feelings, moves them in a positive emotional direction. They lay emphasis on the quality of resonance in the leaders. For them one sign of resonant leadership is that the followers vibrate with the leader's upbeat and enthusiastic energy. Resonance is considered as the glue that holds people together in a team and commits people to an organization.

Goleman, and others (2003, pp. 327-332) describe leadership competencies with respect to emotional intelligence as follows:

1. Self-Awareness:

(a) Emotional self-awareness: Leaders recognize how their feelings affect them and their job performance.

(b) Accurate self-assessment: Leaders know their limitations and strengths.

(c) Self-confidence.

2. Self-management:

(a) Self-control.

(b) Transparency: Leaders who are transparent live their values.

(c) Adaptability
(d) Achievement
(e) Initiative
(f) Optimism

3. Social Awareness:

(a) Empathy: Empathy makes a leader able to get along well with people of diverse backgrounds or from other cultures.
(b) Organizational awareness
(c) Service: Leaders high in service competence monitor customer or client satisfaction carefully to ensure they are getting that they need.

4. Relationship Management:

(a) **Inspiration**
(b) Influence
(c) Developing others
(d) Change catalyst
(e) Conflict management
(f) Teamwork and collaboration.

Conclusion:

We have in this paper described what will be the emerging shape of the organizations of future and what type of leadership will be needed for de jobbed organizations. Our conclusions have been as follows:

1.In future it will be recognized that organizations are communities of individuals not arrays of human resources.

2.It is expected that in future in management field a whole new range of concepts will replace the old conceptual thinking about organizational functioning. The three leading concepts will be:

(a) Subsidiary: Individuals or groups have to be trusted to deliver until it is clear that they cannot do so. The leader must make sure that the individuals or groups are competent to exercise the responsibility that is given to them, understand the goals of the organization and are committed to them.

(c) Earned Authority: In the new organizational set up leaders have to prove their competence.

(d) Virtuality: The new organizations will be dispersed. Workers are employed in many different offices and locations.

3. The leadership in the middle of an organization is a distributed function. At the top it has to be personalized.

4. The necessary attributes of a leader are:

(a) a belief in oneself versus a decent doubt

(b) a passion for the job versus an awareness of others, and

(c) a love of people versus a capacity for aloneness.

5. There are three things that characterize the way we will be getting more and more of our work done in future and that together they would shape the kind of leadership:

(a) the speed of change

(b) the knowledge based work, and

(c) undling the organization

6. The de-jobbed organizations will require more leaders with sophisticated skills.

7. For effective leadership emotional intelligence is highly desirable.

REFERENCES

Bennis, Warren; Spreitzer, Gretchen M.; Cummings, Thomas G. (Eds.) (2001). *The future of Leadership: Today 's top leadership thinkers speak to tomorrow's leaders.* San Francisco: Jossey-Bass.

Bridges; William (1996). "Leading the de-jobbed organization." In *Leader of the future.* Edited by Hasselbein, Frances and others, San Francisco: Jossye – Bass, pp. 11-18

Covey, Stephen R. (1992). *Principle-centred leadership.* Lond. Pocket Books.

Drucker, Peter F. (2003), Reprinted). *Managing for the future.* Oxford: Butterworth- Heinemann.

Ficarrotta, J. Car. (Ed.) (2002). *The leader's imperative : Ethics, integrity and responsibilty*, Mumbai : Jaico Pub. House.

Goleman, Daniel; Boyatizis, Richard; and Mckee, Annie (2003). The new leaders : Transforming the art of leadership into the science of results. Paper back. Time Warner.

Harvard Business Review (June 2003).

Harvard business review on leadership (1998). A Harvard business review paperback.

Handy, Charles (1996). "The new language of organizing and its implications for leaders." In *Leader of the future* Edited by Hasselbein, Frances; Goldsmith, Marshell; & Backhard, Richard. San Francisco: Jossey-Bass. pp. 3-9

Kauzes, James M. and Posner, Barry Z. (2001). "Bringing leadership lessons from the past into the future." In *The future of leadership: Today's top leadership thinkers speak to tomorrow's leaders.* Edited by Bennis and others.

Kamp, DI (1999). *21st century manager: Future-focussed skills for the next "millennium,* Lond. :Kogan-Page.

Lawler iii, Edward E. "The era of human capital has finally arrived." In *The future of leadership : Today's top leadership thinkers speak to tomorrow's leaders;* Edited by Bennis and Others.

Michaels, Ed; Handfield-Jones, Helen; and Axelrod, Beth. (2001). *The war for talent.* Boston: Harvard Business School Press.

Watson, Craig M. (Ed.) (2001). *Dynamics of Leadership*. Mumbai: Jaico pub.

14

CORPORATE SOCIAL RESPONSIBILITY: A REVIEW ARTICLE

S C Vaidya and Parvinder Arora

Meaning and Conceptions:

The role of business in society has been debated for long now. And this debate becomes more important when 51 of the largest 100 economies in the world are corporations and not the nation states. (As per OECD 51 of the largest 100 economies are corporations and not the nation states (1991). Profit maximization or for that matter wealth maximization is no more an only criteria for evaluating a business. This is an established fact that business has an obligation to society that extends beyond its narrow obligation to its owners or shareholders. It is viewed these days that it is not only the shareholders but the different stakeholders who the business has to take care of. This is what is called the basic premise of Corporate Social Responsibility. Corporate Social Responsibility (CSR) is a concept whereby companies integrate social and environmental concerns in their business operations and in their interaction with their stakeholders on a voluntary basis. There are numerous different definitions available on what exactly is CSR. However most of these definitions revolve around one thing that is doing something which affects an identifiable social stakeholder's welfare. A useful report on social reporting by Elkington *et al.* (1998) describes, in a useful way, the various meanings of corporate social responsibility. (Cited from Mohamed Zairi and John Peters, [2002)

In short, this concept covers social, ethical accounting, auditing and reporting;

A little bit more than just philanthropy. The report argues that companies like BP; United Utilities measure, evaluate and benchmark their social activities. Furthermore, they tend to view the community's perception of them as a critical factor for their business success.

Ethics versus social concerns. The interdependency between the two is undisputed. Organizations have, first of all, got to operate with a high code of ethics so that everything else can follow on from this.

It is not just that the CSR is viewed differently by different authors, but the meaning and scope differs along country lines also, may be due to different cultures, environment and circumstances. The idea of CSR is viewed amongst corporate across the globe differently depending upon why they undertake CSR initiatives and what circumstances influence their business prospectus. For example one of the reports has beautifully exemplified the multiple conceptions of social responsibility in different countries. For example, it is philanthropic SR in Chile, its business perspective (reputation) in India and black economic empowerment in South Africa. (Briefing Note: Perceptions and Definitions of Social Responsibility)

Research Issues in CSR

The idea of Corporate Social Responsibility seems to be gaining popularity amongst both the researchers as well as corporate entities. Corporate sector has started reporting their initiatives as well, though in different formats. More than half of the Fortune 1000 companies issue CSR reports (Tsoutsoura, 2004). Similarly, the researchers have ventured into this area with a great zeal of interest and have produced studies covering different aspects of CSR in different sectors and different situations. The researchers broadly have addressed three broader issues viz. what is the quantum of social initiatives taken by different companies, what are the reporting practices (and quality of these) of corporate regarding their CSR initiatives and what is the relationship between financial performance and social performance (if any) of the corporate sectors. There have been various studies which focus on different aspects of CSR. The areas that have been primarily researched by different researchers are measuring the corporate social performance, reporting practices of corporate pertaining to their social initiatives, and establishing relationship between corporate characteristics like size, profitability and industry.

The most important area of research has been to identify if there is any relationship between corporate social performance and certain corporate features as well as certain financial indicators. According to Margolis and Walsh (2002) there have been 122 published studies between 1971 and 2001 to examine relationship between CSR and financial performance. For example, Grey and others found a strong link between disclosure and corporate characteristics such as size, profitability, etc. (Gray et al 2001). Waddock and Graves (1997) found interdependence between financial and social performance. However, their conclusions were questioned by McWilliams and Siegel (2000). Another study conducted in Australia suggests that it pays to be moderately socially responsible rather than be overly concerned with social responsibility involvement (Mangos, 2000). However the results of different studies have been inconsistent with each other. For example, Wright and Ferris (1997) found a negative relationship; Posnikoff (1997) found a positive relationship and Welch and Wazzan (1999) found no relationship between CSR and short - run financial performance. Similarly, Cochan and Wood (1984) located a positive relationship, Aupprele et al (1985) detected no significant relationship and Waddock and Graves (1997) reported positive relationship between CSR and some long-term financial indicators. Another area of research in CSR has been to understand it from stakeholders' perspective. It has been argued by a group of authors that paying attention to the interests, needs and rights of multiple stakeholders of a business is a useful way of inculcating socially responsible behavior among corporations (Goodpaster 2001; Greenwood 2001, 2001; Ruf, Muralidhar et al. 2001; Dawkins and Lewis 2003; Maignan and Ferrell 2004). Freeman (1984) distinguishes between primary stakeholders (owners, management, local community, customers, employees and suppliers), those whose continuing participation is necessary for the survival of the corporation, and secondary stakeholders (the government and communities that provide infrastructure and markets, trade unions and environmentalists), who are not essential to the survival of the corporation although their actions can significantly damage (or benefit) the corporation. Dusuki and Dar (2005) have beautifully compiled the research in the area of CSR with a special focus on the stakeholder. It provides the summary of research studies on CSR with a focus on stakeholder coverage, findings and research methodology instrument used in the literature to date on the perceptions of CSR from diverse stakeholder groups.

CSR Drivers

In the light of such contradictory results it becomes interesting to know and understand what works on the minds of corporate managers while making such CSR initiatives. Is it the financial implications or is it the philanthropy or are there some other motivating aspects which drive them to take some initiatives ? The literature suggests various motivating forces driving the corporate to invest in social sector. Even in one of the studies O'Brien (2001) suggested that social responsibility can be used as a strategic tool to enhance the reputation and public image of the company, while at the same time, prove to be profitable for the company. Companies have been found to increase their ability to attract and retain their employees with a strong CSR commitment (Turban and Greening, 1997). Gnyawali (1996) for example suggest combination of firm specific, country specific and global factors shaping the corporate social performance. Corporate is also viewed as social communities that serve as mechanisms for the creation and transformation of knowledge into economically rewarded products and services (Kogut and Zaher, 1993). In fact the literature suggests reasons behind CSR initiatives by the corporate sector. Different studies suggest different drivers for CSR initiatives. It has been suggested that these drivers would differ from corporate to corporate, circumstances to circumstances and even from country to country (Issue Brief Note, 2004). Some important of those can be listed as:

- Improved Financial Performance
- Reduced Operating Costs
- Enhanced Brand Image and Reputation
- Increased Sales and Customer Loyalty
- Increased Productivity and Quality
- Reduced Regulatory Oversight
- Increased Stakeholder Activism
- More Sophisticated Stakeholder Engagement
- Proliferation of Codes, Standards, Indicators and Guidelines
- Transparency and Reporting
- Growing Government Interest and Action
- Convergence of CSR and Governance Agendas
- Growing Investor Pressure and Market-Based Incentives
- Pressure to Quantify CSR "Return on Investment

These are some of the motivations behind any social initiative or social investment as is suggested by the different studies and writings. However, the validity of these reasons is to be tested in different situations, different countries and different set-ups. Because, companies disclose most of the information concerning social initiatives is in absence of any regulatory or legal requirements. Hence it becomes more interesting to see what motivates them to report this information or for that matter what exactly motivate them to take these social initiatives. Moreover, it would be interesting to know how do social investments/initiatives are viewed by the managers who are responsible for making these social investments. If the recent writings and the information available is any evidence the CSR investments or CSR initiatives are not merely a discrete or discretionary or philanthropic activity. The changing business scenario and the pressures put by the globalization would perhaps not allow the corporate to invest on philanthropic activities to a great extent. Coupled with this, the corporate is under pressure to be socially responsible also at the same time. That means if the corporate have to be socially responsible, they have to make social investments or take social initiatives which make business sense too. What distinguishes today's understanding of CSR from the initiatives of the past is the attempt to manage it strategically and to develop instruments for this. In the competitive business scenario only those corporate social initiatives will make sense which in one way or the other is integrated into their business models of the companies. Any social investment/initiative which is bereft of any link with any business preposition cannot be long lasting in most of the cases. Thus, it makes more sense to study if the corporate have started taking social initiatives which make business sense also. If yes, then it has to be seen how and to what extent companies are integrating the CSR initiatives into the business models. More importantly, it's worth studying if the comparison is drawn between the corporate players belonging to two different nations.

Conclusions

The idea of CSR is as old as the business itself. However, the term CSR has been and is being understood differently by different people and corporations. The firms try to undertake different CSR initiatives for different purposes. The researchers try to understand the CSR and they try to establish the relationship between CSR and different economic parameters. Whatever the results of these different studies by different researchers, one fact is evident and that is the increasing importance of CSR initiatives by the corporate sector. Be it the economic compulsions or social pressures the corporations will have to understand and take CSR initiatives.

REFERENCES

Aupperle, K. E., A. B. Carroll, and J. D. Hatfield (1985) An Empirical Examination of the Relationship Between Corporate Social Responsibility and Profitability. *Academy of Management Journal*, 28 (2): 446-463.

Cochran, P. L., and R. A. Wood (1984) Corporate Social Responsibility and Financial Performance. *Academy of Management Journal*, 27 (1): 42-56.

Dawkins, J. and Lewis, S. (2003). CSR in Stakeholder Expectations: And Their Implication for Company Strategy. *Journal of Business Ethics*. 44 (2), 185-193.

Dusuki, Asyraf Wajdi and Humayon Dar, Does Corporate Social Responsibility Pay-Off? http://mubs.mdx.ac.uk/conferences/bpcsr05/03_measuring_csr/CSR%20Paper%20_Asyraf%20Dusuki_.pdf (visited on 12.06.2006)

Elkington, J. (1999), The Link Between Accountability and Sustainability Theory Put Into Practice, *Conference on the Practice of Social Reporting for Business, ISEA, 19 January*, Commonwealth Conference Centre, London. Cited from Mohamed Zairi and John Peters [2002], The Impact of Social Responsibility on Business Performance *Managerial Auditing Journal* 17/4 174-178

Freeman, R. E. (1984). *Strategic Management: A Stakeholder Approach*. Pitman. London.

Friedman M, (1970)The Social Responsibility of Business is to Increase it Profits, *New York Times Magazine*, 13 September, reprinted in Donaldson T and Werhane, P. (1983), *Ethical Issues in Business: A Philosophical Approach*, 2nd Edition, Englewood Cliffs, NJ: Prentice Hall

Gnyawali, D. (1996). Corporate social performance: An international perspective. *Advances in International Comparative Management*, 11: 251-273.

Goodpaster, K. E. (2001). Business Ethics and Stakeholder in T. L. Beauchamp and N. E. Bowie, *Ethical Theory and Business*, Prentice Hall Int., Upper Saddle River, N.J. 6th Edition.

Gray, R.H. and Milne, M.J. (2002) Sustainability reporting: who's kidding whom? *Chartered Accountants Journal of New Zealand*, 81(6), pp. 66-70.

Gray, R.H. and Milne, M.J. (2004) Towards Reporting On the Triple Bottom Line: Mirages, Methods and Myths, in A. Henriques and J. Richardson (Eds) *The Triple Bottom Line: Does it All Add Up?* pp. 70-80 (London: Earthscan).

Greenwood, M. R. (2001). Community as a Stakeholder. Focusing on Corporate Social and Environmental Reporting. *Journal of Corporate Citizenship*. 4, 31-46.

Greenwood, M. R. (2001). The Importance of Stakeholders According to Business Leaders. *Business and Society Review*. 106 (1), 29-49.

Issue Briefing Note: Perceptions and Definitions of Social Responsibility, May 2004 http://www.iisd.org/pdf/2004/standards_definitions.pdf (visited on 14.06.2006).

Kogut, B. & U. Zander. 1993. Knowledge of the firm and the evolutionary theory of the multinational corporation. *Journal of International Business Studies*, 24: 625-645. cited from *Corporate Social Performance and Multinationality, A Longitudinal Study* by Roy L. Simerly and Minfang Li, http://www.westga.edu/~bquest/2000/corporate.html visited on 25 January, 2006. Maignan, I. and Ferrell, O. C. (2004). Corporate Social Responsibility and Marketing: An Integrative Framework. *Journal of the Academy of Marketing Science*. 32 (1), 3-19.

Mangos, Nicholas and Peter OBrien Investigating Social Responsibility Reporting Practices of Global Australian firms and how those Practices enhance Economic Success. Paper presented at *Second World Congress of International Society for Business, Economics and Ethics* July 19-23, 2000 at Sao Paulo, Brazil.

Margolis, Joshua D., and James P. Walsh (2002) Social Enterprise Series No. 19 — Misery Loves Companies: Whither Social Initiatives by Business?, *Harvard Business School Working Paper Series*, No. 01-058.

McGuire, J.B., A. Sundgren, and T. Schneeweis, 1988, Corporate Social Responsibility and Firm Financial Performance, *Academy of Management Journal*, 31, 854-872.

McWilliams, A., and D. Siegel (2000) Corporate Social Responsibility and Financial Performance: Correlation or Misspecification?" *Strategic Management Journal*, 21 (5): 603-609.

O'Brien, D. (2001). Integrating Corporate Social Responsibility with Competitive Strategy. http: // www .bc. edu / centers /ccc / Media / 2001 _ mbawinner.pdf visited on 25 January, 2006.

POSKINOFF J.F., 1997, Disinvestment From South Africa: They Did Well by Doing Good, *Contemporary Economic Policy*, Vol. XV, January, p. 76-86.

Ruf, B. M., Muralidhar, R. M., Brown, J., Janney, J. and Paul, K. (2001). An Empirical Investigation of the Relationship between Change in Corporate Social Performance and Financial Performance: A Stakeholder Theory Perspective. *Journal of Business Ethics*. 32, 143-156.

TEOH S.H., WELCH I. & WAZZAN C.P., 1999, The Effect of Socially Activist Investment Policies on the Financial Markets: Evidence from the South African Boycott, *Journal of Business*, Vol. 72, no.1, p. 35-88.

Tsoutsoura, Margarita (2004) Corporate Social Responsibility and Financial Performance, *Applied Financial Project*, Haas School of Business, University of California, Berkeley.

Turban, D. B., and D. W. Greening (1997) Corporate social performance and organizational attractiveness to prospective employees. *Academy of Management* Journal, 40 (3): 658-672.

Waddock, S. A., and Samuel B. Graves (1997) The Corporate Social Performance-Financial Performance Link. *Strategic Management Journal*, 18 (4): 303-319.

Wright, P. & Ferris, S. 1997. Agency Conflict and Corporate Strategy: The Effect of Divestment on Corporate Value. *Strategic Management Journal*, 18: 77-83.

15

COMMUNITY PARTICIPATION IN WATER RESOURCE DEVELOPMENT AND MANAGEMENT IN THE SHIVALIK REGION

S. P. Mittal

Introduction

Nearly 97.3 per cent of earth's water is in the oceans and seas whereas fresh water constitutes a very small fraction (2.7 per cent). Of this fresh water, 75.2per cent lies frozen in the polar regions and a further 22.6 per cent is present as ground water. A very tiny portion of planet's fresh water is available in lakes, rivers, atmosphere, soil and vegetation. What is effectively available for consumption and other uses is a small portion of the quantity present in rivers, lakes and underground aquifers. India which has 2.4 per cent of world's land resources, has roughly 4 per cent of world's fresh water resources and supports 16 per cent of world's population. The growing pressure on land for food, fibre and fuel, due to increasing population, has given rise to competing demands for water. The water resources that once appeared to be inexhaustible, have now become a scarce commodity. Lest the scarcity of water hampers the economic growth of the country, it is essential to conserve the limited available water resources through scientific management strategies. Against this background, water resource development and management have assumed greater importance.

Although great strides have been made in agriculture production in the country, particularly in areas which have assured irrigation facilities, about 62 per cent of the total cultivated area of 142 million hectares, is still rainfed. It is estimated that even after exploiting full irrigation potential through conventional sources, about 50 per cent of the cultivated area will continue to remain rainfed and subjected to vagaries of nature. This region contributes about 42 per cent food grain to the national pool.

In spite of best technologies available for dry land agriculture, the average production from this region has remained low. Skewed pattern of rainfall is primarily responsible for this malady. There have been years when farmers did not harvest grain equal to the amount of seed sown. Deficiency of moisture at the grain formation stage of *kharif* crops and at the time of sowing of rabi crops, is the single ubiquitous factor affecting crop yields in this region. Kharif crops may mature to some extent due to monsoon rains, but the fate of *rabi* crops is particularly precarious because there is hardly any moisture left in the soil for germination after the harvest of *kharif* crops. Then, scanty and undependable winter rains play havoc in most of the years. As per records there is hardly any rain between October and December that can help sowing and germination of *rabi* crops. This long dry spell leaves a trail of miseries. Hence, most of the farmers are skeptical to sow *rabi* crops.

The only alternative for sustainable crop production in such regions, is therefore, "runoff farming", i.e., harvesting surplus rainwater during monsoon and use it for providing supplemental irrigation as and when needed. This approach has given a new direction to the management of natural resources for the benefit of rainfed farmers as well as the agro-ecosystem.

Runoff Potential: Runoff has been defined as that portion of the precipitation (rainfall) in a drainage area which is discharged from the area in a stream channel. It can be surface runoff, sub-surface flow or seepage. It is the surface runoff which is of paramount importance. The rainfall distribution of this region is such that about 80 per cent of the total annual rainfall of 1100 mm is received during the south-west monsoon (June end to mid-September). It is estimated that in the Shivalik region of north-west states, spread over three million hectares, out of 1100 mm rainfall, about 30 to 40 per cent not only ends in runoff but causes the problems of floods, sedimentation and damage to agricultural fields and property. This offers distinct possibilities of rainwater harvesting during monsoon for its later use for post-rainy season crops.

Water Resource Development

Water is the most critical factor for livelihood support systems. All the watershed management projects (WSMP), therefore, rely on water harvesting and management. Water harvesting thus forms an important component of WSMPs. Rainwater harvesting is the collection and storage of rainfall runoff from any catchment or watershed, for subsequent use for irrigation or any other beneficial use. Water harvesting can often mean the difference between crop and no crop in the rainfed areas. In Shivalik region , where there is no possibility of developing any other source of irrigation, rainwater harvesting has proved to be a panacea. For the rainwater harvesting programmes to be successful it is essential that moderately large catchments and sufficient storage facilities are available in the vicinity of the villages.

The studies on rainwater harvesting systems based on Integrated Watershed Management concept, were initiated at village Sukhomajri in mid- seventies in community and sate owned lands, by the Central Soil and Water Conservation Research Centre, Chandigarh, with a view to locally develop water resource through rainwater harvesting. It was here that the first rainwater harvesting structure (RWHS), a 12- metre high earthen dam was constructed in 1978 to collect and store 5.6 ha m (hectare metre) runoff water from 9.2 hectare hilly catchment. With the success of Sukhomajri began the era of constructing small water harvesting dams in Shivaliks in the eighties. Consequently, more than 200 such rainwater harvesting dams have already been constructed in the states of Haryana, Punjab and Himachal Pradesh by the Forest, Agriculture and Soil Conservation Departments. The World Bank aided Integrated Watershed Development Project, implemented in the above mentioned sates, has give in a fillip to this programme in a big way.

In the recent years 17 RWHS have been constructed in Panchkula and Yamunanagar districts of Haryana under

Table 1 : Technical details of Rainwater Harvesting Structures

Particulars	*Sukhomajri*	*Bunga I*	*Bunga II*	*Relmajra*	*Bharauli**
Year of Comstruction	1978	1984	1989	1992	2001
Catchment area (ha)	9.2	155	101	59	90
Height (m)	12	16	15	13.5	14
Storage Capacity (ha m)	5.6	60	57	13.5	24.7
Command Area (ha)	16	240	230	32	150

* Constructed by HCFP

Note : One ha m = 10,000 cu m

Community Forestry Project, funded by European Union. These seventeen dams with a combined forest catchment area of 1028 ha and storage capacity of 261 ha m, are irrigating 867 ha of agricultural farms. The height of the dams constructed so far varies from 6 to 16 metres, catchments up to 155 hectares, storage capacity up to 60 ha m and the command area varying from 4 to 240 hectares. The harvested rainwater is conveyed to the agricultural fields through underground pipelines by gravity. Thus, there is no need for electricity or diesel engines. The technical details of some of the rainwater harvesting structures constructed in the region are given in Table 1.

Impact of Irrigation on Crop Yields

Depending on the availability of water, two to three irrigations could be provided to the *rabi* crops. The studies carried out on farmers' fields with limited irrigation from these dams, at critical growth stages of *rabi* crops, use of optimum dose of fertilizer and improved varieties of seeds, resulted in three to four times average increase in yield of wheat, chickpea and mustard as is evident from the following table:

Crop	*No. of irrigations*	*Grain yield (kg/ha)*	*% Increase*
Wheat	Nil	910	Nil
(Triticum	One	2500	174
aestivum)	Three	3150	246
Chickpea	Nil	390	-
(Cicer	One	810	108
arietinum)	Two	1040	166
Mustard	Nil	200	-
(Brassica	One	615	208
juncea)	Two	810	305

In addition to food crops almost all the farmers getting irrigation water have started growing berseem (*Trifolium alaxandrinum*) for green fodder. The average yield of green fodder is more than 300 q/ha. The green fodder is used as a supplement feed for milch cattle. It has given a big boost to milk sector in this region and the milk production has increased almost four times.

Participatory Management of Water Resources

The success of WSMPs depends on community participation right from the beginning. The participation becomes easy if there is transparency right from the inception and people are convinced with the aims and objectives of the project. Before taking up the projects several meetings were held with the villagers. The entire programme and the plans were discussed with them in these meetings. The dire need of irrigation water for the parched agricultural fields which led to manifold increase in crop yields, worked as a *'catalyst'* in bringing about change in the attitude of the villagers. During meetings with the villagers it was emphasized that they must protect the hilly catchments from grazing and illicit cutting of trees if they wanted water in their dams otherwise these would be silted up and they will not get water for their fields. The villagers heeded to this advice and stopped grazing and illicit cutting of vegetation from the catchment areas. This new approach of protection of the forest areas by the people themselves was termed as 'Social Fencing'.

The experience of Integrated Watershed Management Projects executed in this region, strongly suggest technical, economical and social viability of constructing small earthen dams by adopting participatory approach for water resource development and management in the Shivalik region. It was here that the Participatory Irrigation Management (PIM) was first practiced. The availability of irrigation water played a pivotal role in binding the people in to a coherent society. To ensure continued peoples' participation, the entire management of the projects have been handed over to village based societies christened as Hill Resource Management Society (HRMS) or Water Users Society, which have been registered under the Society's Registration Act 1860. These societies have been assigned *inter alia*, the following responsibilities:

(i) Protection of hilly catchments from grazing and illicit cutting of trees i.e. " Social Fencing".
(ii) Distribution of irrigation water from dams among all its members at the rate to be fixed from time to time.

(iii) Maintenance of dams, water conveyance systems and other assets.

(iv) Utilization of society's funds for the welfare activities in the village.

Community Empowerment

These societies made exemplary efforts in managing the projects and the water resources. How far these societies were successful is evident from the revenue these have generated mainly from the sale of water and other natural resources like grass from catchment areas. For instance, the HRMS Sukhomajri generated more than Rs.11.00 lakhs as income and spent Rs.10.4 lakhs on various activities between 1986 and 1999. Similarly, Bunga society generated a revenue of Rs.13.07 lakhs and spent Rs.10.7 lakhs between 1984 and 2000. The Water Users Society, Rel Majra generated Rs.2.65 lakhs as income and incurred an expenditure of Rs.2.58 lakhs. All the Societies used the funds for maintenance of dams and pipelines, welfare and development activities in the villages. WUS Relmajra constructed its own community centre in the village.

Other benefits of rainwater harvesting

Rainwater harvesting and its utilization for crop production has resulted in tangible benefits like productive, protective (ecological), social, economic, and employment generation. The construction of dams in conjunction with treatment of hilly catchments with appropriate soil conservation measures, have helped in checking soil erosion, widening of choes/drains, damage to agricultural fields and communication systems. The most important and visible benefit was the rise in groundwater table. Consequently, the villagers have installed tubewells in many villages. Besides, large chunks of common lands have been reclaimed and put under cultivation amounting to recovering the entire costs of the projects.

These experiences of rainwater harvesting in the Shivalik region have translated in to reality the Guiding Principle No. 2 of International Conference on Water and Environment (ICWE) held in January 1992 in Dublin and endorsed by Agenda 21 of Earth Summit held in Rio de Janeiro in June 1992, that reads as *"Water resource development and management should be based on a participatory approach involving users, planners and policy makers at all levels".* In true spirit of this principle and to ensure efficient and judicious utilization of the limited water resource, the local community was involved in planning, implementation and subsequent management of the projects and its assets.

Lessons learnt

Some very important lessons have been learnt from these projects which have to be kept in mind while implementing such projects. These are:

- People's participation must be ensured right from the inception of the project.
- The needs and the problems of the people must be identified at the outset.
- Unless a project is aimed at meeting their needs, solving their problems and mitigating their hardship, it may not succeed.
- There must be flexibility right from planning stage to the implementing stage.
- The project should have a short gestation period. The benefits should be available to the people in the shortest possible time.
- The emphasis should be on sustainability and equity.
- Constitution of a village society must be a prerequisite.
- Participation of women and the weaker sections of the community should not be overlooked as their involvement can ensure success of the projects.
- Once the benefits from the project start accruing, the people are willing to take up the responsibility of protecting the forests (social fencing), manage the project and maintain its assets.

Challenges of the 21st Century:

There has, of late been a virtual flood of literature, all pointing to a severe water crisis that mankind is going to face in this century. India is one of the most vulnerable country despite being one of the world's top water-rich nation. With the burgeoning population, the spectre of greater water crisis is looming ahead of us. Clearly, the problem has been compounded by the absence of comprehensive regulations and concerted efforts. There is no technology that can manufacture water. The way out is to create awareness amongst the masses to optimize its use and conserve every drop of it.

Broadly speaking, the following aspects will require thinking and sincere efforts to overcome water shortages in the future.

i) Rain water harvesting: (RWH): The successful experiments of the RWH carried out in different parts of the country during the last three decades, have clearly established as the alternaitve strategy of water resources development to meet the challenges of water scarcity in years to come. The potential and prospects of RWH call upon the authorities and the policy-makers to enlarge this activity in a big way.

One estimate puts that restoration of village ponds and construction of small RWH structures can generate up to 10 and 15 billion cubic metres of water respectively. The size of these structures can be decided according to the site conditions and the need. The harvested rainwater is very precious and a limited resource. Therefore, it should be used prudently. Water-intensive crops must not be grown with the harvested rainwater.

ii) Water management: Our irrigation systems (mostly flood irrigation) run at one-third of their operational efficiency. There is urgent need to improve water application efficiency and water use efficiency. The excessive use of water in agriculture needs to be curbed if the production per unit of water applied is to be enhanced. All out efforts are need to popularize sprinkle system of irrigation as its efficiency is almost three times of the flood irrigation.

iii) Community Participation: The National Water Policy revised in 2002, calls for a participatory approach to water resources development and management. That is inclusive of users and other stakeholders effectively and decisively in all aspects of planning, design, development and management of water resources. The right-mix of technology and traditional wisdom would be a winning combination.

Conclusion

The water crisis could precipitate further than expected unless suitable water storage and conservation and scientific water management practices were adopted. The experience of these projects has clearly brought out that the participatory management of water resources presents a strong sustainable approach for the socioeconomic benefit of the society. It is imperative that social mobilization, more decentralization and community empowerment, are explicitly included in Government policies and programmes for the participatory-based management projects.

Be that as it may, the participatory approach in these projects, has established its functional prominence as a model of participatory sustainable management of natural resources which has ultimately resulted in re-habilitation of degraded ecosystems and socio economic uplift of the community.

IT IS SAID IN EPICS

Tanks whose harvested rainwater lasts up to:

Sharad Ritu	-	is equal to donating 1000 cows
Hemanta Ritu	-	is equal to donating gold to Brahmins in Yajna
Shishir Ritu	-	is equal to performing Agnisthana Yajna
Vasant Ritu	-	is equal to performing Atiratra Yajna
Grishma Ritu	-	is equal to performing great Ashwamedha Yajna

Dig the lake for water harvesting and get in turn dharma, artha and karma as reward.

Index

E

U